Racing
IN THE
Slow Lane

By PAMELA JORDAN

PublishAmerica
Baltimore

ISBN: 978-1-61582-855-5 (softcover)
ISBN: 978-1-4489-8682-8 (hardcover)
PUBLISHED BY PUBLISHAMERICA, LLLP
www.publishamerica.com
Baltimore

Printed in the United States of America

DEDICATION

This book is dedicated to Marvin Jordan,
who puts the pizzazz in each day with his constant
supply of fun, support and applause.

ACKNOWLEDGMENTS

Marvin Jordan for prayer, encouragement
and manuscript enhancement.

Sandi Harrington for guidance, wisdom and final editing.

Marcus Parr and his Short Story Writing class for writing expertise and
being my cheerleaders.

Mountain View Christian Church for technical support, prayer
and endorsements.

Julie Bonn Heath for editing and publishing assistance.

CHAPTER 1
WHERE? WHAT? WHY?

I was in the hospital undergoing several days of testing before the surgery that changed my life forever. Some of my time was spent running around with the other teenage girls, watching TV and reading magazines. The plain four-bed ward came alive once filled with rambunctious young girls. Whenever the nurses changed shifts, we snuck out the ward door and down the hall without being noticed. I never knew how much fun exploring a huge hospital floor could be. We actually got to be pretty good detectives.

With all the women's restrooms mapped out, shift change hours memorized and a friend in the laundry room, we were able to make several excursions. Out on the balcony was our favorite rendezvous spot. From that eighth floor balcony, we could watch all the people down below, catch a quick suntan and fill our lungs with a batch of fresh air. Our worst enemy was the giggles. But even that was overcome. With two wadded up paper towels stuffed in our mouths, giggling was seldom our betrayer.

Getting caught in the boys' section was our finale. We hadn't planned it that way, but when the guys got a look at us, they started whistling. We were caught. And, the hospital grapevine alerted every nurse on our floor. Oh well, it was fun while it lasted.

It was a majority vote that we replace our excursions with TV. The vote was three to one. Oh well, I didn't need a scout or crowd to get me down the hall. When the boring part of the movie came, I stepped out for another trip to the balcony.

With a quick peek first down to the left and then to the right, I bolted out the door. I glanced over my shoulder to see what the loud noise behind me was. Wham! The next thing I knew, my freckled pug nose was smashed up against freshly-laundered white something. Stepping back in a daze, I looked up and up. At last, I saw a white mask with friendly eyes looking straight at me. "Hi there," the mask said. "Have we met before?"

"Gee, I don't think so."

"What's your name? And, what might I ask is your hurry?"

"Got to use the women's restroom, our bathroom's full. Do you know where one is?"

"Sure thing," he said. "Tell me your name, and I will show you the ladies room."

"I'm Pam. Thanks."

Wow! That was too close for comfort. I'll just hang out here awhile and give him time to get down the hall and out of sight. In the restroom now, I leaned up against the wall for a brief second.

In an attempt to make it sound like others were in there with me and distract anyone from being concerned about me, I flushed several toilets. I ran water in one, two, three sinks, and yanked several yards of paper towels from the dispenser. Standing close to the door, I listened and listened. Everything seemed quiet until the door swung open and a lady came in. "Pam, are you okay?" she asked with genuine concern.

"Yes, Ma'am, but how did you know my name?"

"Well, you see, Dr. Ramos is standing outside waiting for you. He got concerned and asked me to step in here and check on a girl named Pam."

OOPS! He's still out there. So much for my plans. Now what?

"Come on, Pam," she extended her hand out to me. "We can't keep the doctor waiting now, can we?"

After a special doctor escort down the hall, I was back with the girls. They snickered, but I didn't let it bother me.

Word eventually came. I needed brain surgery to remove a pituitary tumor. And I needed it immediately. I suddenly couldn't even concentrate on the TV.

A short time later, I was resting in my room after lunch when a man came in.

"Hi, Pam. I'm Roger, a lab technician. I've come to get you ready for your surgery."

"Oh, great! Another shot, I suppose."

"No, no, nothing that painful. We just need to cut off some of your hair."

"No! Not my hair! I've worked forever to grow it long like this!" He assured me they'd cut off so little that it would hardly be noticeable. I had always hated liars, but this one quickly became a mortal enemy. Down the hall we went to a small room, the home of one lonely barber chair. With a gesture of courtesy, Roger excused himself. Soon, a broad-shouldered woman with a short, masculine haircut appeared in the doorway. Her stern pale face with thick black eyebrows spelled trouble right off the bat. She began brushing my hair with rough, aggressive strokes. With a loud, double "ouch," I asked her to please take it easy. But, her vocabulary was limited to "sit still" and "be quiet!"

Out of the corner of my eye, I saw clippers in her hand. I begged her not to take off much. But, with two deaf ears turned toward me, she ruthlessly continued cutting and then began shaving. Then abruptly yanking the plastic cape off my shoulders, she left the room as solemnly as she had entered. I quickly swung that chair around to look in the big mirror on the wall. Horrified, I saw a pathetic skinny kid who was bald—absolutely bald! Tears gushed down my face, but only the silent dingy white walls of this tiny torture chamber heard my distress.

I don't remember the surgery itself, but the aftermath was unforgettable. Once awake in my private room, reality hit with a sledge hammering blow. What a shock—I went from hyperactive Pam to an instant invalid! I was only able to lie in bed and sometimes sit up for a meal. That was difficult enough for this livewire to cope with. Yet, it paled immensely to wearing a blindfold around the clock. I was counting the days, hours and then minutes until it would come off and I could see again.

Hooray! The countdown was over! For the first time in a week I could open my eyes, but everything was still as pitch black as when the bandages were on. With my eyes wide open, not even a speck of light was visible, no glimmer of anything. Just black—total black!

"No, No! It can't be true!" *Blind, totally blind. I'll never be able to drive.*

I cried and cried. Ever since fourth grade, I knew what my career would be. I was going to be a grade school teacher. Whenever the student teachers from Parkrose High School came to our school, I watched them closely. They almost always arrived driving their own car and stepped out of it

9

wearing high heels and nylon stockings. That's what I would be doing in high school. I had it all planned to the smallest detail.

Each summer I would get a job and save every penny earned. I would take the written driver's test the very day I was old enough. By my sixteenth birthday, I would have enough money to buy my own car. It was as good as written in stone. I knew that's how it would be.

But it was gone—all gone. Every dream, aspiration and hope for the future was gone! This inner despair haunted me. The horrible words, "Blind, can't do that, what's the use" resounded like the base drum of a rock band pounding over and over in my head.

Soft quick footsteps immediately drew my attention. My ears tingled with excitement. I knew those footsteps. My heart and eyes smiled through the tears. "Oh, Mom, is that you?"

"Hi, Pam. I came right from work to see you. How's my girl doing?"

Her loving arms quickly wrapped around me as our tears mingled.

"Mom, I'm blind. They took off the bandages and I'm completely blind!"

"Oh, Kitten, I'm so sorry. The tumor in your head was very large. They insisted that we say nothing about you going blind. If you got depressed, your chances of living through the operation would be a lot less. The doctors said you barely had a 50/50 chance of surviving surgery, but if they didn't do it right away, you'd only have two months to live."

"I'd rather die than to live like this. It would have been better to let me live two more months having fun and being normal. Now all that's left for me is being a blind beggar just like the one in the Bible."

She gently brushed the hair out of my face. Kissing my forehead, her warm tears caressed my red hot tear-streaked face. "Oh, Kitten, this is not what any of us wanted, but you know we'll stick with you, and together we'll make it through this."

My world became foreign to me and nothing seemed right. Nothing was normal anymore. I knew a sink, toilet and closet were in my room. Yet from my perception, they were only bits of intellectual data way out there beyond my reach. My reality was a black vacuum of nothingness. I felt alone, all alone, like a lost being floating somewhere in outer space. My private room was too private, isolating me from everyone and everything. In that solitude, it seemed as though I dwelt in the darkest of night every minute. This bred fear and inner panic. Nightmares took over my mind and emotions.

I repeatedly daydreamed about smelling the stench of oil reeking heavy in the fog-laced blackness. The tall weathered wooden fence enclosed all the junky valuables with a secure grip. Rust, dents and dirt completely camouflaged the faded shiny glory of their good-ole days. Rusty ruins stretched out like a vast sea of sardines with only enough space between for the ever present guard dogs. Fierce, overgrown German shepherds lunged and snarled at the slightest hint of movement.

Even a mere onlooker would be shaken to the bones with fear. But, such fear would be as child's play compared to this present peril—I was weak and helpless lying atop an old rust heap, a ritzy Cadillac in its prime. The pounding panic of my heart battled against my determination to breathe soft and silent. I dared not gasp nor move lest one of those savage beasts discover me—an intruder. But, my foot slipped and let out a loud shrill squeak as it slid out of control across the wet metal roof. An instant uproar of barking with steel trap jaws and flashing white fangs surrounded me striking just inches from my body. My heart pounded faster than a champion race horse. This terror ended in an ear-piercing scream. Whoever thought that a hypodermic needle would be such a welcome friend? Phew. Relief at last! Or, was it?

Whenever alone, this vision filled most of my waking hours, terrifying me again and again. Thank goodness for the nurses and visitors who entered my room. Without them and my faithful family, I would have lost my sanity.

Grandma and Pastor Wayne visited me often. Although that would appear to be a simple assignment for any grandmother, it was a major project for mine. Ever since I could remember, Grandma had only one leg. Diabetes caused gangrene in her left foot. It would not heal and necessitated amputation above her left knee. When it was time to go outside her home, Grandma would strap on a heavy wooden leg with big steel reinforcement bars. Walking with this was tedious and uncomfortable at best. She couldn't walk alone, but with a firm grip on a companion's arm right beside her, she slowly inched along. Despite all this, my Grandma walked the extra mile often to see me. Pastor Wayne always brought her and stayed to visit, as well.

The two of them filled me in on the important things in life. Pastor Wayne asked, "Pam, do you remember your baptism and the important decision you made just a few months ago?"

"Oh, yes. I decided I wanted to be on God's team and not the devil's."

"That's right. So, Pam, that means you are God's child right now. He will take the very best care of you no matter what happens. You can count on Him."

Opening her Bible, Grandma said, "Pam, did you know God has a special promise for you? It's right here in Romans 8:28. 'And we know that God works all things together for good for those who love Him and are called according to His purpose.'"

I didn't dare argue with Grandma since the pastor stood right beside my bed. But, there was no way I could believe that verse.

Being blind…it could never turn out to anything good! Blindness is too terrible even for God to fix.

At that point, I simply tuned God out of my thoughts and life. But, with loving persistence, the two kept coming and sharing God's words of love from the Bible.

I heard Mom's footsteps the next time she visited and that was a welcoming sound.

"Hi, Kitten. I brought you an extra thick chocolate milkshake. And, here's a book to read. It's called *Pollyanna*. I think you might like it."

Mom snuggled close to me to read, and off I went into the world of Pollyanna. I found the story entertaining, and I liked Pollyanna's charming personality. It amazed me that she came up with something good in every situation. However, there had to be a limit to her winsome way. I felt that limit hit when Pollyanna opened her only Christmas gift. She had so longed for a doll. But, instead it was a pair of ugly crutches. I felt so sorry for her.

There was a Christmas when I, too, had wished for a special doll. My heart was set on that one doll. I was totally thrilled when I opened the gift with my beautiful doll in it. The anger I felt for Pollyanna boiled inside. Before Mom could get to the end of that scene, I already had a solution. Pollyanna ought to use those crutches to knock some sense into the giver!

Well, that's not how the story went. She found something good in this, too. She could walk and didn't need to use crutches. That story drove a sharp impression into both my heart and my brain. If Pollyanna could find something good in all those difficult times, so could I!

So could I!

CHAPTER 2
HOME, SWEET HOME!

After a month of imprisonment within those stale sterile hospital walls, Mom said, "Pam, it's time to go home and the sun is shining for you."

Oh, how I longed to see its dazzling brilliance, but when I stepped outside, the sun was not shining. It was as black as that junkyard night. "Pollyanna," I whispered to myself, "remember Pollyanna." But, I couldn't muster up any good thoughts from my sad inner being. Nothing had improved—I was blind, still blind!

We paused a few minutes in the sunshine and tears promptly started trickling down my cheeks. Mom squeezed my hand in silent reassurance. "Come on, Pam. There's a nice bench close by. You can sit there while I go get the car."

It was a short walk to that bench right beside the doors of the main hospital entrance. Oh, how welcome that rough textured wooden bench felt. Walking that short distance exhausted me. Sitting there by myself, I felt uneasy and so alone. It was about one month ago when Mom and I had walked through those big glass doors to get my eyes checked. But, today, everything was totally different. It felt as though I were in a dank, dark asphalt cave of no man's land. Everything around me was strange, strange!

The loud roar of a busy thoroughfare, clunking automatic doors behind me, footsteps and a variety of noises on my right and left blurred into a confusion that almost made me dizzy. I knew my feet were on flat, solid asphalt, yet this new world of weird, unidentifiable stuff made my inner equilibrium teeter-totter with unsteadiness. Standing up from the bench, I took several steps forward.

If only I could touch the building, a wall, something solid. That would reassure me of my real surroundings. But all I found was more open space, more darkness and increasing apprehension. This was a brand new world I had stepped into but already it was one I hated with a raging passion of anger and despair.

Standing there, the cement quickly got harder and harder. My legs began to bow and feel as rubbery as a baby's yellow bathtub ducky. Thank goodness a car pulled up. It was Mom. And within a breath, she was at my side. Oh, how good it felt to slide across the smooth vinyl seat—something familiar, something good. That was our family's car, filled with all the good feelings of laughter, love and special outings. I'm sure my weary body slipped into sweet slumber because the ride seemed so short. I came to with the familiar crunch under the tires as we pulled into our gravel driveway.

Gravel, oh that lovely gravel! That's the gravel of my driveway!

Each little stone crackled with giggles of fun, reminders of many childhood activities. My little brother, Steve, and I would sit smack dab in the middle of it for hours with our coffee can of water. What a top-notch refinery that big Folgers's coffee can was. It was simple but of the most efficient and of highest production.

We would grasp a handful of that common gravel and hunt intently for any stone that was different. With a couple quick swishes in the big can's cool water, all dust was washed off. The water had a miraculous effect, transforming them into priceless gems, diamonds and jewels. With this valuable cargo, each dump truck full had to be rushed to the bank—my yellow sand bucket in the back yard.

"Hooray!" I was home at last—out of our car into the fragrant air—far from the downtown smog. The cool fragrance of our fresh-cut grass waved to my nostrils with a most pleasant homecoming smell.

And home was so good, just the same as I left it. It smelled and felt like home even though I could not see a speck of it. Stepping through the front door, I heard the familiar low soft blowing of our gas furnace. Its warm currents softly whispered, "Welcome home, Pam. Welcome home." And, my nose came alive with the smell of hot dogs cooking—Dad's gourmet meal that he prepared whenever Mom was not home to cook. He would display his platter of plump hot dogs and freshly toasted hot dog buns as he proudly announced, "Come and get it—we're having ground round tonight."

I was never very fond of hot dogs, but that afternoon nothing smelled more scrumptious than that hot dog aroma.

Later, with the exhaustion of the trip home and my bags neatly lined up along my bedroom wall, I gathered up every ounce of my remaining strength and made a swooping swan dive into the softest, most comfy bed in the whole world.

Three months of recuperating at home, the doctors said. That's a long time to be doing nothing.

But, little did I know that "nothing" was loaded with lots of challenges in store for me. Challenge number one hit me the very first morning at home. It was time to get dressed. What to wear or better yet—where to find what to wear? I got up from bed, and to my surprise and delight, the closet was a snap to find. Then I opened the closet, and a whole new terrain spread out before me.

There it stood—a jungle of entwined stuff, crammed tightly together, defying entrance by anyone or anything. My hands got busy investigating and feeling each fabric. The textures teased my fingertips as I diligently searched for any clue that would trigger color remembrance.

Oh, yes! Here's my favorite wide-wale corduroy burgundy jumper and silky pastel pink blouse with ruffles. But, never mind, where are my jeans? Somewhere in this jungle I have a sweat shirt and a pair of jeans.

Ouch! The sharp fanged wire snake of a hanger attacked my ankle and wrapped itself around my fuzzy slipper.

Finally, I was dressed and ready for the day! This surprise jungle safari sure wore the stuffings out of me.

Breakfast was the usual modest fare and went well until the spoon got into the act. Despite my careful juggling, the shredded wheat went gymnastic tumbling down the front of my sweat shirt. Then the ice cold milky waterfall began trickling down my chin. Good thing I was as thin as Twiggy. Had I been blessed with early voluptuous breasts like many other girls my age (whom I envied), there would have been a milk laden reservoir dead center in the cleavage. Oh well, enough fantasy! Back to the jungle I go to hunt for a clean blouse.

Well, it was out of the jungle and into the fire as the euphoria of being home wore off. I began to resume my "normal" lifestyle. But, quickly I found out that nothing was normal for me. Even the simplest tasks were monumental undertakings. Every time I turned around, another "simple task" was looming up right in my path. Just getting ready each morning was an onslaught of "simple," yet not-so-simple, tasks. Brushing my teeth, for example, was no big deal, I thought, until the tube of toothpaste turned into my brother's Brylcreem. Talk about nasty stuff! It sure did nothing to enhance my smile but definitely knocked my self worth down another notch or two.

Then came the hair-do challenge. Finally my hair grew back enough that I no longer needed to wear a wig. At first, I was ecstatic about this until I was hit with the necessity of having to set my hair in curlers.

My mother, with her supernatural patience, spent hours helping me learn how to do this less-than-ten-minute task. After numerous repetitions of this ordeal, I was ready for my solo run. I made sure I was all alone in my bedroom with the door shut tight. Sitting on the edge of my bed, I began parting my very short hair.

Good, one curler in and now to make a straight second part, oh great! That figures!

As the comb zigzagged across my scalp, it had caught the first curler and sent it flying into space.

Oh well. I have extra curlers. I'll find the stray one later.

My hair was so short that it barely wrapped around the small plastic curlers. No sooner had I anchored a curler in place than out poked strands of hair standing straight up defiantly like sprigs of alfalfa. With each new attempt to neatly put in a curler, frustration mounted. In short order, total anger was raging—already I had been sitting there over half an hour and still had not made one straight part. And there was not one curler in my hair.

That did it! I'd had it! The plastic bin, still full to the brim, instantly went airborne clear across my room. Curlers and bobby pins flew in every direction. I slumped down feeling totally demoralized and worthless. I didn't dare let anyone know what a stupid thing I had just done. Checking to make sure my bedroom door was still shut tightly, down I went on my hands and knees. Crawling around and sliding my flattened palms across the floor, I hunted and hunted for the many curlers and bobby pins. The hardwood floor got even harder, and tears began trickling down my face.

The door knob to my room turned quietly and I froze. But thank goodness it was Mom's hand opening my door. Talk about a first-hand taste of having to swallow one's pride!

"Oh my goodness!" Mom said as she knelt down beside me. "It's okay, Kitten. We'll have these picked up in no time at all."

Those everyday challenges were depressing and most demeaning at first, but my dear mom never gave up on me. And, just like the airborne curler time, Mom never put me down for making a mess or failing at first, second or fifty-ninth attempt. She lovingly encouraged me to keep trying and she worked together with me until we were satisfied that I could do the task both independently and well.

Then there was the basement, that eerie cold place, with so many dark corners. It was always freaky when I could see. But now it was even more foreboding. Just the thought of going down there frightened me beyond words. Standing at the top of that two-flight stairway brought a vivid flashback that gripped me with full force.

The trauma had happened one afternoon when I was home alone after school. Opening the basement door, I headed down the steps. After turning to descend the second flight, I saw my grandfather lying head down at the bottom of the stairs. My heart pounded with panic as I skittishly walked down for a closer look. He was unconscious with blood all over his head.

Remembrance of that scene, displayed with vivid Technicolor in my mind, sent cold chills down my spine. There I stood almost to the edge of the top step. But this time, I could see nothing of the steps—only the image in my mind of their dark, gray, rough, cement edges.

Yah, sure, one more step and I'll end up just like Grandpa.

Mom came to the rescue again with her warm, reassuring hand on my shoulder. She said, "Pam, I have an idea." Together we explored the technique of sliding my right foot forward to feel the edge of the step, then holding on for dear life.

Hold on to what? There are no hand rails.

Next to proceed slowly, and that's just what I did—with the pace of a frozen snail, I made it down the first flight. That was enough for my first attempt.

Just like the basement stairs, step by step, victory came with each new challenge. And with each new victory came more confidence to tackle another, then another obstacle.

Mom was an incredible teacher and knew how to make learning fun. She always invited me to join her in doing things around our home. We worked together a lot in the kitchen, and my favorite project was making desserts.

I quickly learned to identify the different utensils and kitchen gadgets by touch. With the addition of each different ingredient, Mom helped me find a way to identify it by feeling its shape, texture, size and such. Lined up against the back of our counter was a set of four shiny copper canisters. The smallest had tea bags, the second labeled coffee was always empty, the third contained sugar and the biggest can was filled with flour.

One afternoon, right in the middle of making meatloaf, a brilliant stroke of organization hit Mom and me. We were tired of stretching and struggling to reach the top shelf for our bag of salt. That empty coffee canister looked like the perfect solution to our high shelf problem.

"That's good, Pam. Now we have a full lineup of ingredients—tea bags, then salt, sugar and flour." From salads to casseroles, frying meat and baking desserts, we did it all. Soon I had plenty of cooking practice under my belt and I was ready to wing it myself. One day after school, I decided to show off my culinary skills.

Tonight Dad's coming back from California. I'll surprise him and bake a cherry cobbler.

I got right to work carefully measuring and mixing. The recipe called for one cup of sugar. I opened the canister and used my 20/20 vision in all ten fingertips to check its contents.

Yes, that's the sugar.

I dipped the cup in and, just like Mom showed me, smoothed it off level. With the big mixing bowl snuggled up close to the canister, I added my cup of sugar to the butter. Setting the bowl in the sink, I began mixing with our electric hand mixer. What a smart idea of Mom's—to do the mixing in the sink to keep splatters from hitting the wall.

I busily cleaned the counters off and washed the dishes. I wanted to make sure everything was tidy before Mom got home from work. A sense of satisfaction hit as I smelled the wonderful aroma of my cherry cobbler baking. I could hardly wait for my family to get home.

At the dinner table, I forgot every lady-like manner taught me and gobbled down my food. Finally, it was time for dessert. Proudly delivering my still warm cobbler, I set it in the middle of our table.

"Wow, Pam, sure looks delicious!" Dad said with a beaming smile so big that I could clearly see it with both ears. Everyone was served and ready to enjoy. One bite—and out of my mouth flew cherries and cobbler. It tasted horrible! Until that moment, I had no clue that my precisely measured cup of sugar was actually a full cup of salt. Tears of disappointment would have clouded my vision had I had any.

"Well, Pam, it's not so bad after all. You did everything perfect except for that one thing," Dad consoled. With my family's attitude of "no problem, Pam, you'll get it next time," I was more determined than ever to succeed.

The time came to venture beyond the kitchen and onto more "pressing duties." Ironing was next on the agenda. In those days, everything except underwear got ironed. After school one day, as was common, Mom set up the ironing board and brought in an armful of neatly folded clothes. She said, "Pam, sit here beside me while I iron and tell me about your day at school."

Reaching out to feel for a chair by the table, my hand bumped the stack of ironing. "Wow, Mom, that's a lot of clothes. Do all those have to be ironed?"

"Yes, they do. You know, I haven't figured it out—either we are a very clean family or else we're an awfully dirty one. Oh, well, whichever way, we sure have lots of laundry every week."

I wanted to pitch in and help lift some of the load off Mom's shoulders. "Mom, would you show me how to iron?"

"Sure, we can start with something easy. I know…Dad's handkerchiefs. He's almost out of clean ones. Just look at this stack—they all need ironing."

The mere thought of using that hot steamy iron was scary at first, but together we figured out a good system. We first practiced using a cold iron so I could get the hang of it without getting burnt. The next trick was finding a way to get a hold of the hot iron safely. We put our heads together and got it down pat. I always set the iron at the end of the board so the handle lined up with the corner. I could easily reach that same spot and make contact with the cool plastic handle.

Then came the wrinkles. Pleated handkerchiefs were not stylish in those days. Together, we worked through the mechanics of ironing a flat piece of fabric. I would run my flattened hand over the cloth and straighten out any folds or wrinkles. Once I was sure it was all smooth and that my fingers were out of the iron's way, I slid the iron across it. Soon I became the handkerchief expert in our laundry room.

This accomplishment, ever so small, did not go unnoticed. With my first delivery of a stack of freshly ironed handkerchiefs, Dad showed his appreciation with a big hug and genuine praise. With that success under my belt, I got braver with the iron and advanced to more difficult pieces. Dad's white work shirts were the ultimate challenge, and I was ready to tackle those. Dad liked to look his best at work. That meant crisp white shirts that were ironed and starched.

Mom was accustomed to using aerosol spray starch. That sounded simple enough to me, but I was grossly mistaken. I became quickly acquainted with its ways. That can was not at all particular about where nor what it sprayed. After a few episodes of well-starched eyebrows and earlobes, I got the hang of it. I always felt first thing for that tiny hole in the spray cap. Then, I aimed it and sprayed away. With the spray can mastered and a stack of Dad's work shirts, I was all set.

Dad likes lots of starch, so I'll give this an extra shot.

But the result wasn't so good. That week's worth of work shirts had a totally new look. Brown scorch spots appeared wherever extra starch was sprayed. They dotted the bright white fabric to form the most unattractive print. But, with Mom's simple adjustment of the iron temperature and having me slide my hand over the sprayed area, victory ensued.

With practice and my share of bloopers, I learned to do all the household tasks.

Whether laundry, dishes, vacuuming, mopping or cleaning bathrooms, Mom taught it all. Even window washing was on the apprentice list. That always happened on a hot summer afternoon and seemed more like fun than work. Once the squeals of a water fight were heard, we had lots of extra helping hands. Windows got washed in record time.

The three months went by and I was finally strong enough to go back to school. The thought of this was both worrisome and inviting. I was eager to get back to my friends and activities. School was always fun and successful for me. Yes, last year in seventh grade, I did quite well as a 4.0 student. I was in the Honor Society and my clarinet audition was a success. That put me in the top marching band with the payoff of marching in the Junior Rose Festival Parade.

Then there was my Science Fair Project. That, too, was a real success. I took first place in our school Science Fair. Then off to the Oregon Museum of

Science and Industry to display my project, although the most significant part from my perspective was being elected Student Body Secretary. Seventh grade was truly fun and prosperous which I longed to continue as I returned to eighth grade.

Then my mind switched gears and I was flooded with questions and worry—what will my friends think when they find out I'm blind? How will I find my classrooms, read the textbooks, write my assignments? How? What if? How and what if kept plaguing my mind. Those questions kept rotating with no glimmer of any reasonable answers.

CHAPTER 3
OUTER SPACE & THE ALIENS

Ninety days. Eighty, seventy, ten, nine, eight, seven, six, five, four, three, two, one. Finally, my three months of recuperating at home were over and it was time to go back to Junior High. I could hardly wait. It would be so good to see all my friends again. All that enthusiastic anticipation slid downhill like a run-away sled once the reality of my being blind gripped my mind.

What will they say when they find out I'm blind?

My emotions peaked and ebbed like ocean waves heaving and crashing with the force of a harsh winter storm. Oh, how I longed to resume having fun with my friends and be back to normal again. At the same time, I was scared and nervous.

I walked hand in hand with Mom to the front door of Freemont Junior High. With a large lump in my throat and butterflies in my stomach, Mom opened the heavy metal door. One step into the wide hallway and, *where am I? This isn't right. Something's drastically wrong!*

"Mom, are you sure this is Freemont? It just doesn't feel right. We must be at the wrong school!"

"I'm sure it seems strange at first. After all, it's been a long time since you were here. I know you'll do fine after being here a little while."

It felt so disorienting, like outer space—vast, dark, empty with weird, unidentifiable stuff all around me. Standing there, stunned and frozen in my tracks, I tried to figure out what to do next.

I know—listen for my friends. I'll be able to recognize their voices for sure!

I jumped with a start as the familiar bell rang loud right beside me. And like a flash flood, the halls instantly filled with rushing students. The cold, unfriendly atmosphere hit with an icy chill as rude bodies shoved Mom and me back against the wall. No one came up to say hi. No one even yelled across the hall to greet me. I knew my friends had to be there, but where were they? Present like silent thieves sneaking through the dark night.

Had I believed in omens, this would have been one for sure. It spelled out my plight for the next five years of school. I would never wish that kind of torture on even my worst enemy. My feeling of being in a totally different world didn't end with that entrance back to eighth grade. Instead, it grew to monumental proportions. It seemed as though every friend I ever knew had been vaporized out of existence.

Even my very best friend, Carrie, who lived right next door, became invisible. Although we caught the same school bus every morning, there was not even a whisper of her voice or a clue of her presence. I decided to do a little investigating on my own. I asked the school counselor if Carrie still went to our school. He assured me that she was there every day, and even in some of the same classes with me. This shattered my heart into crumbs.

Oh, how I longed for the "good old days" of seventh grade. Those fun packed times were still so vivid in my mind as if they had just happened yesterday. Especially memorable was the last week in seventh grade with all its activities.

Carrie and I were super busy preparing for our big end of the year celebrations. We were a part of Girls League and together we baked cookies and selected a DJ for the dance. Another major project was decorating the gym. Our job was to cover the walls with highlights from the year. Some of those were my favorites, as well.

We started in one corner with pictures from the Junior Rose Festival Parade. They swirled into a colorful collage. Boy, did that ever hit me with a pleasant flashback. I was selected to play my clarinet in that parade. This was a high honor and a big payoff for a lot of hard work. What a wonderful event it was. Even the weather cooperated with blue sky and sunshine. Our band did well, too. The crowds cheered and applauded us several times. Boy, was that a real energy booster. By the end, all of us were hot and exhausted. That didn't stop us from more fun. The Rose Festival Committee served each of the band members a tall ice cream cone and lemonade in the cool shade of Lloyd Center Park. The boys in our band decided to cool down all the hotheaded girls. And, I must say, they were very successful, too. The quiet flowing fountain in the center of that park turned into a free-for-all water fight. Paper cups full of water flew in every direction. Despite all of the screams and protests, we girls truly enjoyed it.

We had just finished the parade display and...Boom! In came the rest of the kids. That was a real blast. We had invited all seventh-grade students to join us in decorating the last bare wall. Lots of creative artists lined up there with posters and memorabilia.

Carrie and the other Girls League Members encouraged me to display my blue ribbon from the Science Fair Project and a picture of me in my band outfit. They insisted I post my campaign slogan for Student Body Secretary, "Remember, dynamite comes in small packages." Without a doubt, I had to include the picture of the Tea Party Dress. I designed and wore it at the Fashion Show. It was for sure one-of-a-kind, never-to-be-replicated, with its hundreds of dangling tea bags. One girl spotted my Honor Society Certificate and said that was a must, too.

Our celebration kicked off in high gear with a great DJ from KISN Radio Station. He danced with several of us girls during his breaks making this day very special. Near the collage were heard many comments and rounds of laughter. What a way to end the school year and usher in summer vacation. And was I ever ready for a break. Those three months were going to be extra fun and free.

Summer vacation turned out to be anything but fun. It was a major disaster with the brain surgery and instant blindness. I survived that summer but things didn't get any better. In the eighth grade, I became a social outcast. My popularity was gone. School life was friendless and void of fun. Instead, I was the target for name calling and mean tricks. It was as though I was surrounded by aliens and hoards of strangers.

I made it a habit to find a seat closest to the classroom door. That way I didn't have to negotiate through a maze of desks and chairs. Although this made it more accessible for me, it also made my purse more accessible to thieves. As the bell rang to dismiss class, kids brazenly snatched my purse off the floor beside my feet. The cruelty stabbed my heart with deep pangs each time it happened. I kept asking myself why any of my fellow students would do that? And why didn't someone identify the culprit? That would have been enough agony in itself, but with each theft, more valuables disappeared. The first time, I lost irreplaceable things like my only picture of Grandma with a precious tactile broach she had given me. What a headache to get my student body ID card replaced and replaced. I had no sooner purchased a new purse, wallet and cosmetics when a thief hit again. But when my brand new winter coat disappeared from my locker, Dad was furious. In a huff of anger, he marched to the principal and ordered a stop to this disgrace! Those were the days of loneliness and tears.

I did not want to bother my family, so I tried to hide it. But, every night behind my closed bedroom door, I bawled myself to sleep.

One soggy pillow night, my mind and body were tossing and turning with restless emotion.

I just can't take it—no friends, no fun, and no future! I'd be doing everyone a favor if I just disappeared off the face of the earth.

I was convinced there was no reason to go on living—it was time to put my plan into action. Many tear-filled restless nights had given me plenty of time to think about how I could end this mess.

Once Dad was snoring, I would quietly open the bathroom window and climb out. I'd walk the short half block to Sandy Boulevard. There I would listen for a semi truck and make sure it was a really big one so that it would smash me and kill me for sure. I couldn't bear the thought of waking up to another day.

Throwing back the covers, I pulled my warm robe off the wall hook, then slipped into my tennis shoes. With a secure double knot tied in each shoe, I was ready. Tip-toeing to my parents' door, I leaned over with my ear snuggled up to the crack.

Yes, Dad's snoring! I'm out of here!

Just as quietly, I snuck to the bathroom. That bathroom window was more of a challenge than I anticipated. But with an extra push and a loud clunk, it was open all the way. Climbing out a window was a first for me, and my clumsy exit was rather a noisy one, too. Finally, my feet hit the ground.

Phew, I made it! Now to find Sandy Boulevard.

I stumbled with skittish steps and made it across our front lawn. The crunch of gravel under my foot told me it was our side street. Pausing with a gulp of fear, I turned left and headed toward Sandy. With hesitance and sluggish steps, I inched through the eerie silence of the bone-chilling darkness. As I halted to wipe tears from my cheeks—the silence was broken with a panicked shout.

"Pam, Pam! Stop!"

It was Dad! And less than a moment later, he was at my side. Wrapping his loving arms around me, he said, "Oh, Kitten, what are you doing out here? I heard a loud noise and got up to check on you."

The only answer that came out was a gush of sobbing tears. Dad's loving arms and secure hug convinced me that there really was something worth living for. With the love and support of my family, I couldn't lose.

The loving support of my family helped so much, but the constant hurt from Junior High deepened daily. Another soggy pillow night, Dad heard my crying. He came into my bedroom and, sitting on the edge of my bed, asked what was wrong.

"The kids are so mean to me," I cried. "All my friends totally ignore me and make sure I can't find them. The only ones that do talk to me are those who call me names or play tricks on me. Today, I got my lunch tray and finally found an empty place to sit. I put my tray down on the table. And, can you believe it! Someone darted right between me and the table and sat down in my spot. There went both my lunch and my dignity.

"You know how hard I try to move through the halls without bumping anyone. But, yesterday in the crowded hall, I barely brushed against a girl. I immediately apologized, and guess what she said: 'You should be sorry, you pig.' Dad, I just can't go back there anymore!"

Dad's wise words came to my rescue. "Pam, I know it's really hard for you now, and it isn't right for the kids to be so mean. But here's how it works: Young teenagers are naturally selfish and self centered. Unless someone older and wiser sits down with them and explains things to them, they don't know the difference. So, don't be too hard on your friends. Just give them some time to grow up, and you'll see a big change in how they act. Honey, just remember that your family is here for you."

I knew Dad was right but it was hard to feel positive. Major losses, rejection, and disappointment caused a constant inner churning of anger and bitterness. It was hard for me to see anything good about my life.

Pollyanna also vanished from my life during the first part of eighth grade. I just couldn't find anything to be thankful for. I grumbled under my breath and then began doing something way out of character for me. Swear words punctuated my bouts of anger and popped out of my mouth without warning. I knew this was not appropriate and definitely not my family's style. Truthfully, I didn't give a rip whether they liked it or not.

Then came insult to injury, or so it seemed—the Commission for the Blind talked my parents into sending a home teacher. I was somewhat okay with this idea, but that was sure not how I felt after her first visit.

Of all the hare-brained ideas! That woman says I should learn Braille and how to go places by myself on the city bus! No way! That's absurd!

When she told me I could walk down our front porch steps by myself, my inner being coiled up in knots of intense fear. That same evening of the teacher's visit, Dad called home from California where he was racing his cars. Thank goodness for Dad and what timing, too! Whenever out of town racing, he called home often and always made a point to talk to each of us individually. So when my turn came, I informed him of the teacher's visit and her disgusting proposal.

"I don't need to learn Braille, Dad. After all, the doctor said I can get some of my sight back. So, I won't need Braille."

"Yes, you could get some of your sight back, and we all hope that will be the case, but for now, why not learn Braille? It will be one more special thing you know that other people don't."

That simple suggestion from Dad put my mind at ease, and I was ready to tackle this new project. Braille was not at all what I expected. I had pictured it as regular print letters written in relief. And, quite frankly, it was more of a challenge than I had bargained for. Memorizing the different combinations of dots making up each letter was a snap for my sharp mind. But, being able to recognize the letters by touch was a real chore.

Braille letters are made up of dots in different patterns. Those letters containing up to three dots were fairly easy to feel. After letter 'm,' the number of dots increased to four, then five. The last half of the alphabet was a real headache to learn to read by touch. I spent several minutes on just one letter trying to feel the configuration of its dots.

Is this an 'r' with four dots or letter 'q' with five dots?

Even though my teacher said not to—in desperation, I used my long fingernail and caught it on each dot in that space. The Braille lessons went on and on, so it seemed, with the teacher visiting our home weekly.

27

Of all things, my homework was to read, "The Little Red Hen." How demoralizing! There I was…soon-to-be teenager and a straight 'A' student struggling to read a super simple children's book. I certainly was not about to let anybody know of this ridiculous endeavor. I was quite put out at first, but Dad's words on the telephone echoed in my mind. "Why not? It's a unique skill. And besides, it's just a steppingstone to bigger and better things."

That pep talk to myself got me moving, but it remained a real struggle. In the beginning, I labored at least a minute to figure out a single letter. Often, by the time I plodded through five or six letters, I had forgotten the beginning of the word. With time, practice and interludes of grumbling, I got to the point where I could read, "The Little Red Hen" almost fluently.

In those days, my sole reason for living was my family. At least they loved and accepted me. Once I stepped through the front door of our home, I was no longer a failure, no longer a misfit. Mom, Dad and my brother, Steve, were what kept me going.

Mom was always there for me. Even with a full-time job, she made sure to get home about the same time Steve and I arrived from school. After a long day at work, there she was, standing beside the ironing board pressing the family's clothes. Those were the days long before the drip-dry, wash and wear clothes. This meant hours of ironing for Mom every week. And every week, at the end of her ironing board, was one of my textbooks. Mom painstakingly read my textbooks and homework assignments while doing her household tasks.

Since I could write Braille at about the speed of a three-legged turtle, it took hours to do simple homework assignments. But, thanks to Mom, my home tutor, I kept up in school and maintained my high grade point average.

On the social front, my brother, Steve, was the most helpful. He was much taller and looked older even though three years younger than me. We were like high school friends. I longed to go to the school dances or out on a date, but this never happened. Things changed when Steve got his driver's license and bought a car. The first thing he did was ask me to go out for pizza with him. It was terrific! And get this—he didn't want me to use my white cane but instead held my hand—like boyfriend and girlfriend. With the onset of pizza, McDonald's hamburgers and just cruising on the freeway with Steve, social enjoyment came back into my life once again. Steve's genuine enjoyment of me as a companion helped me gain that much needed positive view of myself.

The bond between us deepened even more when Dad's disapproval of Steve flared. Dad's traditional conservative ways didn't see eye to eye with Steve's new hippy-like lifestyle. Rejection was nothing new for me. With the demoralizing aftermath of Dad's sharp disgust, my heart ached for Steve. I then made a point to spend quality time with him. As he accepted me, I accepted him. We were pals.

Dad was not on the scene as much since racing took him out of town often. His racing career began on the East Coast where he quickly gained fame. Within a few short months, he was chosen for one of the most prestigious driving positions. The Ford Factory chose him to be one of the drivers on their racing team. His East Coast tour was shorter than he would have liked. Mom was afraid of losing her husband, and rightly so. Just a few years prior, Dad's younger brother was killed instantly while setting a new track record with his Indy car. Mom talked Dad into moving back home to Portland, Oregon.

He followed his love for cars and took a salesman position at Dick Niles Lincoln Mercury Dealership. Mr. Niles was a race enthusiast and knew about Dad's outstanding ability. Dick convinced Dad to drive for the Dealership. That was easier than an adult winning an arm wrestling contest with a newborn baby.

When Dad was home—wow! He was such a positive, cheerful influence, and that was just what I needed. One month back in Junior High left me with a long, long list of things I couldn't do.

One day I could no longer hold in the despair of all my losses. Thank goodness Dad was home and saw my grief. He asked me to sit beside him on the loveseat. With a loving arm around me, he asked, "What's going on?"

"Dad, what's the use of going on! I can't ride my bike, can't play my clarinet in the band and can't find any friends. On and on went the list of all the "I can't do" things. In his loving wisdom, Dad said, "Pam, it's true there are things you can't do, but I'm sure there are lots of things you can do. When you think of something you want to do, let me know, and I'll help you figure out how to do it."

About a year had passed since the surgery and the doctors were right. I did get a little sight back, but much less than anticipated. Nonetheless, I was delighted to be able to see anything. I found something I liked—bright neon signs. The large neon signs showed up well for me in the dark. At least I could see something, and this meant a lot to me. Dad started a tradition that added enjoyment to my life. Many evenings each week after dinner and the dishes were done, Dad would say, "Pam, want to go out for a Coke?" In a split second, my jacket was on and we were headed out the back door to the car. Our destination was 82nd Avenue, where the big bright neon signs were abundant.

Driving just barely the speed limit, Dad would announce each oncoming neon sign. I could see nothing more than a bright glow, no colors, details or shapes. Dad carefully described each one. I would close my eyes to concentrate intently so that in my mind, I could change that bright blob into a lifelike picture. Driving slow was anything but natural for Dad—yet he never complained. Near the end of this neon strip was McDonald's. At that point, it was a quick left turn into their parking lot. At the drive-through window, we ordered our favorite snack—a large ice cream cone for Dad and a diet Coke for me.

It was off to the freeway for more fun. Here is where Dad's racing kicked into high gear. He knew I loved to go fast, so pushing the speed limit as far as possible, we hit the straight-aways and corners in style! Oh, how I loved the feeling of my body being plastered to the car door as Dad took corners. And I'll never forget that one night, Dad and I had just come off the freeway and pulled up to a stop light by Madison High School.

"Pam, there's a high school boy in the car beside us and he thinks he's pretty hot stuff, probably trying to impress his girlfriend in the front seat. Shall we blow him off?"

With bright eyes and a giggle, I said, "Sure, go for it, Dad!"

And that's just what we did! The red light changed to green and we peeled out of there, leaving that hot-shot several car lengths behind. With a neon bright beam, I turned to smile at Dad as he slowed down to the speed limit. "Well, I guess we showed him a thing or two, didn't we?"

"We sure did! Thanks, Dad!"

Dad kept his word about helping me do things I wanted to. When I told him I wished I could ride my bike again, a tandem bike soon appeared in our driveway. I became an instant con artist—conning every one I could into riding with me.

My family was vital in helping the Pollyanna way of life come back for me. With the addition of fun, I was again able to smile. Mom patiently and diligently continued teaching me how to do things at home.

Ever since going blind, any smile on my face was just a mask. Finally, with accomplishments under my belt and fun on my calendar, I was able to smile from my heart. As the thick shell of worthlessness started dwindling, I began to believe someone might enjoy having me as their friend. That belief turned into reality after a couple of years. Some of my fondest summer outings were bicycle rides through the neighborhood with a girlfriend.

CHAPTER 4
OFF TO THE RACES

A brand new adventure had accelerated into high gear the summer after eighth grade. Dad advanced from driving racecars to promoting auto races. Our family bought the Yakima Speedway in Yakima, Washington.

Mom and Dad were dynamic, high-production people. Dad, for example, held down a 40-hour work week as a car salesman and then drove a stock car for every event in the auto racing season. That meant he was racing almost every weekend at least six months out of the year. Much of his other free time was spent working on the car with the race team mechanics. Test laps around the Portland Speedway oval track took place regularly, too. Dad always made sure his car would handle the corners and go fast enough to be competitive or beat the current fastest time set for that track.

Dad was just as fast off the racetrack as on it. One phrase he often used was, "Don't just stand there! Do something!" He was a perfectionist, as well. He sat us kids down at a young age and said, "Remember—anything worth having in life will take work. And, if it's worth doing at all, it's worth doing it the best you can."

Mom was just as active and productive, but focused on family. Outside the home, she held down a full-time job of computer data entry. Inside our home, she was an excellent homemaker and had the best set of listening ears. Steve and I knew that we could always talk to Mom about anything.

Mom's commitment to family went well beyond our close-knit foursome. How well I remember the way she showed love to Grandma Amick, her mother-in-law. Grandma lived next door in a small home. Since she couldn't walk or go anywhere outside by herself, Mom made sure to include Grandma whenever we went grocery shopping or did errands. We kids were instructed to check on Grandma as soon as we got home from school. Mom visited often and put up Grandma's hair in curlers every week so she'd look nice for church on Sunday. I marveled how patient and loving Mom was. She always had so much work to do at home, but never grumbled about including Grandma.

Walking with a heavy wooden leg was a real chore for Grandma. Quite frankly, I was the one who found it hard to be pleasant and patient with that turtle-like pace.

Mom knew how to take care of the family, and she could handle the business of the racetrack just as well. They really worked hard with dedicated diligence until the job was done. Following the footsteps of such productive parents kept Steve and me constantly on the go. The fast-paced lifestyle was no stranger to our family, but with Dad's new position, things revved into a drag strip blur. Right away, Dad informed us that this would be a family business. This new development meant that Steve and I had to give up our night owl excursions. That wasn't the kind of news we wanted to hear. But…5:00 in the morning—that was a real shock to the system!

The first five AM came with a rude and very abrupt awakening. Four bodies wandered through the house in the mental fog of that predawn hour. After a short time of stirring around, Dad, our very own family cheerleader and trail boss, came alive. He was so cheerful and positive.

Despite all the excitement and anticipation of what was ahead, once in the car, we former night owls soon fell fast asleep. Dad motored our shiny metallic blue Mercury Marquis with great skill and excellent speed down the Columbia Gorge Freeway.

He wouldn't own a car without lots of power under the hood, and this one was even better than most. The crew of racecar mechanics at the Dick Nile Dealership specially installed a 440 racing engine under the hood for Dad. With confidence in Dad's smooth driving, slumber was sweet.

Then the car came to a distinct halt and Dad announced, "pit stop." With the Texaco restrooms staring us in the face, we quickly realized what he meant by "pit stop"—our first phrase in Racing Terminology 101. The cool morning air breezing across my face and a quick stretch were most welcome.

Within the blink of an eye, Dad called us back to the car to finish our long four-hour trip.

Finally, we pulled into the driveway of Yakima Speedway. Four severe cases of saddle sores emerged from our car, groaning and stretching stiff muscles. And first out of the car was me.

No way was I going to get left behind. After all, I had more than my share of being left out. Eighth grade had filled the rejection quota to overflowing. No matter what it took, I was going to be a part of this team and a contributing one at that! With a firm grasp of Dad's arm and white cane in hand, we were off to tour the grounds. It was inspector Bill Amick and crew on the scene.

Dad was a top-notch racecar driver and just as knowledgeable in running a business. So, inspection of the grandstand, concession stand, restrooms and, of course, the half mile asphalt oval racetrack was done methodically. After climbing up and down the tall grandstands, walking the half-mile oval several times, and crawling in and out of storage spaces, all four of us were exhausted, sweaty and dirty. That long day ended with oh-so-welcome warm showers at a nice clean motel. Even Steve and I had no complaints about an early bedtime that night.

Six AM came extra quickly the next morning. What a melodious symphony issued in our day—the blaring alarm and a quartette of groaning yawns. Then came Dad's familiar morning greeting, "Okay, everybody, jump in your jeans." We were off to the racetrack again.

During our short four-minute trip from motel to speedway, I reminded Dad, "I want to help out, too." And, not to my surprise, he already had a game plan with specific assignments for each of us. Heavy-duty cleaning and a fresh coat of paint—that was our mission.

"You girls," Dad directed, "can start by painting the inside of the restrooms. I bought some nice fresh mint green paint for you." The boys (Dad and Steve) were off across the property to replace weak boards in the grandstands.

Opening the car door, I stepped onto the coarse gravel parking lot in a bit of a daze. My emotions were mixed wondering how I could paint anything without making a major mess. At the same time, I was delighted to be part of the action. Mom and I each gathered our tools from the trunk of our car and headed off toward the restrooms.

"Mom, how can I paint without making a big mess?"

"Well, Pam, here's a roller. You just paint the center of the walls and I'll follow after you with my brush to touch up any spots you missed and paint around the edges."

Not long into our painting spree, I accidentally bumped Mom's elbow with my roller. A few seconds later, Mom turned around and hit me in the rear with her paint brush. Both were accidental, but we howled with laughter as Mom said, "I'm just evening up the score. You know one green elbow deserves one green hip."

Well, I must say that we were quite productive in our painting, but equally industrious with our non-wall painting. We were just finishing as Dad came around the corner and announced, "It's time to call it a day and go out for dinner." He took one look at us and with a chuckle said, "Guess we'll go through the drive-through tonight."

That prompted Mom to take a good look at herself in the mirror. She burst into laughter. "Pam! You should see us! We're covered with splattered green freckles through our hair and all over our faces. And, you have a green smudge of rouge on your right cheek."

Again, we were in hysterics with laughter. Although we'd never set any fashion trends, we both agreed that at least we had a handle on color coordination—every part of us matched—green, green and then more green.

Mom had an outstanding ability to teach me and help me figure out adaptive ways to do things. Our painting of the restroom interiors, for example, went well. The finished product looked almost professional. And the best part was that we had fun doing it!

I guess Dad wanted to enjoy dinner in a sit down restaurant the next night because there were no more paint assignments for us girls. That didn't mean we were unemployed by any means. We worked just as hard sanding counter tops and scrubbing everything possible in the concession stand. Again, we were all worn out and very happy with a shower and early bedtime.

It was literally "off to the races" (I should say off to the racetrack) every weekend for the next three months. The racing season would kick off with the Apple Cup Challenge Race the first weekend in April. In those months of getting everything ready, it seemed as though we did more racing around than the stock cars.

That meant many challenges and obstacles had to be overcome if I were going to be a productive team player. The brain tumor did lots more damage than just ruining my eyesight. It destroyed my pituitary gland and body thermostat. Without a body thermostat, I couldn't tolerate hot weather. When the temperature rose above 78 degrees, I was not only miserable but at serious risk of heatstroke.

This combination of my heat intolerance and hot summer days in Yakima posed a real challenge. 102 degrees was not uncommon on a summer afternoon. A saving grace for me was the definite sign of impending heatstroke. When I was almost to the point of heatstroke, my face would turn beet red. The blood vessels near my skin dilated in a desperate attempt to cool down my body. One race day, it was beastly hot. I got so overheated that my face looked badly sun burnt. My family always looked out for me with loving esteem, and this time was no exception.

As part of the pre-race routine, a couple of men would go get a load of bagged ice for the Pepsi fountain drinks. Almost like a military marching parade, one by one those huge fifty pound brown paper sacks of ice came through the back door of the concession stand until a miniature mountain much taller than me loomed high up in the corner. Dad was on his usual tour of the grounds making sure everything was going smoothly and on schedule. He stepped in the back room and with one glance at me said, "Pam, you look like a lobster! We've got to get you cooled down!"

Immediately, he went to work fashioning a cool solution to my hot head. Flattening and arranging the ice bags just so, he fashioned a bed for me. Talk about relief! I think a huge cloud of steam rose as I stretched out on that unique ice bed. That race day event was a special one for me. I can't recall who won the race, nor the date, but I'll always remember what a "cool" dad I had.

My job was to work in the concession stand. I was really excited about that. Long before the opening day, I dreamt about operating a cash register and serving customers. The time for opening day grew closer and I could hardly wait for my new job.

What a blast! I'll be right up front working with the other girls, and close to the racetrack. That'll put me in the perfect spot to hear the different sounds as the engines roar down the straight-away.

Well, that is not what happened! Several days before the grand opening, our family got together for a common occurrence which Dad called "strategizing." It was then that Dad outlined how everything would work and where each person was assigned. To my shock and utter disappointment, I would be working in the very back of the concession stand wrapping hot dogs. What a blow! With tears in my voice, I approached Dad with my plea to work out front.

In a very matter of fact fashion, common to Dad's way, he explained that it wouldn't work because I could not see the money. This was double disaster—my dream shattered and my nose rubbed in the fact that I was blind!

Here we go again—more things I can't do! It's not fair! All I want is to be like the rest of the kids. That's not much to ask, is it?

I couldn't hold the disappointment in any longer. So, into the restroom I rushed. After several minutes of crying and swearing behind that locked door, I drenched my face with cold water. Mom's wise words rang again in my mind—"Well, Pam, this sure isn't what I wanted to happen, and it's not what I planned. But, I can't change it. So, let's pick up the pieces and see how we can make the best of what's left." With my pride swallowed and tears dried, I exited the restroom with a new plan of attack. I would find some things I could do and do my best!

I became a master candy bar detective—hunting for bumps, shapes, and any clues to identify the candy bar by touch. This, of course, was a valuable skill since one of my jobs was to stock all the candy bar displays before the concession stand opened. And a "Smooth Operator" too—that was my new self-appointed title. Cleaning the glass and metal counters was another duty of mine.

I could feel the distinct difference that my cleaning efforts made. A real sense of satisfaction and pride filled me as I felt the gritty, dust coated counters disappear into slick, smooth, freshly cleaned surfaces ready for the next race day. I never did work at the front counter. But, with a Pollyanna focus, I found lots of enjoyment laughing and joking with the rest of the gals. Finally, I was a part—a productive part—and that made working in the back A-Okay with me.

CHAPTER 5
PEDAL TO THE METAL

After several very successful years in the race-promotion business, NASCAR asked Dad to be their NW Regional Representative. I thought we were moving fast before, but with this new position, it was truly "pedal to the metal" all the time. We branched out from just owning and operating Yakima Speedway to promoting NASCAR races at seven other speedways in Oregon and Washington.

It was not uncommon for our family foursome to travel to three different racetracks in a weekend. One of my favored tracks to visit was the Monroe Speedway in Monroe, Washington. Every year, Dad managed a full week of stockcar races during their State Fair. Since Mom and I did not need to work there, we were free to tour the Fair. And tour we did! Our fair ground fun usually started off with a freshly baked raspberry scone. By noon, we had worked up enough of an appetite to warrant a stop at both the corn-on-the-cob stand and the hot dog booth. What fun-filled days!

My family always watched out for things I could do and enjoy. What I enjoyed the most was anything that I could "see" by using my other senses. This meant that in the livestock barns, I wanted to pet every animal possible. If my family could get me up close enough to touch something, they were sure to do just that. One year, the smallest horse in the world was on exhibit. And, of course, I had to get close enough to touch him. What a thrill to hold in my hand his tiny little hoof. He was about the size of a black Labrador dog. And when the baby pig squealed, I was so tickled that I squealed with delight, myself.

When it came to the actual races, I didn't get much out of watching them. The general public, on the other hand, felt quite different. The top-name drivers, fast speeds and tense competition drew large crowds. The grandstands reverberated with loud whoops, rambunctious cheering and foot-stomping approval. Loyal fans rallied to support their favorite driver.

Occasionally, to be socially congenial, I would walk with someone outside the concession stand to watch the races, but for me it was boring. Big deal—standing on a gravel bank in the scorching sun just to listen to loud, I mean extra loud, engines recycling round and round. Everything blurred into an indistinct ear-throbbing roar.

But after the race, that was my time. Dad and Steve filled me in on all the interesting details, like who won the race, accidents and such. Then came the best part—Dad would pop into the concession stand and say, "Pam, are you ready to head for the pits?"

"You bet! Just a few more hot dogs to wrap and I'll be there."

It was one quick fold to finish wrapping the last one and off flew my apron. *Yea! It's my turn to have fun.* Down the long flight of concrete steps and across the hot asphalt racetrack we went. With each step, my anticipation and excitement built.

Just a few more steps and we'll be there!

The abrupt asphalt edge yielded to soft gravel, announcing my entrance into the pits. The first stop was the winners' circle. I really enjoyed hearing all the details from the driver, himself. I was totally engrossed until Dad's hand tapped my arm. "Pam, let's go check out the second place winner. He's got a real hot Camaro." *Oh, boy, time for a close up look.* This meant a hands-on tour. I got to feel the intense heat of the hood, dents and newly accumulated scars from the day's events. This made the races come alive for me. I even got several hugs from my favorite drivers and the pit boss. For me, this was more exciting and fun than watching any checkered flag wave the winning car across the finish line.

Probably one of the most exciting events for me happened at our own Yakima Speedway. Steve was practicing his driving so that he could get his license in August. Dad decided that an empty racetrack would be the perfect place for Steve to sharpen his driving skills. It became a routine that before the races, Steve would take the family car for several laps around the empty track.

One morning, Steve entered the concession stand to tell Mom he was going to take a practice lap. Dear Mother, a bit of a worrywart, turned to me and said, "Pam, why don't you ride with your brother? Maybe you can keep him from driving too fast." That sounded great to me! I always enjoyed riding in the car with Steve, and I jumped at any excuse to get a break from cleaning the concession stand.

"Okay, Pam, I'm ready to head out. How about you?"

Steve took my hand and we began our methodical maneuver through the back storage room. We side-stepped around the huge cases of Pepsi cups. Dodging sharp cornered cases of candy bars, popcorn and supplies, we continued weaving through the overpopulated metropolis of cardboard towers. This trip almost always kicked my claustrophobia into high gear. What a gagger—stifling hot air and ink-laden cardboard swirled together with high desert dust. This made the tedious trip draw out like an old overused rubber band that defies breaking and just stretches on and on. A distinct twist in Steve's wrist was my clue to follow directly behind him. It took turning sideways and walking single file to clear the big box fan angled beside the back door.

"Oh, Steve! Fresh, cool air! This is my favorite time in the summer. I really appreciate how you stop by to get me. Just spending time with you is always neat."

"Yeah. We don't get much chance to do that. Dad always keeps us running in every direction."

At the outer perimeter of the huge gravel lot was our family car. In an almost business-like manner, we opened the doors with determination. Fastening our seatbelts, we headed for the track.

Monitoring Steve's driving speed came easy for me. After all, I had lots of practice from the many evening cruises on the freeway with Dad. As we sped along the freeway, Dad would keep me posted on how fast we were going. With no distraction from the scenery, I focused on the feel of the ride, its vibrations and sounds. I became so tuned into its motion that I could often guess what speed we were going.

I suppose it's similar to being a good horseback rider. According to those in the know, a good rider feels with his horse and becomes one with it. I had never experienced that oneness with a horse. However, it seems that I turned into a true auto jock—becoming one with the speed and motion of our car.

Oh, how I loved the feel of the way Steve took the curves. As he drove through the curves, I felt a unique centrifugal force that almost plastered my body against the door. Other than my dad, I'd never ridden with anyone who took the corners like that. And, of course, those kinds of experiences were extra special for me.

"One more lap, and we'd better head in," Steve said. He upped the speed just a tad, and a big smile beamed across my face. Down deep, there was quite a bit of racing blood in my veins and it just couldn't help but pop out every now and then. As we rounded the second turn, Steve blurted out a four-letter swear word. I knew that meant trouble. All I could do was close my eyes (as if that would make any difference), hold on for dear life and pray. I felt the speed accelerate. We were going way too fast and not straight ahead anymore!

Out of control! Out of control!

My heart was pounding much faster than the car was racing. With a loud rear crashing sound, the car came to a jolting stop. Too stunned to move, we both sat silent for a few extremely long seconds. Finally, I worked up enough courage to ask, "What happened?"

"I got too close to the edge of the track, panicked, and hit the gas. I'm getting out to check the damage."

At the moment those words left his lips, my hand went for the door handle. I was out of the car as quickly as my brother. I couldn't sit idly by and let him face that alone. After all, he was my brother, and I was just as much a part.

The only damage was a blown-out rear tire. Like a true racer, Dad took it in stride. "Well, Son, you've just learned a valuable lesson. I'd much rather have a tire ruined than you hurt, so just chalk this one up to experience."

Well, at that moment, I ruled out the option of ever moonlighting as a driver's education assistant. But my love for racing was not affected. It held just as strong as ever.

Many special non-racing events were sprinkled throughout the season— grandiose Easter egg hunts, hot air balloon rides rising up from the pits and demolition derbies, just to name a few.

The most memorable for me was when the famous stunt rider, Evel Knievel, came to our speedway. He was well-known for jumping his motorcycle over a long row of cars lined up side by side. Before his daredevil stunt, Dad took me out to meet Mr. Knievel in person—a real treat. He explained in interesting detail how he performed this feat. His motorcycle's speed on approach to the ramps was crucial and must be exact.

The angle of his approach, direction and velocity of the wind were all major impacting factors, and of the utmost importance, was being able to land with the rear wheel touching down first. The one thing that flabbergasted me was the fact that this VIP actually enjoyed talking to me—just a blind nobody! Wow! Did that ever make my day!

Summer after summer, trip after trip, we went from our Portland home to Yakima and back. I watched Mom and Dad get so weary from all the driving.

How I wished I could drive! Poor Dad is so tired! Just wish I could take the wheel and give him a break.

"Oh, Dad, if only I could drive! I'd love to sub in and give you a break."

Dad said, "You know, Pam, I wish you could drive, too, but there is something special you can do to help. You can be my copilot. That would be a big help."

I quickly learned the ropes of my new job, which meant sitting up front and talking with the driver to keep him awake. Dad told me that it helped the driver stay more alert if they had something to snack on. With that new fact, I went to work. Ahead of each departure, I prepared special finger-food snacks for the front seat people. The two-member back seat crew was welcome to join in, but most of the time, they were engaged in badly needed shut-eye until the next pit stop.

Each summer flew by, filled with lots of action, and an overload of hard work. Being blind does not slow the mind, but it sure decreases the speed of everyday activity. Even the simple routine tasks take special techniques and are much slower than the methods used by a sighted person. The combination of a snail's pace together with my decreased physical stamina meant this fast paced lifestyle was anything but comfortable or easy.

From the time my eyes first opened each morning, I was racing, racing, racing in an attempt to keep up with my dynamic family. My day finished with collapsing into bed feeling beyond exhausted. I knew full well that I had pushed way beyond the limit of my physical endurance. No one ever forced me to keep this pace, but my 200% inner drive would not let me sit idly. I could never be satisfied with anything short of doing my very best.

That inner drive surfaced with much the same effect in Junior and Senior High School. I pushed just as hard in the academic arena. Being new to the world of blindness and unable to read any print, I had to work much harder than the average student. At the beginning of eighth grade, it was almost like working a double shift. Technically, I was an eighth grader. But when it came to reading and writing Braille, it was first grade all the way. It took lots of studying for several months before the Braille was a useful skill. Near the end of my freshman year I finally felt accomplished in doing my studies independently.

The high school principal and teachers were very good to me. They provided a conference room to be used only by me. This became my study hall. When the rest of the students congregated in a large study hall, I met with a sighted reader in my own room. That small 9 x 9 foot room was well stocked. Along one wall stood a miniature library of Braille and recorded books. Lining the full length of the opposite wall was a work table with Braillewriter, typewriter, record player, ream of Braille paper and typing paper. There was nothing compact about any of my equipment.

How I laughed when my Braille teacher handed me my first Braille dictionary, "The Vest Pocket Dictionary." Reaching out with one hand, I expected a think paperback book. "You're kidding," I giggled. "This thing is huge!"

"Wait a minute," Mrs. Sanders said. "Here's the second volume." Each binder was 4 inches wide with 12 x 12 inch hard bound covers. There was no way that was going to fit in anybody's vest pocket.

With time, this plain utility room became much more than just a study hall. When overwhelmed by the crowded halls or hit head-on with cruel comments, I always had a place to retreat. Once inside, locking the door behind me, its quiet safety held me with comforting arms.

Always handy atop my worktable was a large box of facial tissue. And what a friend it became. Without even a whisper of rejection, it softly absorbed my scores of tears. By midafternoon most days, my energy had dwindled to below zero. Nestled between the tall bookcase and large cabinet was my favorite spot. A small chair and pillow in that corner of calmness beckoned with the offer of a reviving catnap—what a saving grace. Even with all that specialized equipment and an extra study hall period every school day, my workload was long and relentless.

Truthfully, not all the blame rested on the shoulders of blindness. I was an outcast and total failure in the social arena. With the haunting heartache of demoralizing rejection, I determined to focus my energy and attention on success in the academic sphere. That was the only way I knew to prove that I was not a worthless heap of trash.

Burning the midnight oil was not uncommon. Whatever it took, I was determined to do. My homework had to be completed, and done with excellence. Even though I knew this was a heavy physical drain, that didn't bother me. Besides, the worst thing that could happen would be to have my body just fizzle out and quit. As far as I was concerned, that wouldn't be so bad after all.

From eighth grade right on to graduation, I lived for each three-month summer vacation. And, finally, graduation with the summer break had come. This one was extra special! The start of this summer meant the end of high school forever! My hard work paid off—I was salutatorian of our three hundred plus graduating class.

Hooray! I can kiss the homework good-bye! I'll have time to rest and do some fun things.

True, the homework was gone, but the work, work, work was soon ahead. We had a very busy race season with more than normal big events. Each special promotion meant a double or triple work load for the family. By the time of the last race, I was thinking much the same as I did at graduation. A break—I needed a true vacation!

With the approach of fall, the race season came to a close. At first, the do-nothing pace was refreshing and most welcome. What a change it was! All summer long I had been literally "racing" around. And just prior to the fast paced summer was that busy senior year. But, this new schedule grew old in short order. That first week I rested and rested, but it was more than enough. By the second week, I had a severe case of cabin fever. I was convinced that vegetating as a couch potato was not the answer for me. I had no clue what to do with my life—much less what job or career was possible for a blind person, if any.

Now what? I can't continue living like this! Looks like I'll be a blind beggar after all. The only difference is that I'll be an indoor beggar, instead of sitting outside by the temple like the Bible beggar. Something has to change. If only I could get a job and work like everyone else! But what can a blind person do, anyway? Oh great! What a future to look forward to. I've got to do something, but what?

CHAPTER 6
OFF TRACK, RIGHT ON TARGET

NASCAR and the Yakima Speedway kept racing at top speed, but for me it was the absolute opposite.

One year had passed since high school, and the busy racing season was over, too. But, my life seemed to be in the shutdown mode. I felt like a caged grizzly bear with nowhere to go and nothing to do. Already grown up and I was still unsure what a blind person could do for a living. The longtime dream of being a grade school teacher still flickered within, but how could that happen? I couldn't even travel beyond my front yard much less to any school or classroom.

Mom and Dad had the best intentions for me, and they figured I was doing so well that I needed no additional training. When the Commission for the Blind sent notices of training options, the flyers flew right into the trash can. At that time, I didn't even know about these opportunities. And, quite frankly, there didn't seem to be a need for them since Mom was an excellent teacher. I was quite an accomplished homemaker due to her persistence and patience.

Independence beyond the home, on the other hand, was not only non-existent but totally nebulous to me. Up to this time, I had never gone anywhere alone except to school or inside my own home. My parents or brother always took my hand and guided me from the car door to our destination and back. My family and I had all been quite content with my scholastic and homemaking success.

But, things had changed drastically. The non-sitter within me revolted with much, much more than 200 percent inner drive. Let's face it! I was just fit to be tied and about to die from that stagnating lifestyle. There was no way I could stand being at home all the time! I felt like a prisoner in my own home. Something had to change and mighty fast!

It was time to check out career possibilities. I contacted The Oregon State Commission for the Blind. Mr. Keddler, a career counselor at the Commission, advised me that with my high grade point average, I should attend a four-year college. That was good news because it fit right in line with my dream. I knew it would take that long to get a teaching degree.

To complete the Commission's evaluation, I had to have a physical checkup. The doctor's report came back stating that I didn't have the physical stamina to work full time. The counselor said that teaching grade school was a full-time job. "So Mr. Keddler," I asked, "what are the options other than four years of college?"

"Well, Pam, it's either college or basket weaving."

Talk about a direct blow to the heart. There went my dream, broken just like a priceless crystal platter shattered into a million irretrievable splinters. That meant back to the boredom and hopeless imprisonment within my own home.

Thank goodness for my relatives. They sprung open my jail door. A perfect example was Mom's sister, Aunt Ginny, and her two young daughters. They lived in Portland. Their respect and love was an essential building block in my struggle to regain self-worth. One of Ginny's comments stuck with me and always brought a warm chuckle with each remembrance.

Ginny, Mom and I were sitting in the car headed for the donut shop. In the course of our conversation, Mom casually mentioned that I was really doing well putting on my mascara.

"Oh my gosh, Pam," Ginny said. "You can do your mascara without watching? That's great! I practically have to poke my nose through the mirror just to put mine on."

Her two daughters, Sue and Cathy, contributed much as well. How timely too—right when I was longing for socialization and acceptance—they pitched in. Sue and Cathy were like close girlfriends. It was so much fun spending time with them. They always welcomed me like a special guest and made sure that I was included in games with the other kids on the block.

Being the oldest in the bunch, they even let me lead the way. After adding several other neighborhood kids, we had just the right amount for group games. I taught them a couple new games, "Beckon-Beckon" and "Who's Afraid of the Big Black Bear." Both were big hits.

Looking back, I probably had more fun than they did. It felt so good having friends to hang out with.

I was grateful, too, for Mom's other sister, Aunt Merl! Although she lived miles away with little opportunity to visit, we had a very special bond. She was very knowledgeable and had lots of visually impaired friends, as well. At birth, Merl had a bad eye infection that caused severe scarring. Her vision was so impaired that she spent first through ninth grade at the Oregon School for the Blind.

It was through my Aunt that I learned of the technical college in Olympia, Washington. Their two-year course in Medical Transcription sounded just right for me. I could have a career and a part-time one at that. Not long after that new development, the phone rang.

Good news—Operation Rescue! Mr. Keddler called me about an opportunity to attend a three-month college preparatory course for the blind happening that summer. "Pam, this will be really good for you, and the Commission will pay for the whole works. Such a deal, don't you think?"

Why not?

And, with each consideration, it looked better and better. I had to do something different and do it soon. In the middle of my excitement, apprehension struck.

Three whole months away from my family! Do I really want to go that far away to a totally strange place?

Mom and Dad were very reluctant, too. They had always been so involved in providing for my needs. If I didn't have the skill to do something, they'd help. Sometimes, however, in the midst of their good-hearted intentions came the over-protection factor. I often thought of Dad as a "Little Red Hen" father. He wouldn't stand for my being outside our home all alone. With even a hint that I was about to venture out on my own, Dad appeared at my side, ready to take me wherever I needed to go.

Both Mom and Dad were comfortable with my career research and contact with the Commission for the Blind. But their comfort turned to worry as they read a letter outlining the program. I could tell that they were uneasy with the fact that I would be so far away from the family. Fortunately for me, my parents were always very practical and wanted the best for both their kids. Having watched my agony about the future fester into hopeless depression, they knew it was high time for help.

Whenever there was a major issue in need of resolving, Dad would call our family together for a brainstorming session. This time was no exception. Putting our heads together with a generous scoop of love, we agreed the summer course would be the next best step. Shifting gears again, I revved into high gear and began packing for a three-month stay at the University of Washington in Seattle.

Good thing I didn't know what was ahead. Because had I known even a fraction of the challenges awaiting—no one could have talked me into going. On June 7, 1969, it was "All Aboard!"

The Commission's shuttle was a small twelve-passenger bus. I struggled up the bus's steps with my arms full. Tightly gripped in my right hand was my brown paper sack lunch with purse and bags dangling from that arm. In my other hand was my heavy blue suitcase. After untangling my purse strap and bags from the hand rail, I settled in the seat right behind the driver. With only three blind high school grads on board, counting me, this little bus seemed really empty and large.

The driver cheerfully announced, "Sit back and relax. Next stop Seattle, Washington."

As the hefty engine turned over, our conversations went full speed ahead, as well. The four-hour trip flew by as we three passengers got acquainted. Nellie sat right across the aisle from me, a Portland girl, too. She was born and raised in Portland just like me. Dan, a Salem boy, sat silently way in the back of the bus. If it hadn't been for a quick turn and his radio crashing to the floor, no one would have known he was back there. His radio slid forward and hit my heel. I blocked it with my foot to keep it from going farther. "Hey, Dan, thanks for the special delivery. Looks like a really nice radio." That broke Dan's silence. Moving forward to retrieve his radio he decided to join us girls.

"Hey, I've got to tell you about this crazy city bus driver," Dan said. "I was the only passenger on board. He saw that I was blind so he had to tell me about the prank he played. He borrowed a white cane from a friend and bought a pair of the black sleep shades. His route had a ten-minute layover in the parking lot of a community center. At the end of his break, he came back with the white cane in hand and shades over his eyes.

When he reached the bus door, he really put on the act. He thumped the white cane extra loud as he slowly went up each step, then whacked it a against the fare box as though he were hunting to locate it. He felt around for the steering wheel. Then he groped a little more and slid his hand up the steering column to find the turn signal. He finally got his key in place and turned the engine over, revving it a couple times. Then he announced, 'Well, everybody, I'm ready. Just tell me when the stop light turns green.' At that point, he chuckled and informed me that all this time the bus had been right in the middle of a huge parking lot, blocks away from any streets."

He had both of us girls almost rolling in the aisles with laughter.

Once Nellie was able to catch her breath, she protested, "Oh, Dan, that can't be a true story!"

"Well, according to the driver it is. But, just so happens I wasn't carrying my lie detector with me that day, so who's to know. There's one fact for sure—we both got a thorough kick out of the whole works."

Dan was quite the comedian. With a captive audience, he kept all well entertained.

Then the driver announced our entrance into Seattle. My apprehension and excitement kicked into high gear.

Wow, we're really here! Just think—forty blind students all in the same coed dorm. Sounds fantastic.

Yet, at the same time, the fear of the unknown and my inability to travel alone hit full force. This gripped me so fiercely that my inner being felt like an over-wound spring gnarled into many tight knots.

Oh my, did I really make the right decision? Not sure I'm really ready for this.

CHAPTER 7
SCHOOL DAYS

My interest perked as the driving pattern changed. Our bus hesitated with a brief stop and then began a long sweeping turn to the left. Its speed gradually slowed, ending in a gliding stop.

"Here we are, folks, the University of Washington," the driver announced. "And, what a crowd! It's worse than a flock of migrating Canadian geese headed south." Taking a deep breath, he added, "Well, we're just going to have to brave the throng, so it's all ashore going ashore. Please watch your step, and just wait at the side of the bus. I'll be right out to get your luggage."

And he was right. There was barely enough room to step out because of all the suitcases, duffle bags and people noisily crowding the sidewalk right in front of the dorm's main entrance.

"Hey!" Dan yelled to the driver, "I think you let us off at the wrong place! This sounds like Grand Central Station!"

To guard my toes from getting smashed, I leaned my back against the side of the bus. I stood there entranced by its magnitude, taking in all the sights with both ears.

This place must be huge. There are people everywhere—as far as I can hear in either direction. Don't know if I'm going to like this.

My distraction was broken by a tall husky voice greeting Nellie. It was her guide, and she parted with a warm good-bye. Then a cologne-loaded somebody bent beside me to pick up Dan's luggage. There went another friend. I stood surrounded by a throng of people—yet a sullen feeling of loneliness permeated my heart.

Mom, Dad and Steve are miles away. This place is way too big for comfort.

After what seemed like an hour, the crowd dissipated as one by one each blind student was escorted to their room by a campus sighted guide. At last, my turn came. Cedrick greeted me with a delightfully jovial welcome. As he offered his muscular arm, I pictured him to be a weight lifter. That was actually a good deal. I wouldn't have to worry about him wrenching his back with my heavy luggage. So, we were off across the long cement entrance and into the dorm. The slick marble-like floor gave way to a carpeted hall and the ding of an elevator ahead. It was up to the third floor with a sharp left and long hall to my room.

As I stepped into my room, I found it was much smaller than expected. That turned out for my good because in no time at all I was unpacked. Once finished, I sat down on the stiff mattress of my narrow cot-sized bed. I was settled in, but it sure was far from homey. It seemed sterile, cold and empty compared to the warm family setting back home.

Learning the layout of the dormitory building was first on the agenda. This was challenging for sure, but kind of fun, too. With thirty nine other kids wandering around the dorm, we joked and laughed even more often than we got lost.

A lengthy novel couldn't hold all our crazy adventures. One such event was when Ben had to call his sweetheart the very first day. Being the independent sort, he was determined to find a phone by himself. And, of course, it had to be a private place—no public pay phone for him! After great effort, an out-of-the-way little room was found. Pulling the door closed, he made that long-awaited phone call. Suddenly in the midst of his steamy conversation, the door swung open. The dorm dean stepped in, wanting to use his desk. Well, by no means did that end Ben's romance, but it did send him on another "phony" expedition.

As for me, my blooper trip would never make the front page, but it was pretty embarrassing just the same. On one noon trip to the cafeteria, I got the brilliant idea that I could expand my study time. Why not review my notes while walking down that long hall to the cafeteria? Skillfully balancing my

Braille notes atop my loose-leaf notebook, I continued walking and began cramming for the afternoon test.

Turning into the lunch room, I digested the last piece of data and proceeded to the buffet line. The line was surprisingly short which suited my growling stomach just fine. In a few moments, a lady stepped right up in front of me. With a rather loud, demanding voice, she said, "You're late! Grab your apron and start another pot of coffee."

"Whoops, excuse me! I'm just here to buy my lunch. I must have made a wrong turn."

"I should say you did! You're standing right in the middle of my kitchen."

"Sorry. Which way is the buffet line?"

Well, she sure didn't notice that I was blind. Guess all my work of trying not to look blind was successful—or was it?

Looking blind was not the image I wanted to portray. Dad definitely felt the same. After brain surgery, Dad began to reinforce this concept. At that time, I resented his constant nagging about my posture. "Pam, you look like a dejected little old lady! Your head is hanging down and your shoulders are slumped forward."

"Okay, Dad," I outwardly responded with respect—but each time he mentioned it—I inwardly grumbled with resentment. I knew better than to even whisper a syllable of disgust toward Dad. His word was law.

Years later, I could truly appreciate his unrelenting wisdom. People at the college had already made numerous comments that proved Dad's diligence paid off. They said things to me like: "You don't look blind" or "Sorry, Pam, I forget you're blind." But, of course, there is always a flip side to every good coin. There were times that this "normal" appearance proved to be a real headache. When in a restaurant or other public setting, my folks would inform the waiter, clerk, etc. that I was blind. My acute hearing would pick up on subtle muttering. With disgust in their voices, I heard comments like: "What a fake" and "Give me a break—she can't be blind. She looked right at me when I asked for her order."

Finding my room, the cafeteria and the girls' shower room was only the beginning of my education that summer. Quite frankly, my first week was a bit more interesting than anticipated. With several practice runs, I gained confidence in finding the shower room by myself. One morning, as usual, I jumped out of bed and quickly gathered all my shower supplies. Juggling my shampoo, bar of soap, talcum powder, wash cloth and towel, I made a bee-line down the hall.

Oh, good! I made it just in time to beat the morning rush hour! There's nothing like a refreshing shower to get the day started right.

Hurrying to get out of there before the throng arrived, I quickened my scrubbing strokes and got almost dry. I gathered up all my stuff and wrapped the somewhat short bath towel snuggly around my body. Intent on keeping the towel's two corners together just above my left breast, I juggled my slippery shower items and headed down the hall.

Next month, I have to buy a bathrobe. They just don't make these towels long enough to wrap around.

Rounding the first corner, my heart sank. *Where is my room key?*

Slowing to a near halt, I frisked my belongings in search of the key. "Oh, no!" my words of panic echoed down the hall, "I'm locked out!" There I was parading around wearing just a skimpy bath towel.

Thank goodness there was a rule of no boys on the girls' floor before eight o'clock. At 7:45 a.m., this thought brought comforting relief for a fleeting moment. Then very loud voices jolted my eardrums.

With an abrupt stop right in the middle of that hall, I cocked my ear for a closer listen. *Oh my gosh! That's a boy's voice!*

I ran down the hall and around the corner, pounding on the first door I could find.

Oh come on! Open the door! It would just be my luck that no one's home!

After standing there for what seemed longer than waiting in a doctor's office, footsteps came toward me.

Brenda said, "Pam, what's going on! Why are you pounding on the stairwell door?"

"You're kidding! The stairs?" *Well, I was looking for a way out, but not that one for sure! How humiliating!*

Not only had the tightly clutched end of my towel slipped from my grip, but I had alerted a crowd of most eager-to-help young men.

This fair Norwegian-Dutch girl certainly was not lacking for color at that moment! If the degree of blushing could be compared to sunburn, I would easily have passed for a lobster's twin. Well, my heart finally settled down, and things got back to almost normal. But, the snickers and grapevine reports took much longer to slow down. I was truly notorious! Despite all this, I was victorious and felt quite pleased with my many accomplishments. I had conquered the shower room dilemma with a long lacy pink robe and a spare key pinned in the pocket.

The four-story dormitory was mastered, too. At least I knew my way to all the important places, like the cafeteria and the boys' lounge one floor up. That small lounge was a perfect spot for a rendezvous with Jason, my brand new boyfriend.

Within that first week, I needed to pick up money my folks had wired to me. This meant a short jaunt off campus. The most economical way to do that would have been by bus. Taking the bus by myself seemed about as possible as making a solo flight to the moon. Despite the hefty expense of a taxi cab, I decided that would be safest for me. I handled getting into the cab with flying colors. To make things even sweeter, the driver was friendly. I gave him the address of my destination, then leaned back to enjoy the ride.

I bet this cabby can give me some valuable information about the layout of the streets.

And, boy! Did he ever! I told him that this was my first time attending the college, and I knew nothing about Seattle or how it was laid out. He responded with this unforgettable formula: "Well, young lady, we cabbies have a sentence that sums up the downtown area. It goes like this—Jesus Christ made Seattle under protest."

"Oh, my goodness!" I gasped and giggled in the same breath. "How does that work?"

"Well, it's like this—all those streets run in pairs. That is, each pair has names beginning with the same letter. The first letter of each word in this sentence is the order they come in. It goes like this: Jefferson and James, Cherry and Columbia, Marion and Madison, Spring and Seneca, University and Union, Pike and Pine."

Well, that funny bone tickler quickly turned into a large lump in my throat.

Oh, man! The dean said I would learn to get around Seattle by myself.

I hope not. This place is too big for me to tackle. Portland's big enough, but this is huge.

I not only survived my first taxi trip but made it back to the dorm and in time for dinner that night. Looking back, it seems like an insignificant accomplishment. But it was a major, major victory for me.

With a successful taxi trip under my belt and learning my way around the dorm, I was feeling pretty confident and ready to tackle more new things. The next step sounded a little scary. But, it truly was a sleeping dragon.

"Pam, five minutes until we have to be at the main entrance," Betty announced.

Although we didn't see much of each other, Betty was a great roommate. We were quite compatible and became good friends, too.

"Oh, you're right! Thanks, Betty. I'm headed for Slate and Stylus class. What class do you have?"

"Good question. Let me check my class schedule. Here it is. Oh yes, I've got English 101. Sounds boring. By the way, Pam, do you have your key?" she asked with a smirk.

With a loud jingle of my key chain, I swung open our door and we were on our way. I flipped up the crystal on my Braille watch. Gently touching its hands and dots, I gasped at the late hour. "Come on, we'd better sprint if we're going to make it." And sure enough, as we rounded the last corner, we heard the elevator doors open.

Jason yelled, "Good morning, girls! I'll hold it for you."

Arriving at the front door of our dorm, we assembled into groups—one group heading for English 101, another going to the Slate and Stylus class and so on. With a vote of confidence for Jason, he became our group scout.

Jason was totally blind, but he sure knew how to skillfully swing his white cane. Nellie was in our small threesome, and I was glad of that. She was the only other Portland girl.

"Well, girls, you'll be glad to know that I did my research. All the turns and landmarks are right here in my Braille notes. We have to take the first sidewalk on our right," Jason announced as he tapped his cane back and forth on the cement.

At first I thought he was awfully noisy with that tapping, but I soon found it to be a comforting sound. It was easy to follow him because I could always hear right where he was. Well, the first pathway to the right certainly didn't pan out. It led us straight to a big cement planter and a solid brick wall. That didn't seem to faze Jason in the least.

"No problem, we'll just try the next one. Besides, that short path probably doesn't even count as a sidewalk." It was an about face as we stayed right behind our dauntless leader.

Wow, this guy is really something! Jason keeps so cool even though this is his third wrong turn.

We did make it to that first class, but we were more than a little late. The teacher, to my surprise, was blind, but also most understanding. It seemed as though her lesson plan already had the first activity as "waiting, waiting" till everyone arrived. Then Mrs. Olsen called class to order.

I wasn't thrilled about learning to use the slate and stylus. In fact, I had avoided it like ice glazed sidewalks. Using my Braillewriter was enough of a challenge, I thought. With much practice, writing on the Braillewriter had finally become a polished skill of mine. This heavy desktop machine (similar to an old-fashion manual typewriter) enables each letter to be written with a single stroke.

Writing with a slate and stylus was tedious at best. The slate is a long metal rectangle with four horizontal lines of twenty-seven little holes in each line. Each hole represents one space and holds up to six dots. The stylus is a hand-held poker with a very small wooden handle fitting in the center of the palm. Just to write one letter requires punching anywhere from one to six dots. The time had come to broaden my skills since the slate and stylus was the only method for taking Braille notes in a classroom setting.

Arriving late came with its penalty. Mrs. Olsen, though very gracious in welcoming us, insisted that we sit in the front row. There my short frame squirmed and wiggled in an attempt to get comfortable at that tall table. The rest of the class was waiting for me to get ready.

Quickly reaching into my backpack, I pulled out my slate. Then came the search for my stylus. This small device was always evading my reach, and this day was no exception. My heart pounded. Where was my stylus! Around my sweater, under the notebook, beside my wallet I felt. At last, there it was, stuck inside my three ring notebook.

"Okay, looks like Pam's ready. Let's get started. First, we'll work on just writing the alphabet. And, remember, you have to start at the right side and write each letter backward."

How awkward! I'll never get the hang of this!

Finally, class was over, and boy was I ready to get out of there. At least I thought I was until remembering the headache we went through just getting here.

With Jason in the lead, I followed along with hesitance. Steps were coming up somewhere soon—four of them as I remembered. Walking up steps was no problem. Thank goodness for the little bit I could see. If the lighting was right, the dark shadowed faces of the steps were visible. Besides, it's a whole lot harder to fall down when walking up steps, but going down them— that was altogether different.

Every down staircase was invisible to me. And to make it even scarier, my balance was not so hot. Balance had been no problem for me until after the brain surgery. Too many times I was strolling along and found myself stepping out into thin air. Fortunately, the only injury sustained was a mortal wound to my pride. So, any hint of a possible down staircase stirred up instant panic that gripped my insides and slowed my feet to a snail's shuffle. This stroll was no exception.

I walked along trying to portray confidence while hiding this gripping fear. The steps did come, and despite diligently dancing the snail shuffle, I stumbled down the first couple steps. With the pounding of my heart in my throat, I swerved into Jason's sturdy arms. Jason held me close until I regained composure.

"Are you okay?"

"Thanks for catching me. I'm fine. The only thing hurt is my pride."

Well, we did make it safely back to our dorm, but lunch was a bit skimpy that day. Possibly, it could have had something to do with the fact that we arrived at the cafeteria five minutes before closing. But if my first day seemed challenging, it was tame compared to Day Two.

CHAPTER 8
HITCHES & GLITCHES

Day two of classes contained hitches and glitches galore! First on the agenda was our English 101 class, and that was held in Building Number Four of the Quad.

The Quad was the central point of that huge university campus. Foot traffic here buzzed with activity like a beehive right in the middle of honey harvesting. Yet, this sunken cement patio courtyard was a beautiful spot. When standing at the top of its staircase, the majestic cascading waterfall right in the center cooled the nostrils with the fragrance of a forest stream. Brilliant red, white and blue Petunias waved their sweet aroma at each visitor. Rustic wooden benches encircling this oasis beckoned the weary soul to stop and take a breather. Standing back in tall, stately manner were the four huge red brick buildings darkened with age and character. These housed many of the campus classrooms.

As our traveling three-some approached the Quad, we were engaged in the usual laughter and joking. With my mind in anything but travel mode, I walked right along behind Jason. I did not detect the changing sound of his cane taps as he began down the steps. I proceeded to step out into thin air. I fell down the stairs, and again, was so fortunate not to get hurt. This time my pride was mortally wounded. It was then, for the first time, I knew I could not travel safely outdoors without a white cane.

With this fourth episode of falling down stairs, both of my friends were very concerned about my safety.

"Pam, you should talk to Mr. Morgan," Nellie suggested. "He's the mobility specialist who teaches people how to walk with a white cane."

Following her excellent advice, I made an appointment to see Mr. Morgan the very next day. And, that same afternoon, I met again with my wise peer counselors.

"Well, Pam, how did your meeting go with Mr. Morgan?" Jason inquired.

"You won't believe it! He said that I have too much vision to need a white cane. So, whenever I think steps are ahead, I should just shuffle my feet."

"Oh, you mean Mr. Monkey?" Jason chuckled. Lots of us have had mobility lessens with him. And we've decided a better name for him is Stone Face Monkey. He's the poorest excuse for a mobility instructor."

"That's absurd!" Nellie chimed in. "Any of us blind students here could do a whale of a better job teaching you cane travel."

"That's it, Nellie! We'll show her the ropes. Do you have a spare cane Pam could use?"

"No, not with me, but I'm pretty sure we can find one if we just spread the word."

From that moment on, I was enrolled in mobility boot camp. The very next day, Jason sat down beside me at breakfast and proudly placed a white cane on the table next to my bowl of cold cereal.

"Here you go. Hang onto this, and we'll get together for some real mobility lessons. It's just too dangerous for you to go outside without a cane."

"Wow! Thanks, Jason." With that long stick dangling awkwardly in front of me, Jason, Nellie and I headed out the door to Slate and Stylus class. Using the cane was anything but comfortable. In fact, it seemed just to get in my way. And, if that weren't bad enough, it almost tripped me as the cane tip stuck in a sidewalk crack. My awkward mishap tickled Jason.

"Oh, Jason, it isn't funny!" But, he chuckled all the louder.

"Okay, Mr. Smart guy, you show me how it's done!"

"Sure thing. I've always wanted an excuse to have you walk close beside me."

With a giggle of embarrassment, I reached out to take hold of his arm.

"Ah, now we're strolling ready! Hold your cane like this—right in the center of your body about waist level. Then, tap it on the sidewalk, first on your right and then on your left. You want to arc it back and forth about the width of your shoulders. This way, you're constantly checking the path right ahead of your body. Now walk along with me and try it."

"Something's not quite right here. It feels like I'm dancing the Fox Trot while you're doing the Two Step. I can't get the rhythm."

"Now comes the tricky part. You tap the cane on the left as you step forward with your right foot. Then, arc it and tap it on your right side as your left foot moves forward. It takes practice before you'll feel comfortable with it, but it shouldn't take long."

Well, it didn't come quite as quickly as I had expected. It seemed that there was much knowledge and practice to be acquired. But, one thing was for sure—Jason was a very dedicated teacher, and he made certain that every day we had a long block of time together for cane travel. Once our first two weeks of classes were completed, we had a much fuller schedule. Still, Jason was diligent in continuing my mobility lessons. He seemed pleased that we had to shift our meeting time to evenings right after dinner.

The summer evenings were beautiful, cool, fresh and romantic, too. How well I remember our first evening stroll. It was on a Friday night, so there was no rush in returning to the dorm. As we laughed and teased about being able to feel the silvery moonbeams, our route became even more nebulous.

"Well, Pam, hate to tell you this, but I haven't a clue where we are or how to get back. But, the good part is, at least we're lost together." Soon his comforting arms held me tight as he whispered with reassurance that we'd be okay.

Those lessons in cane travel hit the top of my Class Popularity Chart. And, practicing with my cane never seemed sweeter. After a few weeks, I felt like a White Cane Veteran.

I must admit that my dating skills were being sharpened, as well. Our rendezvous grew to meeting for breakfast, lunch and dinner. And, after the cane lessons, we would meet in the lounge on the boys' floor to do our homework.

One balmy summer evening, we met as usual. But, our homework assignment was anything but usual. As we sat side by side on the couch, a bout of yawns overtook us. So, I started gathering my books.

"I think we'd better call it quits."

But, before I could get to my feet, Jason took hold of my hand.

"Pam, I know it's late, but sit down just a few minutes longer, please. I have something for you."

And in that rare quiet moment, on the boys' floor, he placed a small box in my hand. Sitting there unsure of what to do, I took a pensive look at its size, shape and plush velvet exterior with all ten fingertips. Opening it, I found a ring.

"Oh, Jason, it's beautiful! Is this for me?"

"Yes, my dear, it is for you. I have never been happier than these past few weeks with you, and I really want to spend the rest of my life with you." Taking my hand in his, he asked, "Pam, will you marry me?"

"You know, that's a huge decision for both of us. Do you think we've known each other long enough to do something this serious?"

"I know that we have something extra special going on between us. It's much too good to let it slip through our fingers. I see our engagement as a commitment to growing our relationship and learning more about each other. And since we still have two and a half months left here in Seattle, it's prime time to do that."

"You know, that makes a lot of sense, but I just need a little time to think and pray about it. Is that okay?"

"Sure, when will you let me know?"

"Tomorrow night, let's meet here in the lounge."

"Sounds good, I'll bring the ring and my homework tomorrow night."

Well, that single, brief encounter really changed my social focus for the remaining Seattle days. By this time, I had gained a good deal of confidence traveling by myself with my second-hand white cane. Even with this newly acquired independence, there were increasingly less opportunities for me to go walking alone.

Whenever our schedules permitted, Jason and I were together. And, of course, it wasn't comfortable walking with him unless we had very close contact. This meant I always held his arm, and he led the way. No chance for practicing my solo travel here. But, who cared about that, anyway? There was a more important curriculum for this summer preparatory course—fun-filled days—that was it! And, fun-packed days truly came our way.

CHAPTER 9
DIZZY DAME

One of my favorite outings took place every Wednesday right after dinner. About eight of us blind students got together for an evening of swimming. We would meet Brian, a sighted work-study student, at our first floor lounge. Brian was perfect for the job, too. He seemed more like just one of our group instead of someone being paid to guide blind people. Wednesday had come again, and we were off to the pool. It was a fair walk too, about a mile.

The chilling effect of the cool evening air quickly vanished once I stepped through the door of the Aquatic Center. The warm misty air and the unmistakable pungency of chlorine welcomed me like a good ole friend. The atmosphere was brimming with the excitement of friends and lots of fun about to burst into full swing.

The friendly receptionist swished quickly through our group, collecting a pool ticket from each of us. Then Brian spearheaded the boys' exit to the Men's locker room. The receptionist was kind and seemed genuinely happy to see us arrive. Without even being asked to do so, she became the leader of the girls' pack. As soon as Brian hollered out for the boys to follow him, Mrs. Layton stepped out from behind the desk. She faithfully guided and assisted anyone who needed help. The sounds of laughter and showers soon filled the room. Once we were all ready, Mrs. Layton quietly disappeared.

I had my own routine, too. Turning off the shower, I made an abrupt about-face. That lined me up with the shower room exit. Then, it was off to the pool door, which was not that hard to find. My wet skin easily detected cool air breezing through that exit.

I was eager to splash and had to remind myself to approach it slowly. There were obstacles and landmarks to negotiate. One slight angle in the wrong direction and I could step off into the deep water. The thought of that made my heart pound. I loved the water but was in no way a good swimmer.

Before our first group outing, I took a tour of the Aquatic Center. I arranged to have one of the sighted attendants walk with me so that I could learn the layout. When we entered each new section, I stopped in the door. Using the door as my point of reference, I asked the attendant to take my right arm and point my hand toward the different things in the room. Once my arm was pointed toward an area I needed to access, I would listen for audible landmarks and figure out a way to get from the door to that area. This took extra time and lots of mental gymnastics, but it was well worth it. I then had confidence, knowing that I could go where I needed to go independently.

Staying in the shallow end certainly didn't limit my activity and exercise. It seemed as though the deep end had an invisible sign displaying "The Boys' End" and the shallow end was reserved for the girls. That didn't last for long, however. Once the guys got their fill of diving and dunking each other, they migrated to the shallow end. That's when the free-for-all began. Instead of floating on our short surfboards, we girls resourcefully turned them into attack sharks and misfit Frisbees. As for the boys, they were into doing cannon balls. The biggest splash possible—that was their goal. The winner of this cannon ball contest had to make the biggest splash and at the same time splatter at least one of us girls. And, of course, moving targets were always harder to hit, so we girls never sat still during their performance.

This group of ten to twelve students had the high priority of doing fun things together. Just as important as the socialization was the unwritten code of comradeship that permeated the whole bunch. No matter the event or its location, we carefully watched out for each other's safety and wellbeing.

This weekly pool event was a prime example of the high level of caring among us. To make sure no one was hurt by divers or the cannon ball invaders, the one about to jump would first yell out "cannon ball." The rest of us would make sure no one was close to that area. The diver always waited for the "all clear" before moving. Wild and zany we were, but at the same time, we kept each other safe.

After forty-five minutes of swimming, joking and teasing, we hit the showers. All that exercise had a heavy impact on our appetites. And nothing satisfied our hunger pains better than a stop at the Continental Pastry Shop. Even before we reached the door, its aromatic advertisement lured us closer. That was a wonderful smell, but once inside, it was sweet tooth paradise. The oily, sugar-laden aroma blended the many delicacies into one harmonious symphony. Even though I couldn't smell any individual flavors, in my mind, I could see the sparkling glass front and shelves of all those delectable choices. The dilemma of which to choose was just as difficult as if my eyes could see everything in front of me.

Now Brian, as I mentioned, fit so very well in our group. A classic example of this took place on our second visit to the bakery. As usual, Brian efficiently guided us to an empty table and made sure all were seated. About one bite into our pastries, Brian spoke up in a stern, quite serious tone. He instructed the guys, "Listen up, men. I mean…gentlemen. I want you to remember this is a public place, so mind your manners!"

A split second later, Brian purposely tipped his chair and fell with a crash to the floor flat on his back. Our round table, filled with coffee cups and pastries, burst into hysterics.

He was a true stand-up comedian. If there ever were a class in the Art of Puns, Brian would have been a straight A student for sure. He always added an abundance of humor and fun to every outing. I have to admit I had a crush on him, but I never whispered a word of that to anyone. After all, I was engaged.

An important location in our dorm was the snack room. This small room filled with stale air and wallpapered with high priced vending machines was definitely not a big drawing card for the students. On the other hand, this forsaken room became the perfect spot for our group of card sharks. This dedicated foursome (Dan, Nellie, Jason and I) met at least two evenings a week.

I had never seen Braille playing cards before, so being able to play cards again was a real treat. Nellie convinced me that I should get my own deck of Braille cards. Buying a deck of playing cards sounded like a simple task, but finding Braille ones was more than just a quick trip to the local store. This, however, was not at the top of my activity list.

Not long after that discussion, Nellie's Braille watch died.

"Well, Pam. Hope you're in the mood for shopping. The Community Service Center is the only place to get a Braille watch around here. That means going clear across Seattle, and I'd sure like to have your company. Besides, you could get your Braille cards there, too."

"Sounds like fun. You bet I'm in the mood. I believe I was born with a shopping bag in my hand. As soon as you find a free spot in your schedule, let me know."

Setting up that trip was a juggling act at best. When Jason and Dan learned of it, they wanted to join us. About a week later, we got it together. That afternoon, two Queens of Hearts and two Kings of Spade all piled into a cab and were off to the Center.

What a fun adventure. I had never "seen" adaptive stuff like this before. In the large Community Services Center, there were all kinds of games and equipment for the blind on display. Like a five-year-old child turned loose in a toy store, I toured with excitement. Everything was so new and interesting that my hands were racing from one item to the next to get a close-up look.

After thoroughly checking out the different styles of Braille playing cards, Jason and I decided the plastic ones would hold up best under all our serious card games.

Right then and there I began making my earliest ever Christmas wish list. There were so many things I was sure would benefit me greatly. Atop my wish list was a Braille Scrabble game. It had both a print and Braille letter on each playing tile. The Scrabble board was so neat! Around each square was a raised ridge. The letter tile fit snugly into each space. That way, as a blind person ran their fingers over the words, the letters did not move out of position.

How cool!

The wind-up timer with large raised Braille dots was a must, as well. But, I had to be practical. What I really needed was a writing tablet. This stiff paper with raised ridges for each line would be perfect for writing letters to my friends and family. So I spent my month's allowance all in one afternoon. I was one happy camper—I mean, shopper.

Nellie found a nice Braille watch, too. Both boys bought boring things— like stuff for their radios and cassette recorders.

That same evening was our card night. I was anxious to get back to the dorm with my new deck of cards. Dinner was inhaled in record time, and off to the elevators I dashed. After pacing back and forth in front of the elevators at least sixty seconds, I dashed around the corner to the stairwell. No time to wait for those sluggish elevators. I bounded to the second floor.

With my ears perked straight up in the air like a vigilant Pomeranian pup, I strained to detect the low humming sound of the vending machines.

I mustn't overshoot the snack room door this time!

I was the first one at the card table. Eager for the other three to arrive, I impatiently wiggled and squirmed in my chair. Finally..."The Gang's all here."

Proudly, I presented my box of brand-new cards. We were ready to play but not ready for the kind of action ahead. Carefully removing the cards from their box, I positioned them in my hand for shuffling. I reached out in an attempt to even the deck with a sharp tap on the table. Before my hand made it to the table, the whole middle fell out and went airborne in a fireworks display across the floor. To this day, I still don't know the name of that game. It wasn't quite Fifty-Two Pick-Up, but pretty darn close.

The summer flew by and came to an end much, much too soon. With luggage, purse and white cane in hand, I walked confidently back to the same sidewalk in the front of our dorm. This was the very same place I had just three months ago stepped onto with fear and apprehension. It was Grand Central Station all over again.

Students, suitcases, and duffle bags were everywhere. But this time, it was even noisier than before. Like a wild collage of vibrant colors sprinkled with random dark hues, so our laughter and hugs with occasional tears painted the tapestry of our dreaded departure.

Just then, Jason's airport shuttle pulled up. "Well, Pam, that's my ride." With a rib compressing hug, he kissed me right in front of everybody. Turning, he whispered in my ear. "Love you, I'll write as soon as I get home."

Prying us apart, the bus driver guided Jason to the shuttle's door. For a moment, I stood there, frozen in a daze of disbelief and gloom. That moment abruptly ended with a loud, sharp smack against my white cane.

"Pam," Dan's familiar voice rose above the chatter, "can't leave without scoring one more point in dueling."

With a squeal and giggle, I swung my cane in his direction, "Oh, Daniel! That's not fair! You snuck up on me! I didn't even have a chance."

"Nellie's right here beside you now. I have to admit; sending you two girls back to Portland together worries me big time. Portland will never be the same again with both of you raising cane down there."

"Oh, Dan!" Nellie laughed, "Portland is much safer with us than Salem ever could be with you on the loose."

Our bus pulled up, and I had to pull her out of Dan's arms. With slow, reluctant steps, we both boarded the bus and found two seats together.

"Well," I sighed with a long ensuing silence. "What a summer! I'm so glad we got acquainted."

"Me too, Pam," she added and reached across to rest her hand on mine. We have to keep in touch when we get back home. I brailed my address and phone number on this index card for you."

"Thanks, Nellie, I really want to stay in touch with you, too."

We recalled many of the special times, and the trip seemed to fly by faster than traveling on a Boeing 707 jet. Right in the middle of reliving last night's farewell festivities, we were rallied back to the present.

"Portland, Oregon, ladies, we'll be at the Commission for the Blind in about three minutes," our driver cheerfully announced. "We're back home safe and sound. Watch your step. I'll be right around to meet you with your luggage."

Gathering my belongings, and with white cane in hand, I made my way between the two rows of seats. I descended the steps with a new sense of confidence. Steve was right there with his strong reassuring hand and a warm welcome.

"Good to have you back. How did it go?"

"Scary, fun and fantastic! Do you have time for lunch?"

"Sure, I'm starved. How about pizza?"

"Good idea. I'll fill you in on my summer, and you can give me the scoop on yours."

We found a quiet table for two in Pietro's Pizza Parlor. The ice cold pop and piping hot combination pizza really hit the spot. Even more satisfying was the time we spent sharing our experiences and thoughts. Steve took a keen interest in the things I had to say. His summer had been a good one, too. He enjoyed several whitewater raft trips, picnics with friends and, of course, lots of trips to the racetracks. Pizza and time with Steve was tops. But, as I later began unpacking my luggage, reality set in.

I'm really not home at all. In less than a month I'll be leaving my family behind again.

With a homesick tear welling up in my eye, I began sorting my things and packing for an even bigger move.

Two years of college in Olympia Washington—that's a long time to be away from home.

CHAPTER 10
BUS STEPS AGAIN!

I truly didn't have anything against buses, much less their steps. But, ever since going blind, climbing up those narrow short flights of steps seemed to mean trouble. How common, how insignificant a set of bus steps should be, but that was not the case for me! They certainly lived up to their reputation of bringing a major change.

But it was too late to back out this time, although I wanted to. My tuition was paid. My apartment was rented and fully furnished. And, the first day of college was just one day away.

I slept during the trip and woke up abruptly to, "Olympia, Washington next stop."

The Greyhound driver was very congenial. "Young lady, may I assist you down the steps?"

"Oh, thanks, I can handle that just fine, but I could use help finding the door into the depot."

Stepping down ahead of me, he asked, "How about luggage? Do you have any?"

"No, fortunately it all got here before me. I start college here tomorrow. Thanks to my parents, all my stuff was moved and settled in last week."

"Will somebody be meeting you here?"

"No, I know my way just fine. Mom, Dad and I took time to get acquainted with the neighborhood. We walked from my apartment to the college, then to Safeway, the Sizzler, and of course, to the Dairy Queen. It's like this—my Dad loves Dairy Queen ice cream. Whenever our family goes on a trip, he has to find a Dairy Queen for our pit stop."

With a firm grip on my new traveling companion, my white cane, I began walking the familiar route to my apartment. The directions that I had so many times rehearsed in my mind kicked into playback mode:

Cross seven streets, walk to the next corner, then turn left. Watch for the second sidewalk with a white picket fence. Ah, got it! This is the place.

I turned down the sidewalk leading to my new front door. Dad's description popped into my mind as clear as a snapshot.

"You know, Pam, the house looks pretty good for a hundred years old. It's light gray with white trim, has white shutters and a white picket fence around the yard."

The wooden porch creaked softly as my foot hit the first step. Stepping forward, a bouncy green sprig tickled my cheek. Dark purple petunias hung in huge clusters on each side of the porch and my nose was filled with their heavenly fragrance. I couldn't resist reaching out to touch and enjoy the soft, ruffled petals. Then my white cane tapped the corner of the weathered wooden bench on the right of the porch. And a smile glowed in my heart as I remembered Mom's warm words, "Pam, there's a nice wooden bench over here. This would be a perfect place to do your homework on a sunny afternoon."

Opening the front door, I paused in the entryway.

Guess I should stop in and say hi to Mr. and Mrs. Cameron first.

My new landlords were nice enough but very sedentary and old enough to be my grandparents. After knocking on their door several times, there was still no response.

Upstairs, I went to my apartment door. My key did its job and I was in my own, my very first, apartment.

With purse and sweater dropped on the small loveseat, I went back to the front door ready for a grand tour.

Yes, here's the kitchen—my kitchen.

The gas stove was directly to my left. Then stretching my right arm forward, I touched the small white enamel sink with its antique like faucets. Two little faucets topped with a short horizontal rounded bar handle were perched like twin parakeets, one in each back corner—cold on the right and hot on the left. How quaint.

Straight ahead, daylight beamed in from the large window. Just to the left was a small square table with two wooden chairs. Tucked in the corner on the other side of the window was the white enamel refrigerator. It was surprisingly small, even shorter than me. Yet it stood tall with pride, boasting its many years of faithful service. Its scarred chrome handle gleamed like the showpiece of an Old West gunslinger with many notches.

The long narrow kitchen had a huge opening in the middle of the left wall which led into the living room. Straight across, an identical opening in the right wall was the entrance to my bedroom. I'd never seen a bedroom constructed quite like this. There it stood, right between the sink and refrigerator, one high step up and I could fall right into my double bed.

This was the perfect layout for me. All three rooms were well defined with landmarks I could "see." The smooth linoleum floor of the kitchen was bordered on the right with that high step into my bedroom cave, and on the other side, the carpet was instantly detectable with one smooth step. This light blue-gray carpet was plush and soft, the perfect spot to stretch out for a lazy book review. The dark gray metal gas heater stood about waist high to my left. Just beyond it on the far wall was the small gold brocaded loveseat from Mom and Dad's living room.

And a loveseat it was for sure. Although it didn't fit in with the antique collection, that gold spot truly brightened my world with love. Sitting on it gave me warm feelings inside as I remembered the love that placed it here. It was one of the most popular pieces of furniture when Steve and I were grade school age. How perfect—it became a fortress when tipped to sit on its back with all four brass feet sticking out like cannons. It was the favorite, first choice spot for every pillow fight, and there were lots of them. As we grew up, this small version couch was my spot to curl up with a bowl of fresh popcorn for a family movie night.

A wooden rocking chair and narrow end table topped with a short lamp rounded out my living room display. At the end of this tour, I paused in the middle of my living room.

My brain told me that this was my home—but although the familiarity of furniture was comforting, my heart couldn't agree yet. It didn't feel like home. Instead it seemed empty, strange and intimidating.

I should call Mom and let her know I got here safe. Right, Pam. With what phone?

With the reality of no phone, the grave senses of being isolated and all alone overwhelmed me. It was as though a dense dark cloud had just moved in and filled my apartment. I knew nobody in Olympia except my elderly landlords, and they weren't home to visit. I couldn't even find comfort by hearing a familiar voice on the phone. I was alone, all alone! That did it! The tears just wouldn't stay where they belonged—first just a tiny drop trickled and then a full-fledged flood came.

Fortunately for me, there wasn't enough free time to dwell on this isolation. I had a bag to unpack, lunch to make for tomorrow and to get ready for my first day in college.

The night of slumber was good and I arose refreshed. All my diligence in arranging and getting everything put away in its place paid off. On the chair by my bed awaited my outfit with shoes and socks carefully positioned beneath it. Then it was onto the bathroom. My toothbrush, mascara, hair brush and cologne were all easily found and truly right at my finger tips.

There I stood right in front of the mirror just like I always did when I could see. But, now my twenty-twenty vision was in all ten fingertips, not in two blue eyes. So with both hands, I took a good look at my hair. Using an extra light touch, I ran my hands across the top of my hair to check for anything out of place.

Good. Hair's in place, my collar's straight. I'm ready and right on schedule, too.

Out the front door I stepped. Excitement filled my heart. This was the first day of a brand new adventure.

The walk to college was especially enjoyable. I didn't even have to count streets because my landmark was the busy main drag of downtown Olympia. That's where my side street ended. I didn't have to concentrate as intently on the route. There was time to let my senses go wild, and that's just what they did. The freshest air of the day filled my nose and lungs. Oh how I loved the cool frisky breeze that danced across my face, clearing out the mental fog. As I strolled along, every so often there would be a wisp of sweet flowers blooming somewhere nearby. Little birds twittered in the trees right above me. Their sweet melody was briefly interrupted as Mr. Crow cawed a hearty good morning to me.

"Good morning to you, too, Mr. Crow. Yes, it is a lovely day!" I responded with a sunny smile.

By the end of this seven-block walk, I was exhilarated and ready to tackle anything. At the corner of that busy thoroughfare, I made the appropriate right turn and switched my mind into serious travel concentration mode. It was time to count streets and pick up clues with my white cane. I crossed the third side street. After crossing the fourth side street, my next landmark was the rubber doormat at the college entrance. This was tricky to detect, and if I walked too fast, I could easily miss it. So, I slowed my pace and stepped up my brainwaves. The vibrations coming up from the tip of my cane changed from coarse ones as it slid across the cement surface to light, almost undetectable, fine vibrations once on the rubber ridged doormat.

Reaching out to grab the handle, I knew I was in the right place. That distinct three bar handle of this old, almost worn out building, was unmistakable. Its shape was very fresh in my mind since Mom, Dad and I had walked from my apartment to this door and back several times. That first day, I knew I was right on target.

Walking through the door, the distinct musty odor confirmed its former lifetime as a Montgomery Wards department store. The wooden floor sloped downward like a long ramp, then turned around a sharp corner into a narrow hall. Making it through the hallway maze was well worth it. There was much more than a small piece of cheese waiting at the end. It was my classroom.

This small rectangular room held more than its quota of desks and tables. Two rows of large gray metal office desks dominoed along its dark wood paneled walls.

Mrs. Stiller's desk headed the room with a long display table spanning the far wall.

"Good morning, Pam. Welcome to our class. Have you met any of the other students?"

"No, I don't think so."

"Okay, class, let's introduce ourselves. Jamie, we'll start with you."

So around the room went the voices: Jamie, Larry, Angela.

I was student number four. The small size of our class came with definite advantages. Getting acquainted with all the kids was easy and the setting most informal. This somewhat quaint classroom was filled to overflowing with most unique equipment and uncommon stuff.

The typewriters, for example, were standard IBM Selectrics. But, most substandard was the way that Mrs. Stiller had adapted them for our use.

This particular model had a small metal arrow that traveled directly above the keyboard. It advanced one space at a time as I typed. Glued to the front of the typewriter were dry spaghetti noodles. These were used for setting margins. When we needed a six inch line for a lengthy business letter, setting the margins was quick and easy. We just moved the metal arrow to the outermost spaghetti noodle on each side and hit the margin set key. What a simple yet thoroughly efficient technique. Each desk was equipped with a Dictaphone, which was a cassette player with a foot pedal and headset.

Once introductions were finished, we got right to work. Mrs. Stiller was very business-like in her teaching and, of course, began with the very basics. First on the docket was to get acquainted with the typewriter. We then moved on to sharpening our typing accuracy and speed.

Mrs. Stiller's goal was to make all the materials and equipment as accessible as possible for students with visual impairments. Her diligence in making adaptations also infiltrated our small library.

The library resembled a long walk-in closet conveniently located right next to our classroom. It housed all of the adaptive books and equipment. All our textbooks were recorded on reel-to-reel tapes. Boxes with one reel in each stood in rigid attention like a long parade of solders saluting their commander. Every inch of space was filled to the max.

Bookshelves snuggly lined the walls like the slats of Venetian blinds. Giant Braille volumes of medical dictionaries and the Physicians Desk References crowded every inch of that space. Wow! I was impressed and fascinated with all of these accessible items. Little did I realize that I was actually mechanically challenged.

This rude awakening hit one Monday afternoon. It was my turn to monitor the library, which meant checking in and out books and supplies. Reel-to-reel tapes were a brand new experience for me. And, to be honest, something I would rather have avoided. Nevertheless, there I was standing all alone right in front of the beast—a huge tape recorder with too many knobs and moving parts.

Oh great! Just my luck! Somebody left a tape that needs to be rewound, and I'm supposed to know how to do that.

Angela had shown me how to thread tape onto an empty reel just yesterday. The process of doing that was about as clear to me as a "pea-soup" fog in London on a winter day. Too embarrassed to ask for more help, I decided to figure it out by myself.

With intense concentration and diligence, I did it. A feather-light touch on top of the plastic reel affirmed that it was turning. Ah, success! I switched it into high speed to get it ready before the morning break.

My concentration was interrupted by noise from the front door. One of the benefits of working in the library was its location. Its door opened into the main hall. Stepping just outside of it, I was strategically positioned to eavesdrop on all the activity of the front reception area. So, even when all my work was done, I was never bored. There were lots of conversations and plenty of jokes to eavesdrop on. As the beast was buzzing, I stepped into the hall for a closer look. Boisterous laughter caught my attention and soon I, too, was part of the joking jamboree.

Right at the punch line, the receptionist tapped me on the shoulder, "Excuse me, but I thought you ought to know there's tape strung halfway down the hall, and it's coming from your library."

"Oh my gosh!"

How can that be? I followed Angela's instructions to the letter.

Sure enough, the receptionist was right. I dashed back into the library and quickly switched off the recorder. Then, to make matters even worse, Larry came out the classroom door. He was always first to exit our room and always resembled a one-man fire squad headed for a four-alarm disaster. Today was no exception.

"Larry, stop, stop! You're about to step on a textbook."

With his cane wildly whipping back and forth, its tip caught in my tape. At that moment, I would have written a million dollar check if only I could have exchanged that reel-to-reel mess for a hardbound print textbook. But, no such luck! Of course, Mrs. Stiller promptly appeared on the scene. "My goodness, Pam, what have we here?"

"Wish I knew. Thought I had everything set up and running just right. Then the receptionist walked up to tell me about the run-away tape, and, well, you know the rest."

As a rule, our breaks between classes seemed short and went by super fast. But, there's always an exception to the rule. On this day, my break was anything but short. It drug on and on, stringing out even longer than the unwound tape. With the help of two other students, we tediously wound the yards of thin tape back on the reel by hand.

Surprisingly enough, this became a landmark reel often referred to as

Pam's Version. Chapter 3 on that reel was damaged with several crinkled sections.

With each student's completion of listening to Chapter 3, teasing darted straight toward me.

"Hey, Pam, I just finished reading Chapter 3. Wish you'd capture that darn goldfish on page two. It's hard to understand the section about the bladder when the reader sounds garbled like a Mad Hatter fish underwater."

There was a good side to all this, however. They never asked me to monitor that beast again. Despite being mechanically challenged, I excelled in all my courses making straight A's. But, all work and no play was no fun.

There must be something more interesting than schoolwork to do here.

CHAPTER 11
KICKING UP MY HEELS

The first few weeks in Olympia were anything but fun. In fact, they were the opposite. They were gray, lonely days. After school, I sat alone in my apartment doing homework. There wasn't enough of it to fill those evening hours. No matter how much dusting, cooking and extra studying I did—still I was alone, sad and isolated. There was no phone to call Mom. I had no friends, just plain old boredom and inner gloom staring me in the face every day.

Thank goodness for Monday morning once again. Bright and early as usual, I beat my instructor to the classroom door. "Good morning, class," Mrs. Stiller's cheerful greeting brought us to attention. "We have a guest with us today. She graduated last term and just got a job working as a medical transcriptionist here in town. I'd like all of you to welcome Connie Wilford."

Little did I know that Connie had the wings of an angel tucked under her soft Polyester dress. At lunch, we soon discovered that we had met some years ago in Portland. That pleasant surprise created an almost instant bond of friendship. Connie invited me to her home for dinner that very night. Of course, I refused because of my busy schedule—not! This brief lunch encounter was the beginning of a total turn-around in my social life. Connie had her own home with her husband and two little girls. She lived in Olympia for many years and knew the surrounding area well. Connie's husband was especially kind, too. He agreed to stay home several different evenings to watch their girls. That freed Connie up to show me around town and introduce me to other college students.

That first month, I had scrimped on my groceries and saved enough to afford a telephone. With the addition of a phone to my apartment, I was living—really living. One ring and I bounced to my feet. It was true music to my ears. With anticipation, I ran to answer it.

"Hi, Pam, it's Connie. Karen and I are hungry for pizza. How about joining us?"

"I'd love to, but where do we go for pizza?"

"Pizza Hut is the best place. That's the hangout."

Tucking the phone receiver between my ear and my shoulder, I reached for something to Braille directions on. "Sounds like fun, but I have no idea how to get there."

"Not a problem, your apartment is right on the way. Karen and I will swing by and pick you up in half an hour."

My clock must have sprung rubber hands because those thirty minutes stretched on for what seemed like hours. Despite my antsy pacing, the girls were right on time. Finally, my doorbell rang.

"Hi, Pam, are you ready?"

"Ready, you bet and hungry, too. Let's go!" As we stepped off my front porch, three white canes started swinging, and we were on our way.

"Pam, stop here. We have to cross train tracks now," Karen directed.

I felt with my cane for the edge of the sidewalk ahead. Positioning my left foot on the curb's edge, I stood poised waiting for the "go ahead."

Connie stepped close and lightly bumped my arm with her elbow. "You probably should take my arm now. This is a real tricky place to cross. We have to go over four sets of railroad tracks. It's such a wide space that it's hard to hear the trains or judge their speed and distance. So, we always stop here and put all our ears together to check for any approaching trains."

With frowns of worry between my brows, my voice wavered, "Oh great! We'll never get pizza tonight!"

Karen just chuckled. "Don't worry, Pam, the trains won't bother us now. Coming back is when they'll get us. That's when we'll be worth hitting. After eating all that pizza, we'll make bigger grease spots."

The three of us roared with laughter. After that first trip, the train tracks had earned a new name, "The Grease Spot Crossing."

It was a good thing I had friends to walk with. Otherwise, this stretch of town was one I would have avoided. Asphalt, semi trucks, train tracks and more asphalt blanketed this industrial area. Definitely not a scenic or inviting route, but the conversation and friends made it an especially fun time. In fact, trips to the Pizza Hut became a weekly event. Several college-age kids congregated there, including Connie, Karen and me.

One thing led to another, of course. Pizza for dinner was never complete without a stop at the Dairy Queen for dessert. The Dairy Queen was dangerously convenient—just two blocks from my apartment.

Pizza and ice cream really hit the spot but certainly were far from lean fare. So we were in dire need of more exercise. Our pizza group numbered about seven, which included three cute guys. The guys came up with a creative solution for this high-carbohydrate diet. Their bowling team would be just the ticket for burning off those extra calories. The Blind Bowlers' League met at the Capital Lanes every Wednesday. And what timing—their team was short of members.

Bowling on Wednesday didn't work out for Connie or Karen. But I was definitely interested. After school the very next Wednesday, it was off to the alley. When it came to bowling, I was a full-fledged novice and had never set foot in a bowling alley.

I followed Connie's directions and arrived there about half an hour early. The automatic opening doors ushered me into a huge, noisy room. Whenever I entered a new place, I used the technique of listening closely to detect a clerk or people talking. That habit usually worked quite well. It gave me a direction to head. Then, I could get assistance or information. This time, however, I stood and stood there listening without a clue. With the loud crashing of bowling balls, shouting and whirring machinery, everything blurred together. It was almost impossible to separate any specific sounds or collection of voices. It reminded me of an indoor racetrack.

Okay, Plan B—I'll just trip the next person that comes my way.

With a cool kiss of fresh air on my cheek, I knew the front door had just swung open.

"Excuse me," I called out. "I'm looking for the Blind Bowlers' League. Do you know where they meet?"

"Yes, Ma'am. Right this way. Here's my arm. I'll take you to the lounge. That's where they meet before bowling."

I gulped. *Oh swell! In the lounge? I don't drink alcohol and sure don't do bars. Doesn't sound too good to me. Well, another first in the same evening—my first time in a cocktail lounge.*

Walking with the security guard gave me a sense of relief, especially since he said he'd be watching out for me. His strong arm guided me right to the booth where the blind folks were. Placing my hand on the edge of the table, he said, "Four of the team members are here scarfing down all the popcorn. Hope you have fun."

"Hi, I'm looking for the Blind Bowlers' League."

"Yes, you must be Pam," Bob said. "We've been expecting you. Here, have a seat and join us."

Bob, Mary, David and Gus gave me the low-down on their League. They were also quite knowledgeable on all the best cocktails. Singapore Sling was their suggestion. Being a novice in this area, I appreciated their help, or so I thought. A bit of information they failed to tell me is that a Singapore Sling was loaded with alcohol. And little did I know that alcohol affects you more on an empty stomach.

Oh well, they say that ignorance is bliss! I was thirsty, but hungry, too.

"Good choice, guys, this Singapore Sling tastes like fruit punch."

With a nibble of popcorn, I guzzled down the rest of that refreshing drink so I wouldn't keep everyone waiting.

"Ready, Pam? Our team is up."

"Sure, Mary, lead the way."

It's a good thing that I had helpful friends on my team. Before our time to bowl, they helped me get acclimated and geared up. First, they showed me the bowling rail. This free-standing chrome rail stood about four feet high like a fence marking the left boundary of our lane. The end of that rail was the spot to start my delivery. Bob worked with me to perfect how many paces I needed to walk before reaching the point of rolling my ball. He proceeded to show me the ball return. Next came selecting a ball for me. Gus helped me select the right weight ball.

Feeling pleased and confident, I took my place on the bench with the rest of the team. In the midst of our laughter and a marathon of jokes, Bob called out, "Pam, are you ready to try it?" Eager to join in, I jumped up. And just as quickly as I rose, my balance left.

"Oh my gosh!" I squealed as I swerved and bumped into Bob's shoulder. "I'm really dizzy!"

A choir of giggles and snickers rang out behind me. For sure, that didn't boost my confidence. But, a soft reassuring voice chimed in with, "That Singapore Sling sure got to you. Just stand still until you get your balance back. Then move slowly, and you'll be okay," Mary coached with concern.

I was ready. With left hand sliding along the rail, I swung my ball backward with gusto. But, before I could finish swinging forward, there went the ball slipping right off my fingers. Moving full speed backward, it headed right for my friends. Talk about a test of friendship. Real friends they were, indeed. They took it all in stride with laughter and encouragement.

"Ten points for Pam. That was a perfect ball—straight and fast." Gus announced with a belly laugh.

Bowling became a highlight of my week. With a good-fitting ball and virgin cocktails from then on, my bowling steadily improved. In fact, later that year, I took second place in our statewide tournament and even won a trophy. I was quite proud of that trophy. Its white marble base with ornate crown of red velvet and gold topped by a bowling silhouette was the perfect addition to my apartment decor.

As the spring weather turned to summer, the bowling alley traded its popularity for the park at Capital Lake. School was out for the summer and the sunbathers were out, too. Karen, Connie and I often walked to Capital Lake for a picnic lunch, swim in the lake and then a nap on our beach towels in the cool green meadow of the park. My apartment was so ideally located. Most everything was within walking distance. The lake was seven blocks away, the bowling alley five, and the Sizzler Steak House was just two blocks away. It was so much fun having lots of friends and so many places that I could easily walk to. No more loneliness for me! It was more like not enough hours in the day, but that wasn't too bad. I could deal much better with the problem of cramming and juggling my social calendar than living with the loneliness.

But of course, all play and no work won't get the job done, either. There were things I had to learn to do independently, and that was both frightening and challenging. The fun of going on picnics, for example, couldn't happen without some groceries. And, those were the days before grocery delivery was even thought of. The closest grocery store to my apartment was Safeway. To me, twelve blocks didn't seem very close, but that's how it was. The walk itself wasn't difficult, just long, but shopping inside Safeway was a whole different story.

My first walk to Safeway was a breeze. Connie's directions were perfect, and

I even walked straight to the main entrance. But, once stepping into that large store, gulp!

I have to do this! I can do this, somehow. Maybe I'll just wander up and down the aisles by myself.

But, how realistic was that? After all, even if I did find the canned food aisle, there was no guarantee that I'd come out with a can of chili instead of dog food. To this day, I still haven't found a recipe I like that calls for dog food. Anyway, there I stood in the entrance, wondering how to get my shopping done.

Contrary to all the news reports, there are lots of kind people in this world. I discovered one benefit of being blind is that it brings the kind people out of the woodwork. Self-centered grumps avoided me like an upset skunk. That actually turned out to be a blessing. After all, I'd rather avoid them, myself.

Standing just inside the main doors, I switched into surveillance mode. This meant that all my concentration was focused on listening—listen, listen until I could isolate the sound of cash registers. Then, I could walk in that direction and find a cashier. Before I had a chance to do that, a kind lady asked me if I would like help. I was delighted with her offer. She actually ended up doing her shopping along with me. That was a real treat.

My delight faded with an abrupt halt when the grocery clerk handed me two large paper sacks.

How could I have bought so much! Two big sacks, and they are both heavy babies.

Struggling with my huge overload, I stopped about every block to reposition them. At first appearance, that wouldn't seem like a difficult task, but I had to carry everything one handed. My right hand was wielding the white cane.

Oh no! That felt like a rain drop. I'd better step it up.

Then the cloud burst wide open. Nudging the bottom of one sack upward a little more with my left knee, I tried to get a better grip on it. Rip! Slip! There went the whole side of my sack, freeing up an avalanche of cans, oranges, apples and my quart of milk.

Oh great! Now what?

I began sliding one foot along the sidewalk, first to my left and then to my right, in search of lost treasures. And they truly were treasures for me with my slim budget. My foot bumped against something, but only long enough to discover a can which promptly rolled away. It was back to sliding my foot around in search of something. Anything would be better than nothing. Chasing oranges down the street in the pouring rain was in no way my favorite activity. Fortunately for me, the next thing I bumped into was a kind person. A young teenage girl came up beside me and asked, "Can I help you?"

"Boy, could you ever!"

She picked up all my runaway groceries and went the extra mile helping me carry them to my apartment.

Stepping into the warmth of my apartment, I beamed with inner contentment as I busily stocked my kitchen shelves. My pantry was full, kitchen warm and cozy. Finally, my small apartment had become welcome, warm and homey. With the addition of a small stereo and telephone, it felt good. It was home.

Soon after that soggy sack disaster, I got a shopping cart with plastic liner. This worked like a dream. It rolled with ease like a trailer right behind me. This cart was great, but costly for me. It drained my cash on hand just as the electric bill came. Expenses, bills and more expenses. That was the never ending barrage. It became obvious that I needed a checking account. And that was another challenge—something I knew nothing about and had never done before.

Thank goodness for Connie, my talking directory for Olympia. It took just one phone call, and the next day I had a competent friend walking with me to the US National Bank. With Mom's instructions in balancing a checkbook and special checks with raised lines, I was able to handle paying all my bills and making purchases independently.

CHAPTER 12
A COARSE COURSE

It was time to expand my territory. According to my classmates, I could save money if I walked to C Mart. That large complex had groceries, clothing, a variety section and restaurant. Even though it meant walking twice as far as Safeway, I was ready for a change.

It was time to get a new blouse. Finally, I thought I was strong enough to make a trip to C Mart. Shopping fever hit one afternoon as I sat in the middle of a boring Microbiology lecture. I was already tired and figured I should postpone that long walk until the weekend. Despite my gut level feeling that I should wait, I headed off to C Mart right after school. Following the specific directions from my classmates, I made the trip just fine. It did have better prices, better selection of merchandise and the store even provided a shopping escort for me.

Natalie was the perfect choice for my escort. She worked there part time and was about my age. We had a ball breezing through the grocery aisles, stopping at every food sample and twice at the tasty ones. Yogurt was on sale, yes! They even had my favorite berry flavors. Non Fat milk and Imperial light margarine completed the dairy section. I found good bargains on tuna and my favorite whole wheat bread. I went wild when we got to the produce department. What a selection of fresh fruits they had. I was fascinated by the unique shape of Star fruit, so I had to try one. Finishing our tour of the grocery section, it was on to the ladies clothing.

Natalie let me really browse. I told her what I wanted. She took me to the first rack where she described all the colors and patterns in detail. I checked out the fabric and styles, but nothing there suited me. The second rack had just what I wanted. The lace and a V-neck definitely grabbed my attention. But, when my fingers saw the embroidery, I was sold.

Popping open the crystal on my Braille watch, I gasped at the time. How could two hours have gone by so fast? It was already 5:45, time for dinner. Natalie escorted me to their in-store cafe. The small eatery buzzed with activity. Its air was still and hot with the prominent smell that broadcasted deep fried foods. Indistinct smells challenged my detective nose culminating in the verdict that this was no culinary kitchen. But at that moment of being famished and fatigued, it seemed like a Caribbean oasis. Natalie assisted me in placing my order then guided me to an empty booth.

"It was fun shopping with you, Pam, but I've got to get back to work."

"Thanks so much, Natalie. I had fun, too. You made my first visit to C Mart extra special."

"Oh, that's good. Hope to see you again soon."

With a warm handshake, she departed, and I embraced the chance to sit down at last. The hard wooden bench was a most welcome spot.

My growling stomach settled into a purr of satisfaction with the basket of yummy fish and chips. As I leaned back to finish sipping my diet Coke, exhaustion hit me full force. I kicked myself for not listening to reason. I knew that this trip would be too much for my reduced stamina. A low blood pressure crisis had hit me about a month previously. That episode left my body void of energy.

Wow, it's almost 7:00, and I still have to walk thirty blocks to get home. Dr. Benson told me not to do anything extra and get lots of rest. What a dummy. Should have waited till the weekend to do this. Just hope I can make it.

As I leaned back to gather a few more minutes of rest, I heard someone approach my table.

"Mind if I join you?" It was a gentleman.

"No, not at all, but I'm just about ready to leave."

It seemed good not to be sitting alone, but even more welcome than this company was the excuse to put off that long trek home. As we talked, I learned that Dick just got out of the Army and was getting settled in Olympia. We soon discovered common ground. "I know you can't see it, but right above your head is a poster with a huge chocolate sundae," Dick said as he continued to describe all the mouthwatering details pictured.

"Chocolate, that's my weakness. If I want something sweet, I usually go for chocolate."

"I'm a chocoholic myself, and that sundae really looks good. How about you, Pam?"

"You know, it sure sounds good. Oh, why not? After all, I'll burn off all those calories with that long walk back home."

Dick insisted on buying the sundae for me. We sat there enjoying dessert and a good conversation.

"Thanks, Dick. It's been nice talking to you, and I really enjoyed the sundae, too." I finally said, "I've got to get going now. I have a long walk ahead of me, and I'd like to get home before dark."

He graciously offered to drive me to my apartment. Although I felt a tad bit apprehensive, I knew that my energy was drained dry. So, I accepted his offer.

Gathering my shopping bags and purse, I took Dick's arm. We headed out to the parking lot, continuing our conversation.

Looking back, I now know that there were plenty of warning signs. I should have known that his frequent comments about my nice legs and such were out of line. Unfortunately, I was too naive to recognize them.

Sliding into the front seat of his car, I began giving him directions to my apartment.

"Okay, Pam, I know where that is, but it's early yet, and the evening's perfect for a drive out into the woods. Don't you think?"

With my protest to his suggestion, Dick's demeanor immediately changed from a kind gentleman to that of a harsh Sergeant of Arms. As usual, I paid attention to the route by keeping track of which way the car turned. But, this time the only information those many turns gave me was the fact that I was lost! LOST! Finally, the car stopped. We were definitely out in the woods.

"Well, here we are. It's a romantic spot, and we're all by ourselves." I rolled down the window and listened. He was right. There was no sound of anything except a few birds quietly twittering and a soft whispering breeze in the tree branches. We were alone! All alone!

"So, tell me, Pam, have you ever had sex before?"

"No, I'm a virgin and plan to stay that way until I get married."

Sorry to say, that was not Dick's plan.

"Well, Pam, that's a noble statement." Then in a deep guttural voice he demanded, "You do what I want now or you won't get back home alive. Do I make myself clear?"

He made himself too clear with a harshness I hadn't heard before. Engulfed by shock and fear, the only response I could make was to slump down in my seat. The cold harsh steel jaws of his death threat gripped my mind like the heavy clamp of a ball and chain on a prisoner's ankle.

Realizing how devastating his harsh words were on me, he tried to calm me with flattery. Those words rang in my mind like empty bells with no clappers.

The door's not locked. I'll just run, run for my life. But where could I go? What's out there? He'd catch me right away and then he would kill me for sure.

As I inched closer to the door, Dick said, "The sooner you get with it, the sooner you'll get home. So, quit fooling around."

Resigned to my fate, I lay there like a limp doll and tried to block my mind from what was happening. His rough hands on me and disappearing clothes stripped me of all dignity. I tried to block my mind from what was happening, but I couldn't. Then, the excruciating pain hit.

If this is the ecstasy of love, I can live forever without it!

I never expected that rape would be part of my college education. But it was, and oh how I wish I could erase it. He did keep his word and drove me home. By the time I got there, it was close to midnight.

Dick carried my bags up to my front door. He thanked me for a pleasant evening and said that he was pleased to be the one to introduce me to the wonderful world of sex.

I couldn't get him off my porch quick enough. With every cell in my body trembling, I struggled to hold the key steady enough to unlock the door. Dragging my bags inside, I quickly shut the door behind me and checked twice to make sure it was locked. Then came the challenge of getting up the stairs. My legs and knees bowed like flimsy rubber bands, and I was shaking with such coarse tremors that I couldn't even lift my foot up to the first step. I dropped to my hands and knees in convulsions of tears and sobbing. Then one step at a time, I painstakingly inched my way to the top. Finally I made it and passed out on my living room floor.

The next afternoon I awoke still curled up on the living room carpet. Stretching and still groggy, I questioned what I was doing there. Popping open my watch, I gasped! It was 2:00 p.m.

Oh no! I slept through class! What will I tell Mrs. Stiller? I can't tell her what really happened.

But, I had to do something. Sitting up, I attempted getting to my feet, but I couldn't even stand. Crawling over to the end table, I pulled my phone onto the floor and made the call. What a relief, Mrs. Stiller was not available. I left a generic message with the receptionist stating that I was sick.

With the call completed, I gathered up enough strength to climb into my bed and slept the rest of that day and night. I called again the next day.

"Hello, Mrs. Stiller, this is Pam. I'm still sick and won't be there today."

"I'm sorry to hear that. What's going on?"

I told her what had happened and that I was having a relapse. The trauma of that night in the woods sent me back to the state of the low blood pressure crisis. Again, my body felt as though the speed of my anatomical engine dropped from a hot rod dragster to an antique putt-putt.

I called home and my family came to the rescue. Only a few hours later, I opened my front door to those reassuring words, "Pam, it's Dad." He greeted me with a comforting hug. My suitcase was ready to go and so was I. Once in the car, Dad asked if I had reported this to the police.

"You know, I hadn't even thought about doing that. Besides, what could I tell them? I don't know what he looked like, the car he was driving, the license number or anything."

We agreed that it would be pointless to contact the authorities. So the remainder of our trip was spent getting caught up on all the latest events. I dozed most of the way. In what seemed to be just a few minutes, I heard that welcome crunch of gravel as Dad turned into our driveway.

Mom must have been watching for us. Before I even got out of the car, she was coming down the front porch steps to meet us, her loving arms wrapped around me to lift my weak body and wounded spirit.

"Oh, Honey, I'm so sorry," Mom said with another warm embrace.

Dad came around to my side of the car and had me lean on his strong forearm as we slowly made our way up the front steps and into our living room.

Oh, the physical and emotional relief that embraced me as I lay down on that old family couch. I was safe at home again. In the midst of my endeavor to relax and regain strength, a sullen sorrow of inner pain gnawed at me. I felt like a heap of trash and mourned my loss of virginity. How carefully I had guarded it throughout my teenage years with modesty and abstinence. Mom came to check on me and saw the teardrops. I told Mom exactly how I was feeling. In a few minutes, Dad joined us.

"Pam, it's normal that you would feel like this. But, the truth is, it's not your fault. If you had been out there soliciting, that would have been a totally different matter. You're innocent and don't need to feel of any less value."

Dad tucked me in that first night. With a reassuring hand resting on my shoulder, he said, "You know; what I'd really like to do is to hunt that jerk down and shoot him myself. But, one thing's for sure: I'd have to beat your brother to him. Just remember, Sunshine, that poor excuse for humanity won't escape God's wrath."

"Yes, I know you're right, Dad," I acknowledged in a whisper. I wanted to say more, but there just wasn't enough strength left to do that. Despite my lack of words, I knew Dad understood, as his warm reassuring hand squeezed mine in the most loving way.

"Better get some sleep. Besides, things will look brighter in the morning."

First thing that next morning, Mom was on the phone making an appointment with the doctor. I had already expressed fear about getting some kind of transmittable disease. Due to a sudden cancellation, they were able to get me in right away. Fortunately for me, the report came back clear. We all breathed a deep sigh of relief.

"Well, we got over the biggest hurdle," Dad remarked. "Now, all you have to worry about is getting well. As soon as you feel better, we'll all find some fun things to do."

My first few days at home were sick leave days for sure. I was too weak to do anything but sleep, eat and then rest some more. My folks' love, encouragement and care was the best therapy ever and just what I needed.

With lots of rest and TLC, I finally started to feel human again. That was good for sure, but the rejuvenation of my mind refreshed the memory, as well. Nightmares and flashbacks hit during the day and night.

Oh, how I wish I could get rid of those terrifying memories, but I don't know where to begin.

The truth is, I did know. When my mind was back to full capacity, I remembered the Christian psychologist's words at our ladies retreat. She said that we can't stop thoughts from entering our mind, just like we can't stop a bird from landing on our head. But, we don't have to let it build a nest there. She gave three steps to help get rid of unwanted thoughts and I was determined to follow them. They were: 1. Be quick to recognize bad thoughts and don't let them linger. 2. Admit I need help and ask the Lord to help me have the right thoughts. 3. Think about and fill my mind with good things.

Whenever the slightest detail of that woodland detour hit my mind, I told myself,

No! I refuse that! It's a bad nightmare! Dear Lord, please help me get rid of this garbage and find the blessings, instead. Yes, I have such a loving family, neat friends in college, straight A grades, and now I'm able to live on my own.

I was clearly surrounded by good things, but the best of all was that promise from God—the one Grandma read to me when I first woke up blind. I could still hear her flipping the pages in her Bible and reading: "God will work all things together for good for those who love Him."

I couldn't believe it back then, but seven years later, I was more than convinced.

It's going to be interesting to see how God can turn this one around for good. Don't have a clue, but I know He will do it.

Another thing I learned from God's Word was to pray for my enemy, Dick. That was the absolute last thing I wanted to do, but it was just the thing that healed my inner fury. Whenever thoughts of anger and hatred for Dick hit me, I didn't let my thoughts dwell on it but immediately began to pray for him. Talking to my Heavenly Father gave me a much better perspective, which had a major impact on my attitude. I began to realize how miserable Dick must have been, searching for something and never getting real fulfillment. I actually began to feel sorry for the poor sap.

It took a full two weeks of recuperating at home. With my energy recharged and attitude adjusted, I was ready to get back to college and my friends. Although saddened by the thought of leaving my family, it was definitely time to pack my bag. That meant off to the Greyhound Bus Depot. The four of us stood waiting for the Olympia bus to pull in. Hugs, kisses and hearty wishes for the best escorted me onto the bus.

Once aboard, I settled in for a long two and a half hour trip. One way to keep from total boredom was to crochet. I carefully positioned my red rose print canvas bag on the empty seat beside me. Then I pulled out my ball of yarn and tucked it between my thigh and the side of the bus.

That ought to keep it in place.

Busy with my crocheting and daydreaming, I was oblivious to anything else, much less that ball of yarn. But, with each little tug of the hook, the ball moved. Then the bus made a wide sweeping turn, and the ball was liberated without my notice. Stretching my legs beneath the seat ahead of me, I leaned back to enjoy a catnap. The peace of slumber was about to settle in when a lady's shrill voice jolted me.

"Oh my gosh! There's blue yarn wrapped around my foot. Where on earth did that come from?"

A sinking feeling hit my gut. In a panic response, I reached beside my thigh and felt for my yarn. Checking the seat, the floor and shaking out my sweater, no yarn could be found anywhere.

Whoops! Could that be my yarn way back there?

Yes, it was mine. What a way to get acquainted with everyone on the bus. Starting in the very back, the passengers, one by one, passed my yarn ball under the seat to the person ahead. Finally, a little tangled and disheveled, it made it all the way up to the front seat and back into my hands.

Well, Plan B—it's going into the zipped section of my bag. That'll fix it.

It was good to get back to my apartment and settled in. I could hardly wait to see my friends again. After getting unpacked, I headed downstairs to visit with Mr. and Mrs. Cameron. They were so glad to have me back and doing well.

"Oh, by the way, Pam, here's some mail for you."

Reaching out, they handed me several envelopes. What caught my attention the most was a small cardboard box. I knew by the size and shape it held a cassette tape. That had to be a letter from Jason.

Oh no! How am I going to tell him what happened?

In a bit of a daze, I headed upstairs. I decided a phone call would be the best approach. Jason was obviously delighted to hear from me, at least at first. News of the current event made him furious. Thank goodness his anger was not aimed at me.

"You know, Honey, this is exactly what I was afraid of. You always see good in everyone, and unfortunately, that's just not the way it is."

My next cassette tape letter to Jason was awkward to make, but after that it became easier. Our relationship grew stronger. Jason coached me on what to watch out for in men. His insightful words helped me stay on guard, "Just remember, whenever you meet a new guy, be skeptical of his every word. You can be kind but don't trust him right off the bat." Before any outings, I reminded myself of this advice.

As I continued healing, I refused to allow fear to set in. I always put safeguards in place like being with a group of friends and never being alone with the opposite sex.

In January, 1971, I was back in college after Christmas break. The time had passed so quickly. What had come even quicker was my graduation.

According to the college catalog, Medical Transcription was a two year course. Its length was actually determined on an individual basis. Mrs. Stiller decided when each student was proficient enough for employment. After a year and a half, I had reached that point. With mixed emotions, I prepared to move back to Portland. My first choice would have been to stay in Olympia. That was not an option because many of the former grads had settled in town. The medical transcription job market was over-saturated.

That meant I would soon be Portland bound. My friends were just as disenchanted about the move as I was. They made sure I knew that. A gala pizza farewell party was held in my honor. It even included my favorite dessert. The warm chocolate cake with vanilla ice cream would have been the Duke's Delight for sure. But, the crowning teardrops diluted Its Majesty. A toast to success with bear hugs and best wishes created an outstanding finale.

Two days later, my moving crew was in motion. Mom, Dad and Steve caravanned north to Olympia. Mom came in the family car. Dad and Steve brought a U-Haul truck. In one afternoon, my apartment was emptied, and it was good-bye Olympia!

Success and sadness warred mightily on the battlefield of my emotions. Reaching my goal of being a Certified Medical Transcriptionist was accomplished—what a sense of satisfaction. On the other hand, Olympia held so many good friends and fun memories. I didn't want to leave them behind.

No sooner had I wiped the tear from my eye when apprehension and fear also hit full force. I wondered how, when and where I would find a job.

CHAPTER 13
ROLL UP YOUR SLEEVES

Well, this homespun Portland girl was back home again and so glad of it! Once I was inside our front door, Mom, Dad and Steve surrounded me with the warmest welcome home hugs. At that moment, my whole inner being sighed with deep contentment. Oh how good it was to be a part of the family's activities again. I had missed out on all the nitty-gritty details in our home for so long.

Steve was busy with his new management position at the Herfy's Roast Beef Restaurant. Despite the long hours on the job, he assured me we would find time to go out weekly together for our traditional supreme combination pizza. My folks were their usual busy selves.

Mom worked part time as a data entry operator outside the home. That was on top of her more than full-time job in our basement. There she single handedly ran the auto racing office. This was no small task, either. During each NASCAR race, the drivers earned points according to their finishing positions. Mom had to keep track of the point standings for the whole Northwest Region. Once it was updated, she mailed bulletins out to all the drivers and sent press releases.

This was long before the days of word processors and photocopiers and the duties were a tedious task. It required manually typing a letter-perfect stencil. She had to line it up exactly on the ink-soaked roller of an old Xerox machine. After finishing that, Mom often commented, "I look like a grease monkey right out of the grease pit." Then came my part, I would hand-crank it and keep count until we had 400 copies. We would sit down with our cup of tea and together fold each bulletin and stuff it into an envelope.

In addition to that time-gobbling task, Mom was Dad's secretary, stenographer and bookkeeper. As for the receptionist, that was me because Dad liked the way I answered the telephone.

My college class in Business Communications came in handier than expected. Dad's least favorite part of the business was doing paperwork. Since he spent many hours driving between the seven racetracks, I suggested he do some of his paperwork then. I gave him my cassette recorder so he could dictate his correspondence, etc. He was delighted with this arrangement and very pleased with my work.

Dad's tapes were entertaining. In the midst of his correspondence would be jokes and colorful travel logs. He really appreciated my skill in phrasing and grammar.

This appreciation was eroded with a flash flood of negativity each time he mentioned my weight. Cortisone was the culprit. Ever since the brain surgery, it was a daily necessity for my survival. While the cortisone did good things like fight infection and improve strength, it caused me to double in size.

Those degrading comments were verbalized often. But, even more crushing were two particular statements. "Pam, you might as well crawl off in a dark corner and curl up and die if you don't lose weight." And, "Pam, I shudder to think of what you could have been if you hadn't have gone blind."

Even counterattacks of Pollyanna positivism couldn't lessen their devastation. Those two comments were indelibly carved right to the very core of my brain and heart.

Settled into the groove of family and Portland, it was time to tackle the next chapter in my life—job hunting. But this was not my preference and definitely not my first choice activity. My brain told me that I should be able to do this on my own, but my gut-level feelings shouted just the opposite. This constant teeter-tottering inside me was anything but a motivating force. In fact, quite the contrary—the more I thought, the more I sat trying to figure out what to do next. This dilemma spun a pair of "heavy duty" cement shorts for me.

Well, I'm getting nowhere fast!

My sedentary quandary finally ended with some professional input. I knew the Commission for the Blind would be the best place to start. I let my fingers do the walking and made a phone call. The receptionist was very gracious and directed me to their Job Placement Specialist, Mr. Grant. Mr. Grant was most helpful. He suggested the approach of mailing out resumes to all the hospitals in Portland.

Feeling confident in my ability to produce a top-notched resume, I kicked Old Blue into high gear. This almost antique baby-blue electric typewriter became my constant companion as I sat diligently pumping out resumes to the many hospitals. Old Blue was no match for the fancy IBM typewriters in college. They were just machines—Blue was my pal. Its individually striking keys clinked with a flowing rhythm like a fine-tuned orchestra.

It made me smile with proud satisfaction. I had bought this faithful helper with my own allowance. It bolstered my self-confidence with a sense of accomplishment. Once again, I was able to write both quickly and legibly to my family and out-of-town relatives.

Several hospitals courteously responded stating they had no openings. But, I continued mailing out more resumes. One afternoon, Old Blue and I were at it again. We hadn't been working long before Mom entered the room with an excited urgency in her voice.

"Pam, there's a man from the Commission for the Blind on the phone for you."

I jumped up to answer it. That familiar voice with its congested wheeze of a year-round cold greeted me.

"Hi, Pam, it's Mr. Grant. Ready to go to work?" He asked in a serious, straight-forward manner. "There's an opening for a part-time medical transcriptionist at McDak. It's a small privately owned business. This is your chance, take it." Interrupting his speech with a raspy cough, he cleared his throat and added, "What do you say?"

"Sounds worth looking into."

McDak was located in the West Hills rising above the heart of Portland. Getting to it would entail a long bus trip clear across town. I was more than worried about tackling such a commute and going to unknown parts. My fear began to dwindle as I took an objective look at the facts.

Well, Pam, it's either the cement shorts or a paycheck.

Knowing I couldn't stand being broke all the time and just sitting at home watching my family members whizzing by, I knew this was the time to step out. After all, this was an ideal opportunity to get my feet wet in the job market. I applied for it, and just two days later I received a call. It was from Barbara, the owner of MeDak. It was good news, too.

Hanging up the phone with an excited clunk, I ran to the washroom in search of Mom. "Hooray! I got the job!"

She dropped the large plastic laundry basket and squeezed me tight with a victory hug. I was engulfed in the world of elation for a split second. Then the icy hand of panic seized me as I thought, *how on earth would I get there?*

Without even thinking, my hand reached for the phone. With a flash, I dialed the familiar pattern of Mr. Grant's phone number.

"Hi, guess what, I got the job. Barbara wants me to start Monday. That's only a week away."

"Well, what do you think? Are you good to go?"

"Chomping at the bit to work, but how am I going to get there by myself?"

He assured me that their Orientation and Mobility Specialist would work with me to learn the route. In fact, on that same call, he transferred me right over to Mr. Oldstead.

The friendly calm voice on the other end of the line soothed my apprehensive fidgeting better than a double shot Singapore Sling. I could see the smile in his voice right through the receiver. That brief conversation filled with laughter and information paved a smooth path for my upcoming adventure.

A minute before seven o'clock the very next morning, footsteps sounded on our porch. Before the doorbell could ring, my hand was on the knob.

"Good morning, Pam. I'm Mr. Oldstead. You sure look nice in that bright floral dress. Lucky for us, we even have a sunny spring day, too. Are you ready to travel?"

"Yes, I'm all set."

"After our phone conversation yesterday, it sounds like you really just need to know how to use our Portland buses. Is that right?"

"Learning the buses is definitely my main goal, but I do have one other concern. I've never had professional training and would appreciate it if you'd check my travel skills."

Mr. Oldstead had me walk ahead of him and go to the corner of my block. A soft puff of breeze swished cool across my face with the sweet fragrance of lilacs blossoming in Mrs. Melheim's yard. At the corner, we turned left and began our four-block walk along Prescott Street. This two-lane residential street was still sleepy in the early morning hours with seldom a car passing.

Mr. Oldstead stopped me at the end of each block. "Pam, can you hear any difference in the traffic sound? Does the pollution smell stronger?"

Each block closer to the high traffic thoroughfare did make a difference. The exhaust fumes increased to an almost gagging stench. At first, the traffic sounds along 82nd Avenue were just a distant low rumble. It got louder and by the last block became distinctly punctuated with the different sized engines and speeds.

Many years of racetrack exposure had trained my ears well. I knew the sounds of everyday street machines compared to the louder hefty full stock racing engines. Whenever possible, Dad and I would take a few minutes and watch the main event together.

"Pam, here comes Hershel McGriff in his flashy orange car. He's leading the pack. You sure can tell his car by the loud strong supercharged engine. It's got power. Now, hear that guy. He's at the end of the pack. Almost sounds like a lawnmower compared to Hershel's."

His enthusiastic commentary created a colorful action-packed movie right before me. It was Dad's gift of fun as we shared the races together.

Whoever thought the racetrack would help me with crossing busy streets, but it sure did. It was time to cross that busy four-lane intersection. Even though Mr. Oldstead stood right beside me, I was petrified.

We stood on that corner for several changes of the signal. I listened with wide open ears as he clued me in on what was happening and how to audibly detect the traffic surges. Using this new information through four traffic sequences, I felt confident in my ability to recognize signal changes. However, that was only one bit of information that I would need to pick up from the traffic sounds. By listening closely, I could detect left turners and much more.

Another important, yet tricky, part was getting lined up for a straight crossing. Without that, I could angle into the center of the intersection. But, Mr. Oldstead sure knew how to get me straightened out. I just had to follow the grass line on my left.

"That's looking good, Pam. You're almost ready. Now, listen closely to those cars stopped in front of you, waiting for the light. You need to keep your mind focused on those sounds so that you can walk just in front of them. Okay, Pam, when you think it's time, we'll cross. I'll have my hand on your shoulder until we step up on the other side."

Well, I made it safely across that busy four-lane thoroughfare and back several times. To my surprise, it wasn't as scary as I had expected.

With the intersection conquered, we were off to find the bus stop. Two blocks and two telephone poles from the corner—that was my map to the bus stop. The loud roar of the bus's engine came clearly into my "view" as it pulled up to the curb.

"Pam, listen for the clunk of the doors opening and head for that sound. Be sure to use your cane to check the distance between the curb and first step."

With his concise briefing, I learned what to tell the driver when first stepping onto a bus. It was essential to communicate both where I wanted off and that the driver needed to announce that stop. Once seated on the bus, I asked Mr. Oldstead for his opinion of my cane travel skills.

"Pam, you look like a seasoned traveler. You are doing a super job." I thanked him with a big sigh of relief and amazement. I was pleasantly surprised and thrilled from head to toe.

It was onward to Pioneer Square in downtown Portland. Arriving there, I learned to find the bus stop for my transfer to the Council Crest bus. Mr. Oldstead accompanied me and made sure I was able to handle each part of this four-bus trip from home to work and back again. Arriving on my front porch, I thanked him for his patience and expertise. We parted with a warm handshake and ear-to-ear grins knowing that we had accomplished our goal.

"Well, Pam, you're doing great. If you ever need help with a new part of town or any other travel tips, we'll schedule another day out on the town."

I was travel-ready and ready for my first day of work. In my purse were two sets of index cards with Braille notes—one set outlining my route and the second containing the bus schedules. No matter what time I left home, there was always at least a thirty minute layover between buses. Sitting on a hard wooden bus bench and twiddling my thumbs in the pouring rain or summer heat didn't suit me at all! I had to find something to do other than warming a bus bench twice a day.

I decided that it would be fun to get acquainted with Portland. First, I got a list of the core area streets. Brailing the list of names was the easy part, but keeping track of them in my mind was a different story. As I contemplated how I could memorize these, a phrase popped into my mind, "Jesus Christ made Seattle under protest." The Seattle cabby's method seemed like a good way to go.

That's it! I'll make up a Portland memory jogger.

I came up with my own phrase. Even though it sounded like a foreign land, it sure helped my memory: "Ba-po-swamy" (Burnside, Ankeny, Pine, Oak, Stark, Washington, Alder, Morrison and Yamhill).

Then came the fun part—getting the chance to explore.

I began just observing as I leisurely walked from one corner of the block to the other. The ornate brass drinking fountain with three bowls of cold running water whispered pleasantly to me. It alerted me that I had reached the middle of the block with just a few more steps to the bus shelter.

Meier & Frank's large entrance made another good landmark. There was lots of foot traffic plus a special swishing sound of the rotating doors. Once I had a good sense of the block from corner to corner, it was time to venture indoors. It took several weeks and a full paycheck to get acquainted with that ten story department store. But, I did it and had lots of fun in the process.

Well, for the most part I had fun. First I familiarized myself with the elevator buttons and then memorized which floors had the departments I wanted. That was a breeze—no problem for me.

A blushing moment hit as I shopped for Dad's birthday gift. For me to browse, of course, meant using my twenty-twenty vision in all ten fingertips. Stepping out of the elevator onto the second floor, I switched into surveillance mode. I listened intently for the sounds of a cash register or the conversation of a salesperson nearby. There was no clue, not even a hint of any impending assistance. But a simple thing like that would never thwart an avid shopper like me.

No problem, I have half an hour before my bus comes. I'll just wander around and check out the men's sportswear department.

My white cane slid across the highly polished floor with ease, and I was shopping ready. I saw a tall dark line at the end of one of the racks.

Oh perfect, a mannequin. It's so much easier to feel an outfit when displayed on a model.

With an air of confidence, I walked over to it and reached out to feel the fabric. I took a close look at the smooth polyester cloth by gently sliding the sleeve between my thumb and forefinger. Moving my right hand, I began to check out the jacket's front. I found an ornate metal button. My fingers were entranced in examining the detailed texture of the button. Then, the mannequin moved! I jumped backward with an abrupt jerk as though my hand had just touched a hot pot. With a faint "excuse me," I spun around without waiting for his response. Well, I certainly wasn't pale anymore. My blush response had kicked into high gear. Fortunately for me, the elevator doors just clunked open giving me an audible landmark. With my ears zeroed in on the elevator and my cane switched into drag strip speed, I was out of there!

Phew! I made it and in record time, too!

As I stepped through the heavy double doors of the Meier & Frank lobby, the smog-laden air and eardrum jarring traffic noise never seemed more welcome. Well, the moral of this story is never touch the belly of a mannequin—they are ticklish.

My half-hour layover between buses seemed shorter and shorter as I found more places to visit.

CHAPTER 14
BRAIN BLUR

The downtown core teemed with lots of little shops quietly tucked in between the larger department stores. The Hallmark store was handy, just three blocks south of my bus stop. The proprietor with her authentic English accent was a delight to chat with. I stopped there often, even when I didn't need gifts or cards. She always welcomed me and enjoyed the company.

Even closer and more attractive was Cress's Dime Store. It became my favorite stop and catered so well to my "bargain hunter" instinct. I spent several layovers just getting acquainted with the sections. The candy counter with its chocolate odor was easy to find and just beyond buzzed the distinct sound of the many compressors of the soda fountain. It was fun to explore and learn a new section or two with each visit.

After all that exploration, my store directory was complete. It read like this: three steps beyond the entrance rubber mat and I was in the personal care section. It took up three aisles. The fourth and fifth made up the greeting card section and so on.

I came face to face with the first drawback when I decided to venture upstairs. I asked an employee for directions to the elevator. It was located in the middle of the south wall. What she failed to tell me was on that same wall were three very similar doors.

Having gathered all my facts, I decided to go for it. As I headed for the south wall, my auditory sensors picked up a noisy obstacle dead ahead. It sounded like a stroller and the giggles of two toddlers escorting it. Instinctively, I took a giant step to the right in an attempt to avoid them. My large canvas shopping bag sideswiped a rack. Instantly, I was showered with a downpour of UFOs. I reached to retrieve the surprise merchandise which was dangling acrobatically from my canvas strap. My fingers were greeted by two floppy ears and stiff plastic whiskers.

Oh great! The weather is worse in here than outside. It's raining not just cats and dogs, but bunny rabbits, too.

Popping open the crystal on my watch, I gasped. I was about to miss my bus. Snatching my bag and cane, I headed out.

True, the elevator door was in the middle of the south wall. But on either side of the elevator were public restrooms. One step farther and my nose cringed with the acrid smell of urine. My forward advance was abruptly halted when a man's voice announced, "Hey, lady, this is the men's room." At that same moment, my cheeks flushed with the intense heat of an all-day sunburn.

Thank goodness kind people really do come out of the woodwork. As I turned to make an about-face, a soft concerned voice spoke tall behind me.

"Here, let me help you."

Before I knew it, I had a personal escort not just out of the men's room but all the way to the bus stop. I must admit, that was a most unique way to meet a guy. However, I wouldn't recommend that approach for any single gal. One important fact I would never forget—there was no elevator in the men's room. That was enough adventure to last the whole week. I was ready to head to the security of my office chair and typewriter.

The four-hour afternoon job at MeDak accommodated quite well my sense of exploration and love of shopping. My job was enjoyable, too. I especially liked Barbara, the owner and director of this small medical transcription company. This pleasant middle-aged lady was fun-loving and easy to work with. As for me, I was diligent in doing my best. I reviewed my medical terminology text from college, made sure I got eight hours of good sleep, exercised everyday and even ate healthy.

Despite everything I tried, things just weren't going well. My work was full of mistakes. My ability to understand the doctors' dictations was poor, as well. Often I interrupted the other typists, asking them to help me figure out what the doctor said.

This ongoing combination of mistakes and interruptions gradually eroded my enjoyment of working. No longer did I wake up and look forward to my job. My inner talk recycled the thoughts of being inadequate and a liability to the company. I couldn't continue like this. Finally, I resigned to the fact that I just didn't have what it took to be a medical transcriptionist.

One afternoon, having worked there almost two months, I drug my heels into the office and spoke with Barbara. She was very understanding and agreed with my decision. She also thought I would have progressed much further by then. At dinner that same evening, I held back the tears just long enough to inform my family of the day's events. They took it in stride but were obviously disappointed, as well. After helping with the dinner dishes, I headed straight to my bedroom. There I knelt and sobbed.

"Dear, Lord, I just don't know what to do with my life! All that time and work in college wasted, wasted! My parents and the Commission spent so much money for my education, and I blew it all! Oh, Lord, I tried so hard. I gave it my very best. What more can I do?"

I was devastated, crushed flatter than parchment paper. Although that was more than a difficult experience, and one I wouldn't want to repeat, it was a pivotal point in my life. Up to that moment, I honestly had no idea that I was leaving God out of the picture. One invaluable fact I learned is that I can do nothing worthwhile in my own strength. God was the powerful force I needed for success in my life.

Ever since going blind, I struggled and worked hard to regain my self-worth and independence. It took a long time, but I made it. I had become confident and proud of my accomplishments. It was that self-reliant attitude and depending on all the wrong things that led to my failure. To make matters even worse, I didn't have a clue how to fix it or where I had gone wrong. Out of desperation, I prayed, "Dear God, I don't know what to do. I just don't know where to go from here. If anything good can ever happen, it will have to be Your doing. Amen."

Meanwhile, my resumes to many hospitals were still out there circulating. About one month later, a letter came from the Portland Adventist Hospital requesting that I go in for an interview. Had I followed my first impulse, that letter would have been tossed in the trash. But a month of boredom at home and a serious case of cabin fever overruled that initial response.

Before making any decision, I knew I had better talk it over with my Heavenly Father. Onto my knees I went. "Dear Lord, thank you for this new opportunity. But should I or shouldn't I? One thing is for sure, I won't be able to do anything good without you. Please give me wisdom and help me."

Knowing that God was my strength, I felt at peace going for the interview. The short typing test, application and subsequent oral interview went well. Beverly, the department supervisor, was easy to talk to. It amazed me that I felt so calm and not intimidated. We parted on a friendly note and within just a couple days, the phone rang with Beverly's cheerful greeting.

"Good news, Pam. After reviewing your application and typing, we've decided that you are the best match for our Transcription Department. And, we'd like to have you start as soon as you can."

Wow, was I ever elated. Then, within a split second, a lump of fear choked my throat with the reminder of my miserable job failure not that long ago. Although I felt it was the right move—it still added to the list of changes that I was experiencing.

That painful lump came at a perfect time. It reminded me of my need to depend on the Lord each step of the way. My morning routine changed so that on arising, I talked to my Heavenly Father. I asked Him to give me the ability and strength to do better than just a good job. What a real turn of events for me—I was working part time, excelling in my field and experiencing a real sense of accomplishment.

About that same time, another turn of events hit. This one was not elating by any means. Jason and I had recently broken off our engagement. With time, I could tell we were obviously growing apart. I was looking for a spiritual leader, a man who really panted after God. This was not the case with Jason. His love was wrapped around his ham radio and electronic equipment. I really enjoyed and loved him, too, but a cool wedge was widening into an icy chasm. With agony and grief, I terminated our engagement.

Summer came, and with it the racing season was in full swing again. This meant that every weekend I was home alone since Mom and Dad were literally off to the races.

Gaining a deeper relationship with God was heavy on my heart. I figured the best way to do that would be by going to church every Sunday. I had been waiting for a time when Mom and Dad could take me, but their out-of-town weekends wouldn't accommodate that. It was obvious that if anything was going to happen, I needed to make the first move. Talking to my neighbors and parents, I found that there was a small Baptist church just two blocks from our home.

Oh perfect! I can walk there—no problem!

As usual, I did my homework and got specific details on the location of the church.

The very next week, on a beautiful Sunday morning, I was up and ready for church. Walking along Prescott, I crossed 84th Avenue. Everything was going well, and I had made it to the corner of the church.

With my cane, I checked for a break in the grassy border (my method of finding a sidewalk). The soft vibrations of my cane brushed along the grass then changed to shorter hard ones. Yes, it was a sidewalk! I turned and followed it to the door.

They said it was a little church, but this doesn't look like a church entrance at all. Just a small cement slab and plain round door knob? I don't know.

Oddly enough, the door was closed. So I knocked. No answer. No sound of anyone around. Gingerly, I turned the knob and opened the door. The delicious aroma of chicken roasting was first to greet me. With hesitance, I stepped in a little farther.

Then soft footsteps came toward me.

"Hi, can I help you?" a kind man asked.

"Yes, would you show me to the sanctuary?"

"Oh, are you looking for the church?"

"Yes, Immanuel Baptist Church."

"Well, you're mighty close. This is the parsonage and the church is right behind us. Would you like me to walk you over there?"

"Wow! That would help a lot. Thanks so much."

Well, it was another "blushing moment" and lots of color for me.

If only I could patent this "all natural" blush, I could give Revlon and Maybelline a run for their money.

I must admit, it was a rather unique way to meet one of the church elders.

After that first Sunday, I had no problem walking straight to the church. That small congregation was just the place for me. They were so accepting and helpful. I had an inner warmth and comfort in their midst.

After attending a month or so, I decided it was time to do more than just warm a pew.

"Dear Lord, please provide something I can do to be of help in church."

One Sunday morning, not long after that prayer, I was sitting in my usual spot on the comfortable gold cushioned pew. My ears perked up as the deacon announced that the position of church clerk needed filling.

After inquiring about the specific duties of a church clerk, it looked like I had the needed skills. I prayed about it first, and then I volunteered. At the next general election, the members unanimously voted me in. Thank goodness for the class I took on slate and stylus. Those writing skills came in mighty handy.

At each Advisory Board meeting, I took the minutes. My very first meeting was an interesting one. Stanley, the Chairman, opened as usual and then welcomed me. The interesting part came when I pulled out my slate, stylus and steno pad. In a matter of fact fashion, I picked up my stylus and began writing a title at the top of my page. The punching sound of my stylus was followed by dead silence which seemed to draw on forever until I piped up, "I'm ready whenever you are."

"Okay, let's proceed," Stanley stated with a hesitant quaver in his voice. As the meeting proceeded, things went well, and we enjoyed just being together.

Reading the minutes from my Braille copy before the whole congregation was another first for that small church. They listened with interest and courtesy, but lots of questions and comments came my way afterward. And, the funny part was that none of the questions had anything to do with church business. Instead, they were asking me how I could read so well and make sense out of all those tiny dots. Once the minutes were approved, I typed them for the office records. Then it was my turn to be surprised. Stanley was astonished at the quality of my report.

This kept me busy but it was an enjoyable time. After two years in this position, I was ready for a change. My days of being church clerk helped me get well acquainted with lots of members. That's when I met Mandie. Mandie was single, my age and lived at home with her parents, too.

We hit it off and in short order became good friends. Mandie graciously offered to read the list of prayer requests to me each week. It was during one of those routine sessions that we noticed the need for someone to teach the mid-week kids' group. We prayed and asked God to find just the right person to fill it. With a hearty "amen" from both our lips, we looked up. At almost the same moment, a light bulb lit up above both our heads. How about us? We started meeting each week at my home to plan the lessons.

Before long, the topic of getting an apartment together was forefront in our conversations. As we talked more and did more together, we were convinced that being roommates in an apartment was the way to go. The next step was planning and apartment hunting.

Mandie was a second grade school teacher in the Portland Public Schools and had her own car. Every Saturday we met for lunch and went apartment hunting. It didn't take long before we discovered Tabor Heights. That small complex was perfect for us in many ways. Not only did the floor plan suit our needs, but it was ideally located just two blocks from Portland Adventist Hospital. Mandie had a short drive to school, as well.

Moving again! Next to job hunting, that was my least favorite thing to do. Mom and Dad loved having me back home. They were anything but thrilled about my moving out. Still, they were supportive and knew it would be good for me.

For the first few months, our apartment didn't feel like home at all. The echoing emptiness of our furniture-free living and dining rooms made it seem more like an empty warehouse. We agreed that the first thing to buy was a dining room table. Standing at the counter to eat dinner at the end of a hard work day just didn't cut it.

"Pam, Levitz is having a big sale this weekend and there are some good looking dining room sets in their ad."

"Sounds good. Let's go."

The next Saturday afternoon, we pulled up in the crowded parking lot at Levitz. Switching off the motor, Mandie turned to me and said, "Okay, Pam, we're here. Before we go in, let's pray."

I nodded with agreement but inwardly the question marks were circulating.

Pray about a dining room table? This is weird.

We prayed, and God answered with an excellent deal on a dining room set that suited our fancy to a T. With the addition of a couch, rocking chair, two end tables and lamp, it was comfortable and homey.

Being single and having our own apartment agreed with both of us really well. We kept busy with our jobs. Our extracurricular activities often took us in different directions but whenever our schedules permitted, we spent time together. I usually got home earlier than her. This gave me the opportunity to cook dinner. Mandie's appreciative attitude made cooking fun. She always let me know how good it was just to come home, drop her heavy load of books, sit down and enjoy a home-cooked meal. Dinner was especially meaningful. We used this time to talk and pray about things that had happened that day.

I learned so much from her. She was an excellent teacher. Her second grade class at Lents Elementary School was a role model for good behavior. Those two years of teaching Sunday school with Mandie gave me the skills of a Master's Degree in teaching. What a valuable time that was, and a fun one, too.

Of even greater benefit were the spiritual lessons that her life taught me. Already eight years had passed since I made the decision to become a Christian. I loved God and always tried my best to live like a child of God. But I never had any idea that there was more to being a Christian than just going to church and living right.

From the moment of that prayer about buying our dining room table, my spiritual eyes started to really see. For the first time in my life, I heard about having a personal relationship with God.

Every Saturday we spent anywhere from one to three hours working together on the Sunday school lesson plan and crafts. Those planning sessions were fun and gave me a close-up look at God. I learned so much about my Heavenly Father. The more I learned, the more I grew to love and enjoy time with Him.

Single and satisfied—that was our motto—but God definitely had other plans for Mandie and for me.

CHAPTER 15
A REAL RINGER

Our days were very full from beginning to end the whole week through. Saturdays were extra busy, but fun, too. First on our agenda was our Sunday School lesson plan. One of the most memorable lessons happened one spring morning. Mandie sat scanning the teacher's manual at our dining room table. She loved how cheery and bright the sun's rays lit up our room. I chose to sit where the comforting sunbeams came through warmest.

"Wow, Pam, this is cool! We're supposed to get a glass canning jar and put all kinds of yucky stuff in it. After we get all that junk in it, we get cooking oil and color it red. Then pour it on top to show how the blood of Jesus covers all our ugly sins. Then, we set the jar on the floor and look down into it just like God looks down on us from heaven. The oil is supposed to cover up the mess and look bright red like a ruby. First let's do the part of putting junk in it."

With two giggles in almost stereo, we searched our kitchen for treasures. Into the jar went an empty catsup packet, rusty bobby pin, wadded up napkin and a chicken bone.

"That's a good start." Mandie said. "Let's look at our directions for the next step. Yes, here it is—now we need to add dirt, rotten leaves and yucky stuff."

Down the stairs we bounded to scoop up a trowel of dirt. We gathered some other treasures like a few pieces of gravel and even a dead slug. Candid Camera should have been on the scene. Mandie would have been a real hit. We both agreed that the slug was a necessity for our collection, but the real bug-a-boo hit when we realized we'd have to pick up that slimy thing.

"It's perfect!" Mandie exclaimed with delight. "Nothing could be more disgusting than a slug."

"Great idea, but how are we going to get it from this flower bed upstairs and into our jar?"

Mandie stood in quiet puzzlement for a second trying to figure out what to do. "Pam, why don't you go get the dust pan, and I'll look for something to pick it up with." She began her search as I headed upstairs.

"Here's the dust pan."

"Good, we're in business. I found a sturdy twig just right for the job. I'll pick it up with this. Pam, stand right here and hold the dust pan still."

It was so comical watching her. She was determined to stay as far away from that slug as possible. I squatted down to position my dust pan beside the curb edge of the planter. By the sound of it, her nose must have been almost touching the dirt. There she stood with her feet firmly planted on the asphalt right beside me and her slender body stretched out across the curb like a McDonald's golden arch. Carefully sliding the twig under the slug, she gingerly balanced it on the twig and just made it to the dust pan.

"Got it. We did it, Pam."

Proud as great white hunters, we returned to our kitchen to complete our assignment. Like two dedicated chemists, we added the water and stirred with anticipation of how our experiment would turn out.

"Oh, Pam, it really does look awful!"

Satisfied with our masterpiece mess, we started on part two.

Mandie went down the hall to get the cooking oil, and I was off to the cupboard to find our red food coloring. Climbing up on the stepstool, I stretched to the top shelf for the food coloring. With my hand just off target, my little finger brushed against something and—crash!

"Oh no!" I yelled with panic and anger. "What was that?"

Heavy footsteps came jogging down the hall.

"Are you okay?" Mandie asked as she rounded the corner into the kitchen. "Whoops, I'll get the broom."

"Sorry, Mandie! What was it, anyway?"

"Just the tall glass vase. Well, if anything had to break, I'm glad it was that one. I was getting really tired of climbing up on the stool every week to dust that thing, anyway."

Our schedules continued to be jam packed, but took a whole different swing when two fellows entered the picture—Jake and Henry. It all began for Mandie at our church ice cream social. She just went over for a scoop of rocky road ice cream and came back with an infatuated guy. Even I could see the stars in Jake's eyes as they talked and laughed that first encounter. Not long after that, Jake was a regular guest at our front door. They were going out more often and seemed to be getting kind of serious.

As for me, my romance began at the white cane repair shop. Henry just so happened to be in town from Florence, Oregon, waiting to pick up his cane. I was there to drop off my broken folding cane. We both ended up waiting about an hour in the small coffee shop next door. With only a table for two, we found ourselves having a snack and sharing our experiences. This rugged outdoorsy gentleman had just the kind of personality I enjoyed immensely. He owned his own home. And of all places, it was in a small town on the Oregon Coast. I had always dreamed of living at the beach.

Before this, I had several different quick flames, but nothing steady. At work, the gals in Medical Records teased me, "My gosh, Pam, another boyfriend. You have more boyfriends than any gal around here," they would say as we chatted about our weekend activities.

Thank goodness for Mandie and our close friendship. We, of course, had to talk often about our romantic times. These conversations helped both of us keep God's values in the forefront as we dated.

A perfect example of that was my infatuation with Henry. One statement at our dinner table straightened me out. Mandie said, "Pam, whatever you do, don't settle for anything less than God's perfect mate."

I knew she was right, but Henry was just the kind of guy I enjoyed being with. We seemed to have so much in common, so many good points going for us. I told Mandie about all this and that I really felt like I was falling in love with him. She listened intently and then, with real conviction in her voice, said "You know that Henry is not a Christian, so this couldn't be right for you. Besides, just think, if Henry's not the one, God has someone even better for you."

Her words rang true. Still I had to tell him that it was not God's will for me to marry him. I agonized over this as my emotions and will battled within me like two huge Dobermans in serious tug-of-war, growling and snarling with each forceful yank. What a heart-wrenching task that was. I tried to ease the pain by telling him that we could still be good friends, but Henry responded, "Pam, that won't work. I can't stand to be around you if I can't have you."

"I understand how you feel. I feel the same, but I know getting married won't work for us. I have learned that following God's road map for life is the only way to experience true inner satisfaction. And, since we differ in our view of God, it just won't work. I know it seems hard to believe now, but in the long run, you will be much happier without me."

Good thing I had a job. Keeping busy helped get my mind off of Henry.

Working as a medical transcriptionist this time around was turning out much better than I ever expected—what a contrast from my days at MeDak. Starting each day in prayer was the key. Not having to depend solely on myself was a big relief and confidence booster. I knew that if I couldn't handle it, God could.

Portland Adventist Hospital was a great place to work. They were so considerate and good to their employees. Every employee received a gift and birthday card signed by the hospital president. This was thoughtfully delivered right to their work station on their birthday.

Each Christmas, they had an incredible staff buffet. The feast happened in the hospital cafeteria. Once stepping through its doorway, the splendor of Christmas whisked away my breath with one large "oooh" of amazement. Sugar plumb music from the piano danced around us as we approached the salad bar. This lengthy table was just as beautiful as its mouthwatering dishes. Fresh evergreen boughs lightly dusted with snow wove between its platters like miniature woodland. A four foot hand-sculptured figure stood majestically in the center.

My colleagues from the Transcription Department were doing a super job of describing the statue in detail. The more they described it, the more I knew I had to get up close and take a good look with my 20-20 vision in all ten fingertips. The large penguin was incredibly detailed and life-like.

I always liked to get an idea of the big picture first, then zero in on the details. With both hands, I skimmed from the top of its head to the bottom of its feet getting a picture of the full figure. Then my focus shifted to examine its sharp pointed beak, small beady eyes and the intricate details of the feathers.

I would like to have looked longer, but the salad line was already backed up far enough. Balancing our over-sized dinner plates, we moved on. Just a few steps away was the huge roasted soy turkey with all the trimmings.

There it stood, in all its golden brown grandeur, almost defiantly challenging our stacking skills. No matter how we piled the food on, there was never enough room for even a small nibble from each scrumptious platter.

Servers in festive attire constantly refilled our coffee and goblets of sparkling punch as we leaned back and enjoyed the live Christmas music. What a gala affair!

Of course, it wasn't all play in my work environment. Soon after I began working there, a bonus plan for our transcription department was initiated. Each transcriptionist received extra pay for every line typed above the base amount. With each pay check, I earned a bonus, as well.

Those benefits were very enjoyable. Even more satisfying to me was the fact that I was able to help the other transcriptionists. They had so graciously assisted me as the new kid on the block. Finally, it was my chance to return the favor. My well-trained ears proved to be a big plus. After working there a few months, I got familiar with the different doctors and their style of dictation. Soon I was able to understand difficult-to-hear words and sort through the syllables as doctors dictated in the midst of eating. Often I was asked to slip on the headset of a veteran transcriptionist to listen and help figure out the word they couldn't understand.

Things were going well for me and Mandie's life was moving in positive ways, as well. Jack had proposed and their wedding date was set. This was certainly a match made in heaven and I was happy for her. Mandie asked me to be her maid of honor and I was honored. What a treat it was to be part of the planning, preparation and ceremonies.

Without my loyal roommate, I couldn't afford to keep the apartment. The thought of getting another roommate had crossed my mind but Mom and Dad were eager to have me live with them. Weighing all my options, I chose to move back home.

Just one day after the moving ordeal, Dad was talking to his neighbor. I beamed with a glowing inner warmth as I overheard him say, "Well, Alex, our daughter has moved back home and we're so glad to have her with us. I hope she never moves out again."

It seemed as though I had just settled in when summer was upon us. And with summer came the racing season again. Mom and Dad were out of town more than home. I didn't want to spend my week of paid vacation staying home alone. So I decided to go to the McKenzie Camp for the Blind.

This week-long camp was held at a Catholic lodge way out in the woods. As a lifelong city girl, I jumped at any opportunity to get out of town. I longed for and loved spending time at the beach or out in the country. With eager anticipation, I packed my bags and was ready for the trip. The Lion's Club charted a Greyhound bus to transport all the blind folks to camp. Our bus turned into a chat-room on wheels as the annual reunion of campers headed southward. Although the amount of miles we traveled was considerable, the time seemed to race by. Much sooner than I expected, the bus stopped and we were at camp. Stepping off the bus, I stood entranced in that majestic mountain woodland. After dinner the first night, the dance band arrived.

How perfect! I just got here, and we'll be dancing.

I was one of the first campers to arrive in the recreation hall. People began gathering and I knew I had a few minutes before the band would start. That gave me just enough time to dash to the ladies room. And dash I did. I wasn't about to miss even the first beat.

In my hurry to return, I cut the corner a bit too tight and before I knew it, I was nose to nose with a stranger.

"Oh my, excuse me," I apologized.

A soft timid voice responded, "That's all right."

"You know, I don't recognize your voice. Have we met before?"

"Probably not. I'm new here."

"Oh, neat! I'm Pam. What's your name?"

"Rex."

"Welcome, Rex. Would you like to join the festivities? We'll be having a dance and live music in the Rec hall tonight."

That simple "bump" really got things rolling. For starters, we shared a lot of common ground in our past histories. Rex lost his vision with a brain tumor much like the one I had.

His gentle, fun-loving ways attracted me like a magnet. We both enjoyed dancing, walking to the little store, and of course, hosting Night Owl snack parties in my room every night. One afternoon, he asked me to play pool. That was a first for me.

"Sounds interesting, but how do you do it? I can't see the end of the pool cue, much less figure out where the ball is."

"Step this way, my dear, and I'll show you how it's done."

What a novel idea he had. We didn't even need pool cues. Instead, standing at opposite ends of the table, we used our hands to block balls from ending up in the pockets nearest us. At the same time, we furiously rolled balls toward our opponent's pockets to score points. The element of danger heightened our excitement. With all those balls bouncing and flying in every direction, fingers were at high risk of being smashed. Each ball had to be handled like touching a hot potato. At the same time, it had to be skillfully aimed for the well-guarded far end pockets. Once I got my feet wet in this pool duel, we branched out. Tournaments of "the girls against the boys" popped up on the events schedule many afternoons.

Friends, fun and excitement made a winning combination for all participants. The remarkable part is that our fingers survived many pool games with few battle scars.

By the end of that week, we hit it off so well that Rex asked me to go steady. In considering his offer, my mind was immediately hit with a message much like a pop-up window on a computer screen.

"IMPORTANT, IMPORTANT," it flashed in bright bold letters. "Make sure this guy is a Christian."

Earlier that same year, Mandie and I had attended a Basic Youth Seminar which taught Biblical principles for everyday life. There I learned that it was essential to find out first thing if my date was a Christian. I made sure to check out his stand as soon as he hinted of more than a friendship interest in me. His genuine response of, "Yes, Pam, I love God" was a brilliant green light for me.

With each new day of camp, we spent more time together. Our laughter and enjoyment of each other steadily increased, as well. The last night of camp, long after the dancing was over, we sat in front of the glowing fireplace, just the two of us. Rex reached out with a warm hand on my knee and asked me to go steady. I was not ready for this. I told him I didn't want to get serious so fast.

"I agree with you, Pam, but we sure have had a terrific time together this week. I believe we have something extra special started. By going steady, we'll be making a commitment to getting to know each other better and explore the possibility of engagement." His response made lots of sense. And, since Rex had assured me that he was a Christian, my answer was a hearty yes. We parted camp with hugs and the commitment to stay in touch often.

CHAPTER 16
THE WORK FORCE & THE WALK FORCE

Dating Rex after camp was sparse at best—much less than we would have liked. He lived in Salem, about a two-hour bus ride away, but that didn't hinder the deepening of our relationship in the least. Although this was not dating made easy, he came to Portland about twice a month. Since he was not employed, Rex did more of the commuting. Each visit he brought something special—fragrant flowers in ornate vases, sparkling jewelry and an occasional box of chocolates—but not too much candy, I warned him. I loved chocolate and that was precisely the problem. I'd eat every bit of it.

We both enjoyed eating out and walking through the neighborhood. Rex had already come to my home three times in a row. On this fourth visit, we had a superb day for walking.

There was no debate. Going for a walk won hands down over a fancy dinner or trip to the mall. I knew just the perfect place for it, too. It was the bike path near my home. This wide cement path paralleled the Mall 205 freeway, creating an oasis right in the midst of intensely populated suburban Portland. The spring sunshine had coaxed sweet flowers into bloom, and what a fragrant treat it was. We strolled arm in arm with our senses totally intoxicated. The brisk breeze cheerleaders led the procession, followed by squads of lilac dancers and bands of gaily chirping birds. The warm neon glow of near noonday sunshine lit the set of this gala affair like a Broadway stage in its glory.

Walking with a white cane required intense concentration and was certainly not conducive to meaningful conversation. The smell of freshly cut lawns lining both sides of our path lured us to its soft cushion. Sitting on that plush green carpet, we laughed, dreamed and caught up on past events.

"Oh, Rex, this is absolutely delightful, and I really appreciate that you took time to make the long bus trip up here. It looks like it's about my turn to go down your way. What do you think?"

"I'd like that. Mom and Dad have been asking about you often and would like to see you, too. When can you come down?" We settled on a date two weeks away.

As usual, the days flew by much too fast. Before I knew it, the time had come to head south, my third trip to Salem. I was looking forward to my trip. Just like me, Rex lived at home with his parents. They were a very nice couple and all four of us enjoyed visiting together whenever I arrived. This visit was no exception. The four of us were casually conversing over lunch when Rex said, "Pam, why don't we go look at engagement rings? I know you haven't accepted my proposal yet, but it won't hurt to look and get ideas."

"Okay," I agreed, "but let's be sure just to look and not buy anything today."

We all piled into their compact car and headed to downtown Salem. Zales Jewelry Store was the closest so that was our first stop. His parents thoughtfully offered to shop somewhere else so that we would have time alone to tour the rings. We gratefully accepted their offer. As we stood waiting at the counter, I slid my fingers across the slick glass surface and felt warmth coming up from beneath.

Lighted displays, I thought to myself, must be a high-priced place. And, I was right, too. Finally, a saleslady came our way and escorted us to the wedding ring counters. Reluctantly I followed, still in a daze from the whirlpool of dollar signs spinning in my head.

"Rex, maybe we should start shopping somewhere not so high priced."

"Won't hurt us to look here, will it?"

"You're right. This is as good a place to start as any."

The clerk was very accommodating and brought several rings out for me to try. She was very thoughtful and seemed sincere in coaching me as to the appearance of each ring on my finger.

Then she slipped a heart-shaped diamond ring on my finger.

I gasped with delight. "This is beautiful but how much does it cost?"

I was convinced that we should not spend that much. On the other hand, Rex could tell I liked that heart-shaped diamond best so he insisted. Before I knew it, we were walking out Zales' front door and my finger sparkled.

That visit was nice but certainly not as planned. A couple hours later, I boarded the Greyhound bus homeward. Settling back and ready for the long ride, I pondered over the day's events. My fingers slid over the large diamond and I cringed with guilt.

How could I be so stupid! We were only going to look at rings, not buy anything! It's such a gorgeous ring—but I just don't feel right.

It tore me apart as I thought how I had allowed this to happen. Rex spent all that money on my ring and I wasn't sure I even loved him.

What a dumb thing to do. Oh my goodness, there's no way I can show Mom and Dad the ring, not yet. I'd better put it back in the box.

Squirming several times to get comfortable, I tried to catch a nap with the hope of easing my pain. But the bus seat was unusually hard and the trip seemed extra long.

At last, I made it home. Boy, was I ever sick. Cordially greeting my folks, I told them I was exhausted and still felt carsick from the long trip. So I was off to bed. That night, it was as though I had a severe case of the flu. Feverishly hot and aching all over, I tossed and turned the whole night long. I knew Rex really loved me and I had led him on. Although I did not intend to do that, I couldn't justify my stupidity. How could I do something so terrible to such a kind, caring guy?

He says he's a Christian and I'm certainly not the one to judge that. On the other hand, he prefers going to the pool hall and bars instead of church. I can see it all now—every Sunday will be a tug of war for sure. He'll want to sleep in after his Saturday late night on the town and I need my spiritual boost for the week at church. We seem to be going in opposite directions. It's not going to work! Just like Mandie said, I shouldn't settle for anyone other than God's best. The Bible says a husband should be the spiritual leader. I'm sure God would rather have me single than married to a spiritual deadbeat.

The next day was Sunday and I didn't have to go to work. That morning, I was a basket case and couldn't hide my dilemma any longer. At breakfast, Dad cheerfully greeted me and asked how my trip was. With understanding ears and the kindest of hearts, Mom and Dad listened to my whole story.

"You know, Pam," Dad spoke in a more serious tone, "I know you're concerned because lots of girls your age are getting married. But whatever you do, don't get married just for the sake of being married. Marriage is a wonderful thing unless you marry the wrong person. Then, it would be like hell on earth." After our discussion, I went straight to the phone.

Forcing myself to pick up the telephone receiver, I began dialing: 1-306 and…click. I hung up.

I'd better pray first. Dear Father in Heaven, please help me with this and especially help Rex, Amen.

The very next day, Rex's parents made a special trip to Portland to pick up the ring.

An inner ache stayed with me for many days after that. I struggled in a desperate attempt to get back to my normal cheerful self. But it was not happening. I was moving ahead about as fast as a jogger trying to run a marathon with a ball and chain around his ankle. After a few weeks, I was able to smile from my heart instead of wearing a mask.

This occurred when I decided to believe God's Word—He still loved me, forgave me and would take the best care of Rex despite heart-breaker, Pam.

Life went on, but seemed so empty without Mandie. We had always been busy and did lots of fun things together, as well. Now my social calendar was almost empty. And, to make matters even worse, all the staff in our medical transcription department were old enough to be my grandmothers. They were nice to work with, but certainly not candidates for after-work outings.

This bleak existence suddenly burst into panoramic color with the brilliance of a glowing orange sunrise. Sandi was hired to fill a vacant position in our transcription department.

She filled a lot more than the empty chair in our office. Talk about filling the desires of one's heart! God promises that if we delight ourselves in Him, He will give us the desires of our hearts. And boy, did He ever! Sandi was better than any friend I could have prayed for.

She was about my age and single, too! We hit it off instantly and began doing things together after work. Since we both enjoyed walking, we decided to sign up for the hospital's fitness campaign. The goal was for each participant to walk 76 miles in 1976. Almost every day after work, we went walking together. This was clearly not a chore. With Sandi's delightful personality and good sense of humor, the miles whizzed by.

The hospital's location atop Mt. Tabor provided excellent surroundings for leisurely strolls. Down the North side of that hill took us on a nice jaunt to my parents' NASCAR office at 81st and Burnside, about a five-mile walk. This was a favorite route of ours. Not only was it downhill most of the way, but it took us by Tabor Heights Grade School. Often the children would be playing on the grounds as we passed. Their vivacious laughter and cheering tickled the youngster inside me. Those lively sounds added a youthful bounce to my strides.

Another enjoyable route was walking down the East side. This quiet residential area was much more challenging to negotiate. It did not have wide smooth cement sidewalks. Instead, the old narrow sidewalks ribboned the street's edge with sunken portions and large tufts of hearty weeds poking through cracks. Those stubborn intruders loved to catch the tip of my cane and disrupt the rhythmic flow of my steps.

Despite those obstacles, it was a nice change from the busy thoroughfare and noisy grade school playground. Seldom did a car pass through, and often a local neighbor would stop their yard work to greet us. The fragrant smells of fresh cut grass and nearby flowerbeds heightened the enjoyment of this exercise routine. We walked, talked and laughed.

Our walking routine was closely guarded and rarely interrupted. Something had to be pretty important before interrupting this schedule.

However, a couple of pretty important reasons to forgo walking were two new boyfriends. One was Marvin, a guy Sandi met at her church youth group. And two was Andy, an excellent pianist, whom my pastor introduced to me.

The days of summer and fall were spent juggling our walking commitment with our dating interests. This was some balancing act at best, but we did it and met the walking goal. We decided to celebrate our success by taking a trip to Kah-Nee-Ta. That sounded like the perfect a la mode to our victory.

This time, the Greyhound bus was headed for a totally different get-away spot, not a rustic, rugged campground but a fancy resort on a high desert plateau in Central Oregon.

We couldn't get off that bus fast enough. Sandi and I were filled with anticipation and excitement as we walked up to the hotel reservation desk. Quickly we checked in and unpacked. We had a full weekend ahead of us and couldn't wait to start exploring.

The decor was so lavish even its atmosphere felt ritzy. Soft classical music filled the hall and footsteps were silenced by the plush thick carpet. The hotel's restaurant broadcasted its gourmet menu with the aroma of elegant spices and charbroiled steaks. A soft cascading brook flowed symphonically along the far side of the immense lobby.

What a place—we were really living!

This Indian resort was famous for its hot springs and warm swimming pools. True, it was in the dead of winter, and the pool was outdoors. Still we had to try at least one swim. Wrapped up in towels like two Indian princesses, we dashed to the pool.

"Ah, this really is toasty warm, almost feels as good as lying on a warm sandy beach at the ocean." I smiled.

"Does feel really good," Sandi agreed. "Now aren't you glad I talked you into it?"

We paddled, floated and thoroughly relaxed in the comforting warmth. But, in my mind, I dreaded the impending exit. To get back to our hotel room meant a considerable trek across the open-air courtyard. With our fingertips shriveled like over-dried prunes, we climbed up the pool steps. Immediately, we were surrounded by a tribe of icy wind warriors attacking from all sides.

"Run, Pam! Faster! Faster," Sandi yelled as we raced across the icy cement landscape at a pace almost faster than my footing could keep up with.

Well, that was enough! That one trip to the pool filled our quota for winter swimming. In fact, after that, indoor activities never looked better. We were very content relaxing in our warm room with TV, eating out and browsing in the gift shops.

One activity took priority throughout the whole weekend. Whenever there was a moment to converse, Sandi talked about Marvin. "Pam, I just don't know if Marv is the one for me. He's definitely a solid Christian. I can see his love for God in everything he does. He's a pretty neat guy, but I don't know."

"Well, Sandi, just relax. Give it some time and God will give you the peace. One thing I've learned is that whenever I have that unsettled teeter-tottering inside, it's time to keep praying and not make any major decisions."

Thank goodness for such a neat girlfriend. We both benefited as we shared our current dating experiences and God's words of wisdom.

Our a la mode trip was a double scooper for sure. However, our vacation was winding down. With reluctance, we had to face returning to the work world and our old routine.

CHAPTER 17
SOMEBODY PINCH ME

Working and walking right along, that's how it was for Sandi and me. We continued to be good friends and got together as often as our schedules would permit. She was still dating Marvin and wanted me to meet him in person. We found an open Sunday afternoon and agreed that she and Marvin would stop by my parents' home to visit. With a pot of tea steeping and a plate of cookies on the kitchen table, I was ready for company.

One ding of the door bell and off came my apron. A couple quick steps and I opened the door.

With a warm hello, I welcomed them. Seated at the kitchen table, the three of us had tea and cookies along with an enjoyable visit.

Later that same day, the phone rang. It was Sandi.

"Hey, long time no hear! What's up?"

"I just want to know what you think about Marv."

"Well, Sandi, he seems really nice. It looks like the two of you enjoy being together, but I think you need more time dating before you even consider getting serious."

I was happy for Sandi. She had a neat Christian boyfriend. At the same time, I was busy trying to figure out my own dating relationship.

Andy and I had been dating for several months. He was blind and a very accomplished pianist. It was his piano music that brought us together. He performed at my church. Afterward the pastor, Mandie, Jake, Andy, and I all went out for dessert. That began our dating relationship.

Andy lived in Tacoma, Washington so it was another long-distance relationship. Long-distance phone calls became a routine and we met often in Portland.

On one of his visits to my home, Andy arrived with a beautiful big bouquet of red roses.

"Oh, Andy, these are beautiful! You are so thoughtful. Thank you! Thank you! I'll put them right here in the center of our table for the whole family to enjoy."

"Pam, come over here on the couch and sit beside me."

Moving over extra close to me, he took my hand and said, "My life has been so much happier and more meaningful ever since spending time with you. I would like this to continue the rest of my life. So, Pam, I want us to take the next step and get engaged. What do you think?"

"Andy, I really like you and enjoy being with you, but I'm not sure I'm ready for such a serious commitment."

"That's okay. Just think about it and let me know, okay?"

Ever since the delivery of those beautiful roses, I had been thinking and thinking.

A few days later, I called Andy and told him that I needed more time just to be friends.

He seemed okay with my decision. Truthfully, he was more than ready to put a ring on my finger, and not just an engagement ring, either. He told me in no uncertain terms that he believed it was God's will for us to get married. So, while I was thinking and thinking, he was pushing and pushing.

"When will you know that you are in love with me?" He asked often. On each repetition of that question, all I could say was, "Honestly, I don't know. There is no way to determine when or if I will fall in love with you."

With this pressure, my mind and insides bounced around like an over-caffeinated youngster turned loose on a trampoline.

Why can't I feel some love for him? He is a solid Christian and has lots of good qualities. Besides being an excellent pianist, he has a good government job and owns his own home. He's well off financially.

I tried to keep all those good points in the forefront, but the negatives kept clamoring all the louder. He was so harsh, exacting and had a bitter outlook toward life. I just couldn't relax or feel comfortable around him.

My dating relationship was not the only unsettled thing. There was a very unsettling event looming in the future. Sandi had accepted a position at the hospital in Seaside. This meant a promotion for her. I encouraged her to go for it, but inwardly I was discouraged about the distance it would put between us. Seaside was on the Oregon Coast, about two hours away from Portland.

Well, Sandi got the job and was packing for the big move. She was understandably apprehensive about this new adventure in a far-off land. As we talked, I felt her uneasiness. It brought back memories of my first days in Olympia when I was so lonely and depressed. I couldn't stand back and watch my best friend go through something like that—not if I could help it. I offered to take a week of my vacation to help her move. She was delighted and thankful for my offer.

The time had come to make the move to her cute one-bedroom apartment. It was within walking distance of the hospital and downtown Seaside. Since Sandi had to start work immediately, I spent the daytime hours unpacking, stocking the cupboards with groceries and cooking. She was gracious and took me out for dinner often. She also stood true to her promise and made sure I had several walks to the beach.

Oh, how I loved to drink in the beauty and majesty of the ocean. I could spend hours just listening to the crashing ocean waves, catching the cool breeze on my face and filling my lungs with fresh salty air. My senses swooned with enjoyment. After each dose of saltwater delight, I was invigorated and ready to go back to unpacking.

Remembering my lonely Olympia days prompted me to check out opportunities for socializing. Sandi agreed that getting connected with a good Bible teaching church was the number one priority. The next day, while she was on the job, I went to work making phone calls. My fingers were racing across the dial with Directory Assistance as my phone book. By the time Sandi arrived home from work, my research contained three good options. She chose the First Baptist Church. It had a young adults group.

With the mission accomplished and my week at its end, we exchanged a bear-hug good-bye and I boarded a Greyhound bus for Portland.

Back home I returned to working and to wondering—wondering if I would ever have love in my heart for Andy. Finally, the teeter-totter stopped when I accepted the fact that we were just too different. I had a heart for people—he did not. Having such extreme opposite driving forces would cause nothing but friction. I knew that Andy and I were not a match made in heaven. Peace settled in my heart, but then came the pain of telling him. I agonized and prayed, prayed and agonized.

Why does it always end up on my shoulders? Every time, I've had to be the one to say, "no." It would be nice if my boyfriend would figure out it's not working or not God's will. I hate, hate, hate having to tell them!

It had to be done, so I picked up the telephone receiver and dialed. As I told him my decision, my insides churned with sorrow for him. I knew Andy genuinely loved me and was deeply hurt by my decision. But the love for him just wouldn't come, no matter how hard I tried or wanted it to happen.

Hanging up the receiver, I sank into a limp mound on our couch. Lying there exhausted and dazed, I pulled the afghan off the back of the couch. Snuggling in its warmth, I felt the comfort of Mom's love so tenderly knit in each soft stitch.

This is love—a warm glow of peace and goodness all around me and clear through to the core of my heart. Yes, I made the right decision.

With that weight off my shoulders, I was ready to move on. But, move on to what? I was already 29 years old and there was no sign of marriage any time soon. I knew it was time to switch my goals for life. Up to this point, my number one plan was to get married. That became seemingly more and more unrealistic. After all, I had been engaged twice and had many others wanting to marry me. There is no doubt I had given the option of marriage a good try.

It was time to face the fact that maybe God wanted me to remain single. That was a possibility, but not one I had seriously considered.

Well, being single wouldn't be so bad. If that is God's plan for me, I know I'll be happiest single.

On my knees, I talked to my Heavenly Father. "Dear Father, I'm here again with lots of questions. I want most of all to be like the blind man Jesus talked about when he said that the man was blind not because of sin but so that your works could be displayed in him. That's how I want to be. Please guide me in the way you want me to go."

A seminar I took on setting goals said that it was wise to vividly picture how you would like life to be five years in the future.

It was time to do just that. In the quiet of my bedroom, I thought about how my heart's desire would look in real life. I imagined and vividly pictured myself single, living in my own small modest home. I was standing on my patio in the sunshine reaching out to a little neighborhood boy with a plate of homemade cookies. There we sat, laughed and talked. Happy with this picture, I was ready to work hard on my new goal of being single and satisfied.

Sandi and I kept in close contact with frequent phone calls. She was doing well on the job and socially, too. The Baptist Church group was a good fit for her, and she even met a neat guy there. An interesting side-note is that I had already met her new beau before she did. While spending that week in Seaside to help Sandi get settled in, I shopped for groceries at Safeway. And, it just so happened that the kind gentleman who helped me shop was Frank. When Sandi told Frank about her blind girlfriend, he remembered helping me shop.

Sandi was off to a great start in Seaside, and I was feeling good about my new "single and satisfied" future.

I continued working at the hospital, but there was an obvious void in the office. Work seamed much more hum-drum without Sandi's presence.

Fortunately for me, that position did not stay vacant very long. And, better yet, it was filled with another young transcriptionist. I was delighted with this new development. Paula was single and about my age. In short order, we became good friends. After work we enjoyed shopping, eating out and doing handcrafts together. What a great friend I was blessed with.

One real difference was that Paula was single and unsatisfied. She so wanted to get married and have a family soon.

On the home front, things were going well. I was very content and comfortable living with Mom and Dad. The three of us got along so well. My folks had transitioned out of racing and into the Dairy Queen business. It was so nice to have them home more. This meant we got to go to church as a family every Sunday.

One Sunday morning, we were on our way out the door. Dad looked at his watch and said, "Oh, my gosh! We're ready half an hour early. We can't get to church that early. I know—I'll take you girls for a cup."

That three letter word, "cup," always meant we'd stop for a cup of coffee and a sweet treat. Ever since I can remember, Dad had the biggest hyperactive sweet tooth imaginable. He was brilliant at coming up with excuses to go have a "cup." And no cup was complete without a sweet side dish.

This Sunday was no exception. Dad decided we would stop for a cup at Eve's Buffet, a restaurant on our way to church. Inside, we chose a booth and sat down to enjoy our goodies. Just a few bites into my cornbread, a familiar voice greeted me.

"Hi, Pam, it's Marvin. John and I stopped here for breakfast on our way to church. I spotted you and your folks sitting over here so thought I'd come and say hi."

"What a surprise," I responded and proceeded to introduce him to my parents. "Mom and Dad, this is Sandi's friend, Marvin Jordan. He's the one who helped her move to Seaside almost a year ago."

After the exchange of introductions, Dad asked Marv if he'd like to sit down. I slid over to make room for him. We shared a short but pleasant conversation with the main topic being updates about Sandi. Then Marv said, "Well, I'd better shove off, it's almost time for church to start. Sure was nice seeing you again, Pam. You folks take care. We'll meet again, if not here, for sure when the rapture comes."

As he moved to get up, I slid my hand to bump his and then gave it a squeeze. "God bless you, too."

Mom, Dad and I agreed that unexpected visit was a nice treat. Marv quickly vanished from my thoughts as I busied myself with the activities at hand.

As usual, the days whizzed by and Saturday had come again. That was my normal day to do laundry and cook some entrées for the coming week. Right in the midst of chopping celery for a pot of chicken noodle soup, the door bell rang.

Who on earth could that be? I'm not expecting anyone.

With an abrupt turn, I dried my hands and headed for the front door. Expecting a door-to-door salesman, I unlocked the bolt lock and opened it hesitantly.

"Hi, Pam, remember me? It's Marvin."

"Oh yes, would you like to come in?"

First thing in the door, Marv handed me a gift. Little did I know then that this behavior was a preview of the coming attraction. He placed a tall bottle in my hands and purposely said nothing about what was in it. He quietly stood there waiting for me to feel and figure out what the gift was. I securely held the heavy glass bottle with my left hand. Then, my other hand got busy investigating. At its top I closely examined the embossed foil cover which was so typical of a wine bottle.

Is this wine? Oh dear, what should I say? Some Christians don't believe in drinking any alcohol. I don't want to offend him by guessing it's wine.

Giving me ample time to squirm with embarrassment, he then said, "I brought this for you and your folks. It's nonalcoholic sparkling apple juice. Hope you'll like it."

"Thanks," I responded while attempting to hide my sigh of relief.

Then we sat and talked. The conversation went smoothly until he shocked me with, "I might as well tell you, I'm hooked on you."

At that moment, my feet were completely swept out from under me. I could scarcely believe my oh-so reliable ears. He spent just a short time with me that day, but the impact of his visit was huge. After he left, I ran down the hall and squealed with excitement.

I don't believe it! That handsome Godly man is hooked on me.

I had often heard the phrase "swept off your feet," but I had no idea of what it meant. Much less had I ever experienced such a thing. But that day, it was as though a whole band of cupids arrived with heavenly brooms a-swishing.

SOMEBODY PLEASE PINCH ME! I must be dreaming.

With my mind in the dream world and my ego soaring, that next week flew by. I was still having trouble getting my feet to touch down on solid ground.

My internal alarm of excited anticipation woke me half an hour earlier than my radio clock was due to ring. Humming and singing out loud, I got ready for my first official date with Marv. We were going to go bowling. He was due any moment and I was pacing with nervousness and excitement.

The door bell rang, and I dashed to answer it.

"Hi, Pam," he reached out and held my hand. "Are you ready to go?"

"Yes, all set."

Marv offered to carry my bowling bag and we headed for his car. He placed it in the back seat and then opened the passenger door for me. But, before stepping aside to let me in, he said, "You know, it's such a beautiful day, would you like to go for a walk instead of bowling?"

That was so neat because I had been thinking along those same lines myself. With the warm sunshine on my face, fresh air and melodious birds, the thought of spending the day inside a stuffy bowling alley all of a sudden lost its appeal. We left our bowling balls in the car and started off walking hand in hand down my street. Even more impressive than the beauty of spring in full bloom was my date.

It was incredible. He was a natural at guiding me. I asked if he had ever guided a blind person before. He assured me this was his first time. As we walked along, he began describing the surroundings. "I don't know what you can see of it, but this tree is sprouting out with brand-new leaves all over."

"I can see an indistinct darkness as I look up there."

"There are a few low branches close. Would you like to feel the leaves?"

Amazed and delighted all at the same time, I jumped at the chance. He showed me, by touch of course, the tight little nut-like nubbins where the leaves were just forming. Gently, he moved my hand to the next stage where the hard nubbin was softer and a little fuzzy. On to the one with a few little ends popped out and then the brand new finale.

"Oh, wow, thank you so much. What a treat for me to see spring actually happening."

"I'm so glad you liked that. I really enjoyed it, myself. It's easy to just glance at the tree and not see the details. God is so wonderful in how He designs things. Getting up so close like we just did helps me appreciate his creation lots more."

That was amazing. Marv actually had fun doing it, enjoying my world with me. That was a first. My family was great in helping me get up close to touch interesting things, but they never got involved much in experiencing it with me.

After our walk, Marv suggested going out to lunch. That was A-Okay with me. As we sat in his car and started fastening our seatbelts, he hit me with another shocker.

"You know, Pam—I'm not going to promote this relationship. If anything good happens, it will be God's doing."

I couldn't believe my ears at first.

Wow, this guy has his head screwed on straight!

What a relief for me. I had just ended a relationship loaded with gut-twisting pressure. My spirit let out such a huge sigh of relief that it must have been heard clear across the heavens.

Marv then asked me to go steady, which he explained meant he wanted me to go to church with him every Sunday. I liked this plan of growing together spiritually. But at the same time, my heart was saddened. Many years I attended church all by myself. Just recently my parents had joined me. It felt so good having them sitting in the pew with me. But Marv's request would change that right away.

No doubt in my mind that he was worth it—so going steady we were.

This "somebody pinch me" experience was certainly a mountaintop high. Another wonderful development arrived April first that very same year—a beautiful baby girl born to my brother, Steve, and his wife, Fran. For the very first time, I was an aunt and truly delighted with my new role. Holding that tiny warm bundle in my arms was such a treat, and when she wiggled, I giggled.

Steve and Fran lived in Bend, Oregon, about a three-hour drive from our home. As a result, we didn't get to see that little bundle very often.

The long distance didn't slow down our love or bonding. Baby Bria grew up knowing her Aunt Pam and soon-to-be Uncle Marvin. Steve and Fran showed her our pictures often and taught her to say our names. April first was a day to remember. That's the day when the parade of heart warming, fun-filled times began marching into our lives.

I had to give up counting blessings on my fingers. By that time, my arms were loaded with two new sources of incredible love, Marv and baby Bria. And I hugged them both for all I was worth.

Things were looking good—mighty good. But, of course, life is never all straight-aways. Unknown to me, not far ahead lay some pretty scary hairpin S curves.

CHAPTER 18
SMILES AND TRIALS

Dating and fellows—those were the topics of the day. Paula and I talked often about my new beau. I was still in the dating high but at the same time felt saddened to see Paula so discontent. That, however, didn't slow down my dating in the least. Marv and I got together as often as our work schedules would allow. Marv lived in Hillsboro, about a forty minute drive. Despite the long treks, he never seemed to mind making that commute.

Saturday had come again and we were off to Taco Time for lunch. In the middle of my Super Natural Taco, I decided to fill him in on my concern about Paula.

"I certainly don't want to play matchmaker. I know that's God's job, not mine, but Paula sure needs to meet a nice Christian man. Do you think it would be out of line to introduce her to your roommate?"

"I don't see any harm in introducing them. As long as we just stand back and let God do the rest."

"John sure seems like a nice guy but I really don't know him. Would you mind filling me in?"

"We've known each other about a year and decided to save money by rooming together. He is a good solid Christian but not so good when it comes to housekeeping. He dumps his freshly laundered clothes in a pile on the bedroom floor and does the same with the dirty ones. I've never seen anyone quite like that. In the morning, it is comical to watch him pick out an outfit to wear. He goes through the piles sniffing each item to decide if it's clean enough to wear."

Marv's agreement to have John and Paula meet was all I needed to hear. The very next weekend Paula, John, Marv and I went for a picnic. Blue Lake Park was the perfect setting. We girls pot lucked the lunch. Our homemade potato salad and freshly baked chocolate chip cookies were a real hit.

We chose a table close to the lake with a full view of the swimming area. The essence of fresh water drifted right into our picnic site. It was generously polka dotted with hints of cocoa butter and other sun lotion fragrances.

Marv and Paula teamed up to describe the fun and activity before us. It was so nice of them to do that and I was instantly pictorial again. The water created a brilliant blue backdrop for this collage of colorful floats in every imaginable size and shape. I had a dazzling display of splash contests, squeals and giggles popping up in a variety of tones. We were well entertained and all had a good time.

As the daylight dwindled, we packed up our belongings and headed for the parking lot. Even Marv's little blue Honda was smiling with contentment as our foursome headed homeward. After dropping Paula and John off at her apartment, I turned to Marv and asked, "That seemed to go well, don't you think?"

"I don't know. Neither of them talked much."

"True, but it was their first date. One thing they have in common is a love for children. Did you notice how they both laughed with hysterics when that little boy in diapers shared his bucket of sand all over Paula's white tennis shoe? That's a good start."

"Right, Pam, and it's up to God now. We've done our part."

The next Monday, Paula and I took our lunch break together. Our conversation was supercharged with excitement. Paula now had a boyfriend, too, and she was pleased with their first date. I was excited to see her happy.

The work week whizzed by and Saturday was here again. I could hardly wait for Marv's arrival that morning. One activity we both enjoyed was walking and hiking. In the cool of that lightly overcast summer morning, we decided to drive to Multnomah Falls. And a bit of a drive, it was. The ride, itself, would be fun, I knew. I was confident of that because any time spent with Marv had proven very enjoyable. But, little did I know that I was really "in for a ride" this time. We had just finished plodding through the metropolitan region with its many stop lights. Marv informed me that we were turning onto I-84. That was the freeway we took which coursed along the Columbia River.

Marv really wouldn't have had to announce I-84 after all. His car did it for him. He picked up the speed and swung into a long sweeping curve. As we came out of that turn, the car hit a straight stretch, but my head was still spinning. Once I caught my breath again, I said, "Marv, that was terrific! How did you learn to drive like this? Have you ever raced before?"

"I did race a hydroplane once, but not automobiles. Why do you ask?"

"That's so unusual. I've ridden with lots of different drivers and, besides Dad and Steve, no one else swerves through the curves like that. Now you know one of my weaknesses. I love to go fast and all the more when hugging the car door."

"That's okay with me just as long as you have hugs left for me, too."

About twenty minutes later, we pulled into the parking lot of Multnomah Falls. This beautiful display of nature's power rose up to majestic heights far above the Columbia River.

As we began our climb up the switch-back trail, Marv checked with me to make sure it was cool enough for me to hike. By then, we had been dating several months and Marv knew about my intolerance to hot weather.

"It's nice and cool. I'll be just fine, thanks."

And, fine I was, at least in the beginning. We walked arm in arm up the switch-back trail, making frequent side trips. Knowing that I loved the hands-on scenery, Marv made sure to show me some of the forest's beauty. Just as dense as an Amazon jungle, this lush green blanket covered nature's sleepy shoulders.

I was especially fond of ferns. They were on display everywhere and Marv made sure I got to see all kinds of them. Tall stiff dudes with prickly leaves mimicked tin solders standing staunchly at attention. More mild-mannered fellows waved at us and fanned out as far as they could stretch. My favorites were the frilly soft puffs that felt like feathers. To my delight, they worked just as well as feathers to tickle Marv's cheek. Just ahead, a rustic wooden foot bridge crossed the river right in front of the falls.

We were only one step onto the bridge when I tugged Marv's arm with a special request, "Do you mind if we stop here in the middle of the bridge? I can get a panoramic view by hearing the different sounds of the flowing water when standing there.

Without the slightest hesitation, he halted in the center of the bridge. The real shocker came when Marv closed his eyes and listened right along with me.

"Ooh, Marv! Listen, did you hear that extra crash way up there?"

"I think so."

"It's so neat that you are willing to stop and just listen to experience what my world looks like. That's rare, you know. Sighted people I've been around usually won't take time to enjoy their other senses in detail."

About halfway up the trail, we stopped to sit on a bench nestled in a miniature cove of lush greenery. A soft branch of the nearby bush seemed to be dancing to the wind's tune. It just so happened to gently thump me on the head. This didn't faze me the first time. But when it recurred several times and then started tickling my ear, I knew something very un-natural was happening.

The truth, however, was that this was a very natural "Marvin happening." With his next tease, I was ready. Snatching the branch I returned the tickle. Once we both had our fill of tickles, it was time to head for higher ground.

We had no sooner started walking again when the blazing sun burnt every hint of clouds from the sky. It began baking everything around, especially me.

Marv noticed my body thermostat climbing much faster than our steep path. With this onset of two red stoplights for cheeks and hot hand, he turned to say, "Boy, your hand is hot! Are you okay?"

"You're right. I'm getting pretty hot. How much farther do we have to go?"

"Not much. I'd say about two more short stretches. Would you like to stop now? There's a shady spot not far off the trail?"

This guy was so thoughtful, so attentive to my needs instead of his own. He paused in the shade and looked for a way down to the river.

"There's no safe way to get down to the water here, but we're very close to the top. I think there's a place where you could wade in up there."

Wading! That sounds like heaven right now. I can make it that far for sure.

"Let's go for it," I smiled with a bounce in my step. "Cooling down in the river sounds like the best solution."

After our third date, I learned that Marv's body thermostat was incredible.

Mine refused to work, but his seemed to work overtime. He could handle very hot days and cold temperatures without being affected much.

The moment we crested the top, he found an easy route down to the water. He did not need to cool down, nor was he particularly fond of wading. Yet, there he went, wading right into the middle of the icy water. His attitude was cooler than the freshly melted snow we stood in. Without as much as an under-the-breath grumble, he stayed right there with me. A small splash of cold water hit my elbow. At first it was just a few sneaky drops, but once I squealed with protest, he took his job seriously. That first small splash was followed by slightly bigger, then bigger ones. I returned fire, and Marv hollered, "Wait just a minute! You're the one that's hot, not me."

"Well, you should have thought about that before you started splashing me."

Laughing and dripping, he reached out and wrapped his arms around me. There we stood—right in the thigh-high water—entrenched in a most delightful bear hug.

That cold water and hot hug refreshed me in a way I'd never experienced before. I had always enjoyed hugs immensely. This hug was effervescent to my soul. It was so hard to step away from Marv's warm embrace. Hiking down to his car was no sweat with our brand-new wet suits.

Outdoor excursions, picnics, going out to eat and an occasional movie rounded out our summer dating.

Paula and John were seeing each other more often, and definitely becoming more romantic. I, of course, got the inside scoop before anyone else and enjoyed every juicy detail. I was delighted when they announced their engagement. Their wedding date was set for the end of November, just a few months away.

Paula and John were not the only romantic couple in town. Marv and I were also growing closer, but not as fast. At the beginning of our relationship, I informed Marv that I needed to spend time getting to know him. I explained that in previous relationships everything seemed fine at first. But, with time, major concerns and differences cropped up. Marv was willing to take the needed time, and what a relief that was.

In the fall, we did make it to the bowling alley a few times. The real thriller came not in the bowling alley, but during a quiet romantic dinner. The dessert that night was nowhere to be found on our menu, but absolutely decadent. He was just supposed to hand me a spoon for my scoop of orange sherbet. Reaching his hand across the table, he did have a spoon. He let my fingers barely touch the handle and promptly slid it aside.

"My spoon, please. Sherbet is not finger food, you know."

"Well, Honey, there's a bit more to our dessert than sherbet tonight."

Gently placing my hand in his, he proposed. This time I didn't need to think about it, I already knew my answer. With stars in my eyes and my hand resting warmly in his, I said, "Yes, yes, I'd love to be Mrs. Marvin John Jordan."

Meanwhile, Mom and Dad had been just as busy. With Dad's new position of General Contractor, they decided to build their own home. Since they still owned and operated the Gresham Dairy Queen, they wanted to live nearby. Diligent scouting exhibitions led them to a new subdivision on the far Eastern border of Gresham. It was a peaceful setting and still had a little touch of country left. Five blocks away was an open pasture with three horses and a nearby field of grazing sheep. Although it was a great spot for them, it was not the best for me. It was far away from stores, public transportation and all my friends.

I decided it would be best to get my own place. The Felicia Apartments were not far from Portland Adventist Hospital. A one-bedroom upstairs apartment was my choice. What a perfect location. The Tri-Met bus stop right in front of the apartment, and just three blocks away was a small shopping complex. It had a Safeway with pharmacy, ninety-nine cent store and restaurant. This was ideal. The Village Square fit the bill, a reasonably priced restaurant with a homey atmosphere. I found it just right for a juicy hamburger and tall diet Coke.

While the apartment was still empty, Mom and I got busy doing the preliminary work. None of the thermostats or appliances were user-friendly for me. We began the process of adapting one dial at a time.

A strip of plastic labeling tape was glued on the knob to serve as a pointer. Then on the flat surface surrounding the knob, another strip was placed at the 70-degree mark. By turning the knob around until the two strips lined up, I knew the heat was set to my comfort level. The kitchen appliances were much more time consuming to label. Nevertheless, the dishwasher, refrigerator dial, stove burner knobs and oven dial all had to be marked so that I could handle everyday life by myself.

With my apartment in order, Mom and I were off to find the laundry room. Across the complex to a basement of another building was our destination. It entailed memorizing not just the route, but many details like turns, toe-catching curbs and more. A worrisome feature was no hand rail at the top of the stairs. The rail did not begin until the third step down. Misjudging its location could result in tumbling headlong into the laundry room. That was one acrobatic stunt I never wanted to attempt.

Ever since my many down-the-stair traumas at the University of Washington, I battled the fear of falling. Just the knowledge of descending stairs ahead caused my insides to clench like the fist of an ardent boxer. For years, I had worked to rid myself of this spontaneous reaction but without success. I just had to pause, take a deep breath, and talk to myself.

Relax, Pam, you've done this hundreds of times without falling.

Letting out a deep sigh, I pictured the Lord holding my hand each step of the way. The calmness that came over me was incredible.

Once in the laundry room, Mom showed me the dials on each machine. In those days, it was not acceptable to put Braille markings on things used by the general public. That meant I had to do a lot of creative figuring and even more memory work. To set the washer, I first had to locate the biggest knob on the far left and very carefully turn it just five clicks. Each of the three knobs on the washer had a different number of clicks for the setting I needed. What a load of mental gymnastics it took to do an everyday load of laundry.

Then came the fun part, we were off to the outdoor swimming pool. Finding that was a must. One important criterion when hunting for an apartment was a heated pool. After memorizing the turns from my front door to the pool gate, Mom helped me get familiar with the layout. I needed to know things like the pool's shape, how to find the steps and how to avoid various potential toe-catching spots.

Once moved and settled in, I really liked my new place. Even more enjoyable was the fact that Marv and I were seeing each other more often. Marv's good nature and fun-loving ways heightened my enjoyment of everything we did. How well I remember our first movie. Before the picture started, he leaned over and bent down close to whisper in my ear.

"Yesterday at work I told the guys I was taking you out to the movies. Tom shook his head and asked me why I would take a blind date to see a show. I told him that is the good part about having a blind girlfriend. You have to sit really close and whisper what's happening on the screen."

Although I could hardly believe what I heard, my heart took it all in. The little girl inside me happily bounced, clapping her hands and giggling.

I was so comfortable doing things with Marv that I felt at ease enough to do more. It was high time to make a home-cooked meal for him.

CHAPTER 19
SOMETHING'S COOKING

The time had come to test my culinary skills. This would be the first meal I had cooked for Marvin and I had it all planned. Tonight was no exception. In fact, I was extra careful to have all the foods dished up and placed in the order of the meal. That gave me time to relax and enjoy my guest.

A shrimp casserole was in the oven. Two bowls of tossed green salad waited on the top shelf in the refrigerator. Two large scoops of vanilla ice cream sat on a plate in the freezer ready to a la mode the warm homemade apple cobbler. Two tall glasses with ice were in the freezer door ready for filling with Marv's beverage choice. The meal was ready. It was off to the living room. A quick click of the power button and soft instrumental music set the atmosphere just right. Then, I dashed to the bathroom to check my hair, put on lipstick and my favorite perfume. I was ready.

The door bell rang. Marv was right on time. With a bounce in each step, I headed for the door. With one twist of the knob, open arms embraced me. There we stood on my front porch as I melted in the warmth and security of those strong arms. We sat down to pray and began eating. Serving dinner went like clockwork, just as planned. Everything was going along smoothly as we talked about the day's events. With a pause in the conversation, he leaned back with a satisfied-sounding sigh and said, "My, this sure is musty."

"Musty!" Oh, no, was the cheese moldy or maybe the lettuce brown?

In quiet pondering, I sat puzzled for a few embarrassing moments.

The silence of my quandary was broken when Marv, in a matter of fact way, said, "Must have more!"

"Oh, Marvin Jordan, you scallywag!"

Jumping up, I took a giant side step to the refrigerator and snatched my two oven mitts. With a pivoting twirl on the ball of my right foot, I immerged punching. Trying to look serious and mad in the midst of giggles was the toughest part. Then I boxed him on both shoulders simultaneously just for the sake of making sure I knew where his ears were. The beating came as I, oh-so gently, tapped his ears with my boxing gloves.

Marv retaliated with a jumbo size napkin spit wad initiating an outburst of laughter and hugs. Mischief, teasing and puns were not on my dinner menu, but from that evening on, they popped up at each meal, and not just when we ate but were ever present everywhere.

God's promises rang true again. He promised that if I delight myself in Him, He would give me the desires of my heart. And, wow, did He ever! I never would have thought to pray for such a master in puns and fun, but that's the very thing I needed.

Many dates and home-cooked dinners followed. But right in the middle of our engagement, our relationship took a turn for the worse. I couldn't figure out how or why that happened, but we just were not communicating well. There was a growing block, and I had no clue how to fix it.

Interestingly enough, Marv was oblivious to this. Even when I brought it to his attention and explained my concern, he couldn't see any problem. Soon, our conversations dwindled both in quantity and depth. Then discord and distance set in.

He's such a wonderful Christian man, so much fun to be with. But, it's obvious that we're not as close as we used to be. Sure wish it was obvious to Marv, also. Something major is wrong.

I knew it would be impossible to have a lasting good relationship if we couldn't communicate. The agony continued and I tried not to let on that anything was bugging me. Bugging me, that was putting it milder than mild. I couldn't sleep well at all and had trouble focusing at work. I thought ending each of the past nine romances was hard, but I hadn't experienced hard until agonizing over this.

What should I do! I just keep hitting my head against this huge cement communication wall.

This heart-wrenching struggle affected everything I did. One day on the job, I fell asleep in the middle of typing a doctor's operative report. But, even stranger was the fact that when I came to, my fingers were still typing.

Oh, my gosh! What on earth am I doing? I must have been sleep typing. There's no way to tell what I wrote, and I feel too stupid to ask anyone to read it back to me. Oh great! What a waste. I'll just have to start the whole report over.

Well, it was high time, actually past high time, to use my hotline to heaven. As usual, I kept praying and kept waiting for the teeter-tottering within to subside. As for Marv, he still thought things were going along just fine.

Near the end of July, I told Marv how I had been praying for a month about our communication problem. That is when I hit him with the bomb.

"This is really, really hard for me to say, but I have to break off our engagement as of today."

He hung his head and said, "I don't understand what's going on. I still love you. Don't you love me?"

"I love you, yes, very much, but there is something seriously wrong in our relationship. An icy wedge seems to have grown between us. When we get together, it's more like two tomcats in fierce competition for their territory. This is no way to live together. If we can't resolve it now, things probably will get worse once we're married."

My days were empty and sad for quite awhile. To make matters even harder, I was an active part of Paula's wedding preparations. November 15 was her big day. I was to be one of her bridesmaids, and Marv was supposed to escort me down the aisle. How awkward that would be, but I couldn't back out and spoil her wedding just because of my personal problems.

Unknown to me, Marv had told John he didn't want to escort me in the wedding.

John informed him, "That's tough, Marv, it's too late to change that now."

Paula and John's wedding day had arrived. There in the women's restroom, I dressed and primped with the rest of the bridesmaids. All of us were nervous and excited but the aching in my heart could not be curbed even in the midst of this joyous entourage. The show had to go on. I finished my silent prayer with a deep sigh. Trying to swallow the large lump in my throat, I quickly wiped away a tear from the corner of my eye just in time to join the wedding procession.

One by one, each bridesmaid stepped forward to join her escort. My turn came next, and Marv came up beside me. He greeted me with a soft, sullen "hi."

Trying to act cheerful and cover up the pangs of my aching heart, I smiled in his direction and said, "Sure is good to see you. How are you doing?"

"Terrible," he responded followed by a sullen silence.

Clearing the lump in my throat, I asked, "You mean because of our broken engagement?"

"Yah, I don't like it at all."

Silence prevailed for a few steps forward when Marv whispered these shocking words, "You know, I sure would like to walk down this aisle some day with you."

What a blatant nudge from our Heavenly Father and a direct blow from cupid all at once.

Being close to him and hearing that he still wanted me was all it took. The love flame I had tried to suppress burst into a vibrant warm glow of desire. I picked up the phone the very next day and dialed Marv.

"I'm so glad you're home. You know, I've been thinking. It's a good thing we had to walk down that aisle together. The timing of that was no accident, you know. Anyway, I've been praying a lot about our relationship ever since yesterday. We have so much going for us with just one problem. One thing I'm sure would help us a lot is premarital counseling. If you'll go with me, I'll consider continuing our engagement."

Marv was hesitant, stating that Christians should be able to find all the answers to their problems in the Bible.

I agreed with that and added, "True, but God has given each Christian different talents and expertise. We are supposed to seek wise advice. A good Christian marriage counselor could be just what we need." Marv was silent for a moment, then responded that he would be willing to try one session. On the inside, and probably on the outside, too, I beamed. He desired to honor my wishes and do whatever was needed to build our relationship. My heart swooned with a giant sigh of relief.

It took one visit with the counselor. Cedrick had just the advice we needed. When charting our personality traits, much of the graph showed many very close points. There was a sharp difference in one particular area. We both agreed that difference could be lived with. The real eye opener for me came when Cedrick said that I was expecting Marv to be a mind reader.

Both Marv and I were glad for the wise counsel and our engagement was back in full swing. Our relationship blossomed and deepened like never before. Soon plans for getting married took the forefront in our thoughts and conversations. Marv left it up to me to choose the wedding date. Since I loved flowers, a spring wedding was my preference.

"I've figured out a date for our wedding, May first. It falls on a Saturday. What do you think about that?"

"Sounds good to me, Honey. As the bride, this is your big day. I'm leaving it up to you to plan things the way you'd like them."

"Thanks, dear, you're so thoughtful. May first will be perfect. I can use a May Day theme with lots of bright flowers."

"Mayday! Mayday!" Marv piped up with a distress sound in his voice.

I stood back wondering what was wrong. As usual, after giving me a few moments to squirm and ponder, he said, "You know, May Day like the distress call of a ship going down."

"Oh, Marvin Jordan!" I squealed in protest. "Whatever am I going to do with you!"

"Well, you could marry me for a start."

Wedding plans became top priority on my agenda. Mom and I were eager and excited to plan the wedding, but a little nervous about getting everything done in just four months. Thank goodness it would be a small church wedding. That would make it possible if we really got busy. And, busy we were.

Everything was going along normally until an unanticipated turn of events hit me full force. That dark gray afternoon, I had just arrived home from work. The walk from my bus stop to front door was a short one, but already my coat could have passed for a backyard sprinkler. Everywhere I stepped, it left drops and puddles of water. Once inside, I couldn't peel off my wet layers quick enough. What a relief to be home, out of the rain and noisy traffic. I sat down with a smile as the warmth and comfort of my apartment surrounded me with a welcome home hug.

Leaning back, I sank into the plush cushions of my favorite rocker and daydreamed.

The soft, easy listening music had just begun soothing my nerves when a news flash hit straight from my memory bank.

Oh no! The potluck after work tomorrow. I told Paula I would bring a seven layer salad.

Not particularly excited about the task before me, I inched out of my rocker and began scouting my cupboards. As suspected, salad dressing and water chestnuts were nowhere to be found. Picking up my umbrella and shopping list, I grumbled. The walk to Safeway, though short, was anything but pleasant in the pouring rain and intense rush hour traffic. It had to be done, so zipping up my rain coat, I was out the door.

Sure wish I'd done this yesterday. It's almost pitch black and raining tigers and wolves. Won't be easy to hear the traffic in this loud pelting rain. Good thing my umbrella's hot pink. It should make it easier for the drivers to see me.

I walked to the corner and positioned myself with the sidewalk edge making sure to cross straight. Switching into serious concentration mode, I stood there like a British sentinel listening and listening. With both ears, I carefully watched all four lanes of intense traffic. I waited extra long just to make sure I actually heard a break in it. Then, jumping off the curb, I began my dash across to the far side.

One New York Second later, excruciating back pain jarred me into consciousness. I moved slightly and my whole right side screamed with sharp pangs.

I hurt so bad! Where am I?

A soft unfamiliar voice said, "Oh good, Pam, you're awake."

"The pain," I cried as tears choked my voice. "It's horrible! What's going on?"

"You were hit by a van and brought to the Emergency Room several hours ago. You've been unconscious the whole time until now."

A short catnap followed until the doctor's entrance woke me. He gave me the full report. "Your right leg is broken. We will be putting a plaster cast on. It's going to be a long one, from your hip to ankle because the break is in the middle of your knee joint. That means you'll need to stay here in the hospital several days."

Oh great! I can see it all now! I'll be hobbling down the aisle in my wedding gown wearing that heavy plaster cast.

In the next breath, I asked the doctor how long it would be on. In a flash, my brain began calculating the timeframe. It would come off around the end of March. Relieved, I settled down and lay back in my bed with the comfort of knowing that I would be a cast-free bride.

Marv and my family rallied around me during that hospital stay. What a constant source of comfort they were. They thoughtfully brought cheerful gifts of flowers, fuzzy little critters and tasty treats. But, of even greater comfort was the love I felt each time one of them walked into my room.

When it came time for my discharge, Mom was right there to take me home. She and Dad had decided that I should stay with them while recuperating, and was I ever thankful for that. I had been concerned about getting up and down the stairs to my second story apartment.

Learning to function wearing that heavy awkward cast was a major project all by itself. That was bad enough, but then there were the crutches. Walking with crutches was more than difficult. I certainly could not use my white cane with a crutch in each hand. This left me feeling vulnerable and uneasy since I had no way to check the path ahead.

Much worse than that awkward, exhausting way of walking was the new trial of living with severe pain. I couldn't stand anything touching my back. Even the soft fuzzy fabric of the plush rocking chair created excruciating pain with the lightest contact.

There was no way I could make it up the stairs of their tri-level home to the bedroom or bathroom, but that didn't stop my family from giving me top-notch care. They turned their first floor family room into my private suite, complete with soft bed, room service and a commode.

A full week of convalescing at Mom and Dad's went by before I began to feel human again. It took even longer for my murky mind to clear enough so that I was able to look up.

"Dear Father in Heaven, you promise that you will work everything out for good for those who love you. I think I'm wearing out that promise. I sure can't see any possible good coming from this ordeal, but you proved your faithfulness before with the brain tumor. I know you can handle this one, too."

Well, good stuff was right around the corner. Dad hired an extra employee so Mom could stay home with me the whole time. Our dilemma of finding time to plan my wedding was solved! And the overdue rest for my faithful hard-working Mom was here at last. Oh how she welcomed that break from the long hours of fast-paced work at the Dairy Queen. Having something fun and exciting like planning the wedding was real therapy for both of us.

For starters, we began perusing bridal magazines.

There I was, still weak with barely enough strength to sit for short spurts.

But that didn't hamper our progress with wedding plans in the least. Mom was quite the Pollyanna, herself. She quickly found the good things and figured out ways to overcome obstacles. She was always so positive.

"You know, Pam, your accident was a terrible thing for sure, but it has done us a real favor. We never would have had so much time freed up to plan your wedding."

When it came to problem-solving, Mom was tops! Even though I only had enough strength to lie down, Mom found a way to get things done. She would pull a chair up beside the sectional couch which had become my bed, and read bridal magazines to me.

Together we dreamed, laughed and planned. What a unique and powerful therapy that was. I was productive, entertained and encouraged all at the same time while lying weak and helpless.

Once I gained enough strength to sit, Mom would bring a TV tray and the Brailler to my bedside. She sat beside me and read the planning portions that we had previously marked in the magazines. The wedding timeline, planning checklist and other pertinent information were added one page at a time to my wedding notebook. This three-ring binder separated into chronologic sections grew in size and value. It soon became my wedding day-runner.

On to the guest list we went. Shopping came next. We worked out a technique for Mom to guide me while I walked with the crutches. This was tricky and almost dangerous at times. She walked on my left side giving verbal communications, which worked fine most of the time. The dangerous part dwindled as we perfected our maneuvers. But at first, it was scary. I misinterpreted Mom's direction and proceeded to turn the wrong way and, swinging my crutch, I hit her leg. Thank goodness she didn't trip or tumble. But, she was a little worse for the wear with a black and blue souvenir on one ankle.

Although Mom and I were busy, busy, my schedule was never too full for time with Marv. Even at a moments notice, I would willingly drop my project midstream to be with him.

One thing amazed me about my sweetheart. Of course, it was a given that the bride would keep close track of the days, hours and all the details. But when Marv made the statement that there were only ten days left till our wedding and he could hardly wait, I was shocked.

Wow, he's actually counting the days! For a man to do that…it's got to be really important to him.

As I contemplated his deep and genuine enthusiasm, a glowing inner satisfaction warmed me through and through. He didn't stop at the ten-day mark either. Marv was my talking calendar and turned into a talking stop watch as we got to the hourly countdown.

Full of fun, encouragement and help—that was my man!

Despite many obstacles, the planning and wedding preparations were completed and right on time, too.

We were ready, really ready to tie the knot!

CHAPTER 20
TWO "KNOT" HEADS

That first day of May in 1982 was an unusually warm one. Bright sunlight beamed down on the brand-new leaves of spring. Even more unusual was the hub-bub in the parking lot of Emmanuel Baptist Church. On an early Saturday morning, it buzzed with activity like a beehive in the middle of honey harvesting.

Mom and I should have been wearing jogging shoes instead of white high heels. We were running everywhere, so it seemed. Mom, with checklist in hand, was making the rounds.

First on the list was the sanctuary. Reaching out to hold open those large swinging doors, I paused a brief moment to let my fingertips enjoy the soft well-worn wood. A low squeak from its hinges proudly whispered decades of faithful service.

One step inside and it was breathtaking. My senses swooned with the floral fragrance. It was as refreshing as a backyard garden in the early morning dew.

This spring time pageant blossomed with big bouquets on each side of the stage. They held a full array of pinks and purples, from pastel shades to the deepest rich hues of hot pink and royal purple. Each pew smiled with its own floral garland of white, pink and lavender flowers. Even though there wasn't much time to dally, I had to go up close to those huge balls of splendor for a twenty-twenty view.

With the sanctuary meeting Mom's approval, we headed downstairs. There the ladies of the Hostess Committee were dashing around with pots of tea and coffee. Lace tablecloths, glowing candles, fresh flowers and bright ribbons almost magically appeared in precise array. Those once drab school-like tables were transformed into festive elegance.

I, of course, had to inspect the decorations. As my fingers examined the floral wreath and lacy ribbons surrounding elegant glittering candles, my face beamed with approval. Then Mom spotted Marv standing near our wedding cake. The moment she mentioned his name, I was drawn to him like a magnet.

"Hi, Dear, how are you doing?" My words whispered with concern.

"Great, Dear," he responded with an audible beam, "and how about you?"

He reached out to hold my hand and gave me the most comforting squeeze of reassurance.

"Things are shaping up just fine thanks to our wedding coordinator here," I responded with a nod toward Mom.

"Have you seen our wedding cake yet? It turned out really nice."

"Wedding cake! Oh, Marv! I forgot that the bride is supposed to feed her husband the first bite of cake. What are we going to do! I can see it all now. You'll end up with a purple mustache and probably pink frosted eyebrows," I said giggling in an attempt to cover up my panic.

In the calmest imaginable voice, Marv said, "Don't worry, Dear, just hold the fork still, and I'll come to it."

Such a super simple solution that was, yet what a profound sense of relief. Even more flabbergasting, he came up with it in a split second. With a deep sigh of relief and a crocodile wide smile, I said, "Oh thanks, Babe, I can do that!"

Mom tugged at my arm with her eye on the clock. The checklist was complete and it was time to get dressed.

Like a mother hen, Mom gathered all the bridal chicks under her wings and herded them toward the ladies room. With all four attendants, plus Mom and I in that small restroom, it was definitely a full house. Soon pink and lavender floor-length gowns sprang up in every corner. Once each of them was dressed, all attention turned to me. Love in action filled that place. I felt like the Queen of England as helping hands surrounded me. Mandie checked the slip length while both cousins straightened my veil. Mom (my faithful talking mirror) did a last-minute makeup check. Each lady took a tour in front of the mirror for a few final touches and we were ready.

Standing erect and as tall as 5 foot 2 could ever be, I stepped forward into the hall with confidence and excited anticipation. Dad walked up to me. Reaching out, he squeezed my hand and said, "Pam, you look great! Ready to go?"

With a nod, I placed my hand on Dad's arm. As I stood there poised and ready, Dad leaned close to whisper, "Marv just walked up on the stage and he's looking mighty handsome in his tux."

Immediately a vivid snapshot of Marv popped into my mind. At that moment, I felt like running down the aisle and leaping into the arms of my soon-to-be husband.

Nice and easy, Pam, take it slow. Chin up, shoulders straight—here we go!

The joyous organ music began and our procession moved forward with celebration in each step. The church sanctuary was full and overflowing. Smiling guests watched from the lobby and side doors. Mounting the three steps to the pastor's podium, we took our places and faced the audience. Once up on the stage, my excitement instantly changed. I couldn't believe it! My whole torso began to quiver with uncontrollable coarse shaking.

I shouldn't be, couldn't be nervous! Not now! Oh great! I'll never be able to say my vows shaking like this. Calm down, just breathe deep.

That didn't help matters a bit. In less than a minute, rescue came when Pastor Anthony asked us to turn and face each other. Marv reached out and lovingly held my hand with a reassuring squeeze. I could feel the endearing gaze of his soft hazel eyes focused on me. Everything vanished but my groom. The very moment he took my hand, my nervous shaking disappeared. Warm, calm contentment infused my whole being.

The sound system gave out just as Pastor Anthony began speaking. But, not to worry, even that didn't faze me. Marv and I were so ready and so in love that everyone could hear both of us as we confidently said our vows. The best part came when we finished our vows by answering in unison with an emphatic "we do!" Promptly, the pastor turned to the audience with a boisterous, "Is there any doubt?" A wave of soft chuckling swept across the sanctuary.

Then he announced, "I would like to introduce Mr. and Mrs. Marvin Jordan."

The organ burst forth with triumphant chords of celebration and we joined its merriment with our own procession of ecstatic joy.

The reception went super smooth. Even sweeter than the cake and candy were the many hugs and kisses showered on Marv and me. As for the cake-feeding, giving a bite of it to Marv was no problem. His suggestion worked better than the well-greased bearing of a winning stock car.

Our family and friends had honored my request by not decorating our car with any disgusting stuff like Limburger cheese or shaving cream. Those restrictions, however, did not hamper their creativity in the least. With streamers and balloons, they transformed our little blue Honda into a near Rose Festival float. We pulled out of the church's parking lot and slowed to a stop at the first side street. Instantly, an avalanche of multicolored balloons floated forward, bouncing everywhere. Just as abundant as those balloons was the outburst of our laughter and smiles.

We headed to our home, a modest two-bedroom apartment on the west side of Mount Tabor. About two months before our wedding day, I had moved there and got it all set up for our new life together. Marv's parents were at our apartment waiting to take us out for a pre-honeymoon meal. In an attempt to be a "quick-change artist," I headed straight to my bedroom to get out of my wedding gown. Intently focused on hanging up my dress and slip, I stepped from the walk-in closet to my dresser. My ears picked up the sound of a door opening. Panic hit and my heartbeat quickened.

Who could that be? Oh, must be Marv's Mom. Neither of those Godly men would just walk in without knocking.

The next thing I heard was a male voice. Instinctively, I grabbed my blouse in an attempt to cover my bare body and made a mad dash into the closet.

"Honey," his calming chuckle came as the door closed, "we're married."

In an instant, my cloth shield dropped to the floor and I turned to hug my man. That moment of panic and embarrassment was a God thing for sure. I needed that ice breaker to usher me from my many years of extreme modesty into the arms of marital intimacy.

We cannot boast of a lengthy Caribbean cruise or a ritzy Hawaiian resort, but our short two-day honeymoon in Lincoln City on the Oregon Coast was more valuable than mountains of pure gold.

I was so relieved and at ease because of Marv's thoughtful, caring ways.

A few weeks prior, we had talked about our first night together. I was very open and honest, letting him know I was not sure how intimate I could be. He assured me that just being together and married was satisfaction enough for him. With my mind at ease and my guard dismantled, wedded bliss hit in its full splendor that very first night of our honeymoon. That was a miracle of God's love come down to earth.

The next morning greeted us with the sunny splendor of Oregon's coast. It was perfect weather for beachcombing. Like two young teenagers we held hands, leisurely strolling and enjoying everything around. There were more stars in our eyes than in the sky. The hours flew by even faster than our hearts were fluttering, and soon it was time to go back to Portland.

At home we settled into the humdrum of everyday life which meant it was back to work for both of us. I still worked part time at the hospital. However, my homemaker role suddenly took on a whole new sparkle. I was a wife and very pleased with my new position.

Throughout all those past years of dating and singlehood, I had earnestly prayed that God would make me a true prize for the man I'd marry. Desiring to be a Godly wife and real helpmate for Marv, I took my wifedom seriously.

Things were going along pretty well and normal for us. That is until one evening. We had just finished dinner. To this day, I can't remember the topic of our discussion, but its impact became embedded in my brain. By the end of that conversation, the tone had sharpened considerably. Marv stood up and, with disgust in his voice, started to go into the living room. Noticing his irritation, tears began streaming down my cheeks.

Seeing my tears, he stepped toward me and said, "Honey, what's wrong?"

"Oh, Marv, I'm supposed to be a helper, not an irritator."

Wrapping his loving arms around me, he said, "You know, sweetheart, it's kind of like two porcupines living together. It's like this—they want to be near each other. But, the closer they get, the bigger the risk of getting poked with their partner's quills. What I'm trying to say is—no two people can live together without grating on each other once in awhile. But, we have a lot of good things going for us. If we concentrate on the good stuff, we'll do just fine."

The biggest Pollyanna beam spread across my face and dried up the many tears almost as fast as they began.

That was the next set of bricks laid in our rock-solid foundation.

This guy—my guy—is wonderful! How could I be so lucky to get such a neat man for my husband? Yes, I do know how—it's you, dear Father. Thank you for giving me the man of my dreams.

With Marv's lead in focusing on the positive, I was a born follower.

CHAPTER 21
TWISTS AND TURNS

The foundation of having a positive outlook was working quite well until two years into our marriage. Second birthday in a row and no gifts, not even so much as a birthday card from Marv.

What's wrong with this guy, anyway? If he really loves me, you'd think he'd show it at least a little bit. It's certainly not asking too much. I don't want lavish gifts—just a little remembrance of some kind.

Two Valentine days and two Christmases had also come and gone with no gift or card from Marv. This was a real shock to my system. What a major difference this was compared to my previous nine suitors. Each one had showered me with lots of flowers and special gifts. I couldn't even begin to count the many roses I was given by my former boyfriend in just a short time.

Andy knew roses were my favorite, so he was always very thoughtful to bring roses, chocolates, jewelry or some gift with his every visit. Not having that show of affection left a big empty spot in my emotional closet. Meanwhile, all this time, I had been diligent in remembering Marv with gifts and cards on every special occasion.

On the surface, this wouldn't seem very significant and certainly nothing to worry about. After a few months, however, this had grown to be a major problem. My focus had shifted and slipped downhill from a twinge of disgust into the gutter of resentment.

The downhill shift in my attitude was so subtle that I didn't even notice it at first. I tried communicating to Marv the significance of a birthday card and such. I told him that it didn't need to be an expensive gift but just something small or simple to let me know he valued and loved me. But, after another Valentine's Day had come and gone with absolutely nothing from Marv, the bitterness reared its ugly head with startling fury. As I thought about his blatant ignorance of me on this special occasion, disgusting thoughts about Marv began flooding my mind.

Ooh, I didn't like that negative churning within me. If I tried to ignore it and stuff my feelings, the resentment would continue to fester and grow. Something had to be done and done right away, but what?

By this time, I knew right where to go for the true solutions. On my knees. "It's me again, dear Heavenly Father. You know how mad I am. I know this is not how you want me to feel, but the truth is, I do feel that way and can't figure out how to change. Please do something to change Marv or change me so that I'll be satisfied without another trinket from him."

As I rose from my knees, the word trinket turned into a huge hammer and thumped me a good one. Trinkets they were. Yes, indeed, all those flowers, candy and the like were merely trinkets. They were designed as a way to show the real gift, a heart full of genuine love. What little value they held compared to Marv's love for me. So often, even several times a day, he would take extra time out of his own agenda to enhance my world. It might be a quick side detour in the grocery store to get my hands on an unusual item or a pause to show me holiday decorations. He made sure I got in on the good things around. Anything cute, pretty or wholesome always was brought into my view. As I thought about the many ways he showed his love to me, an idea hit me literally "out of the blue."

I know! Every time Marv goes out of his way to do something special for me, I'll just consider it as if he had handed me a lovely fresh rose.

The very next day, Marv did something extra-special for me. Setting aside his project, he took time to do something I wanted. Marv walked with me to Seaton's Pharmacy, the neighborhood drugstore. Inside that small pharmacy was one of Portland's few remaining old-fashioned soda fountains. What a quaint setting—six stools lined the short curved counter. Genuine hand-scooped rich milk shakes were proudly served in the tall shiny metal containers. This was a real drawing card for many local city folk. And that was what drew me there. I was hungry for a milkshake.

It was a sunny afternoon and perfect weather for being outdoors. We chatted and enjoyed our leisure stroll along this very familiar route—the same way I walked to work every day. Despite its familiarity, I still loved the setting. Here small homes lined one side of this busy two-lane street. Even though this residential strip was a short one, it was tall on the neighborly atmosphere of the "good old days."

Friendly neighbors and back yard chats were a regular occurrence. Small front yards waved their refreshing hints of greenery. Right above my head, birds twittered with petite voices. Lingering there, my ears twitched in delight with the cheerful serenade. Standing so close made it much more enjoyable. It was similar to hearing the individual instruments in an orchestra.

Then, my nose flared to Jimmy Durante size as I inhaled and savored the cool freshness coming special delivery by the breeze.

One step farther took me out of my sensory delight and into the concrete jungle. The loud roar of a Tri-Met bus rumbled right beside the curb's edge, putting an abrupt halt to our conversation. There it sat idling at the signal, pelting us with dark blasts of disgusting exhaust. We couldn't get across the street and into Seaton's fast enough.

What a relief to step inside that small drugstore! Appetizing aromas of sizzling hot dogs and grilling hamburgers broadcasted the fountain's sandwich menu. The counter was lined with customers. Casual conversation mingled with the quiet crunches of chips and popcorn.

Our friend, Cora, piped up with a hearty welcome from behind the counter while flipping hamburger patties. Off to my left in front of the candy display, a young boy was practicing his salesmanship. Turning to his older sister, he said, "Look, Angie, licorice, red licorice. Mommy always lets me get red licorice."

"Oh, good, we're in luck," Marv tugged on my arm drawing my attention back to the task at hand. "There are two empty stools at the end. This way, my dear, here's one for you."

"Oh yes, this is perfect!"

With one hand placed on the counter, my fingers slid along its outdated chrome edge. It had long ago lost the slick surface of shiny metal. The lengthy lineup of scrapes and dents crowded between well-pronounced rusty screws recorded many years of serving customers.

"I'll share a shake with you if that's okay," Marv suggested.

"Sure thing. How about chocolate?"

He agreed and I proceeded to order a chocolate shake with two glasses.

"Excuse me," he interjected, "could we have just one tall glass with two straws, please?"

Marv and I sat side by side on the stools sharing that shake. What a very special, very romantic moment. As I sipped that yummy chocolate shake, my cheek brushed softly against his. It was then that I realized Marv was truly giving me a gift—a gift much more valuable than any rose in its prime.

Marv always had an extraordinary ability to capture the moment and he seldom missed an opportunity to do something fun, romantic or encouraging. That was so meaningful to me, but even more amazing was the fact that Marv enjoyed it, himself, right along with me. From that experience on, I was careful to make note of any time Marv went out of his way to do something special for me. To my sheer delight, within the short span of about one week, Marv had, through his special acts of love, handed me so many roses that I already had a large bouquet.

When out doing mundane errands like grocery shopping and such, he would say, "Honey, you've got to see this!" He would escort me over to something touchable, cute or fragrant. How insignificant and mundane that would seem for the average sighted shopper. But, for me, it was totally different.

Since I had normal vision the first twelve years of my life, I knew there was so much around me that I was missing. Whenever Marv took time to show me things that I could enjoy in detail, he made my world come alive.

Without this input, my surroundings were merely a blank Picasso. After all, a blind person's world in detail exists no farther than the length of their arms. I could, for example, tell a refrigerator was nearby because of being in the kitchen and hearing the motor running. That did not give me any clue as to its size, color, texture of the finish and so on. Until reaching out my arm to touch it, all the details were missing.

But when Marv moved me aside for one of his unique detours, the beauty of my world came into full view. One of those simple, yet most enjoyable, detours happened right in the kitchen of my brother's home. "Honey, you've got to see this," Marv said as he gently took my arm and moved me to the nearby refrigerator. There, stuck to the front, was the cutest decorative magnet I'd ever seen. It was a tiny ornately textured vase where my sister-in-law had placed a miniature bouquet of real flowers. He always gave me the chance to touch, smell and enjoy whatever was at hand. What fun and beauty his abundant gifts added to our lives.

Another source of positivism in our lives was how Marv loved to tease and please me. We were walking down the frozen food aisle in Safeway. I was concentrating on reading my Braille shopping list and pretty much oblivious to the surroundings. On the other hand, Marv was totally observant of everything around. He spotted a stuffed bear displayed high on top of the freezers. All of a sudden, something flew through the air right over my shoulder and almost hit my nose. I jumped backward with a start. Marv had skillfully knocked it from its lofty home and smack-dab in front of my nose.

That UFO no sooner lit in the child seat when it began growling as Marv made it come alive with his special sound effects. With laughter and an inexpressible joy, I turned to deliver a bear hug to my great guy.

Totally in context with my character, I had to see that black blob myself. Reaching into the shopping cart, I took a close look at that fuzzy bear and couldn't resist squeezing its soft cuddly body. Turning to show my proud catch to Marv, I said, "Thank goodness you did that. The poor critter was pretty lonesome up there and really needed a hug."

During an afternoon lunch out, Marv gave me another special treat. We had just finished our meal at Skipper's Seafood Restaurant.

On our way to the parking lot, Marv halted and said, "Honey, you've got to see this!"

With that familiar short phrase, the little girl inside me jumped up and down with excitement just like a child stepping into a candy shop.

Off the sidewalk and right across the front lawn we walked to a tall plant. Towering stately above my head like a proud African warrior, it stood with vigilance guarding his land. Marv gently moved my hand to one of the blades, and what a treat. How well I could feel the coarse ridges. Its broad stiff grass-like blades with jagged edges ended in a sword piercing point.

"Yes, Dear," Marv said as he moved my hand slightly to the left, "that is neat, but here's what I really wanted you to see. It's blooming, and look at the flower."

"Oh, my goodness! How neat! It's really different. Wow, kind of feels like the silky tassel on a graduation hat, but of course, lots bigger. Oh, Babe, I love it! Thank you! Thank you!"

"I was hoping you'd like it. God's creation is sure amazing. Here you have the extreme opposites. There's the frilly delicate flower in the center of such stiff wide blades. And the color contrast is striking, too. The green blades are really dark, and the bloom is snow white."

As I reflected over the week's events, it amazed me how many roses Marv had given me. Carefully arranging them in my mind, they created a gorgeous bouquet. I wanted to share my idea of roses with Marv but was hesitant at first. There was no guarantee how he would take it. He might think I was foolish, even a bit delusional. On the other hand, it might be a big relief for him to know I wasn't so upset with him anymore.

Oh, why not, Marv's so understanding and kind. I really don't think he'll put me down.

One Saturday morning, we sat enjoying a relaxed breakfast and I explained my new idea of the roses. To my surprise, Marv accepted it and was really pleased. He was quite impressed with my attitude change.

Several weeks went by with no mention of roses. However, they were alive and well in my mind. As for Marv, he continued handing me roses again and again. One evening, we sat together on our living room couch just talking about the usual topics of our work day and so on.

"Oh, Honey, remember awhile back when I told you that whenever you do something special for me, it's as though you'd handed me a rose?"

And he did remember.

"The first rose you gave me was at Seaton's Pharmacy when we shared the milkshake. Ever since then I've been collecting a rose each time you do something special for me. And guess what, now I have a lovely bouquet of roses. It's beautiful!" With a chuckle in my voice, I added, "These roses never wilt or die. Pretty unique, don't you think?"

Marv was more pleased than ever with this new development. In fact, it seemed to improve his enthusiasm and eagerness to share more of the special things around us.

Life in the city—that's the way it was—and not too shabby overall. But it was far from pressure-free. In fact, the pressures were mounting up and taking a toll on me. I couldn't put my finger on any specific thing causing the insomnia, but this new development was most revolting. It seemed to take hours before I could unwind enough to fall asleep.

A real help came when a seminar on relaxation was offered for the hospital employees. I was able to attend it and so glad that I did. I came away with one very helpful idea. The technique was to clear my mind of the day's stresses by imagining myself in a tranquil setting, somewhere I enjoyed being. That same night, in the midst of restless tossing and turning, I pondered the new information.

What place would relax me the most?

I thought and considered, considered and thought. Finally, I got smart and prayed.

Then it came to me.

I love the fragrance of roses, and I should have a gazillion of them by now!

Yes, why not—a rose garden!

I lay there beaming and began creating my very own garden. A white picket fence surrounded it. A rose covered arched trellis displaying our wedding colors stood majestically over a swinging gate. The shades of pink and purple were accented with white roses and frilly ferns.

Before I could step through the swinging gate, sweet slumber swept me away.

The next morning, I was elated to arise refreshed from a full night of restful sleep. That started a trend, and a fun one at that. Before long, I had a breath-taking garden with soothing waterfalls gently cascading into a tropical pool. Whenever my racing brain refused to settle down, I retreated to my private tropical rose garden.

I loved to sunbathe at the pool's edge. Or relax beneath the whispering willow tree and recall the day's events. That was fun, but the best part came one evening when Marv and I had just retired for the night. Noticing that Marv was still awake, I rolled over and whispered, "I have something extra special to share with you if you're not too tired."

"No problem, Dear, go for it."

"Remember not too long ago when I told you about the beautiful bouquet of roses you had given me?"

He answered with a yawning yes and a question mark in his voice.

"Good! Guess what, I've continued saving each rose you've given me. And, now, I have a rose garden! I know this sounds crazy, but I'd like you to lean back, close your eyes and imagine yourself walking with me in our rose garden."

What a good sport he was, and that night proved it. He walked with me to enjoy the vibrant colors and tantalizing smells. As our heavy eyelids began to close, Marv whispered in my ear, "I'm so glad you decided to share your rose garden with me. It's so good of you to do something like that. It's pretty unusual, I think."

With the addition of my special mate and best friend, it had become even grander. It was our rose garden. Marv never promised me a rose garden, but my Heavenly Father sure knew my heart's desires. He filled that desire to full and overflowing for sure. This firsthand experience reminded me of the reality of God's ability to turn the trials into good.

How good to know without a doubt that God even cares about the little everyday things in my life.

What a giant confidence booster that was and how timely, too. I was more convinced than ever that no matter what the future brought, I could walk with courage knowing I would never walk it alone.

CHAPTER 22
SHIFTING GEARS AGAIN

I still enjoyed working at the Portland Adventist Hospital and was well engrained in the humdrum of the work day world. As far as a typing job went, mine was superb. Yet my heart still yearned for a people-oriented position. I felt as though I were tied to a typewriter. So, I prayed, "Dear Father in Heaven, I sure would love to have a job working with people."

It seemed like the best approach would be to find a people-oriented activity for my days off. I didn't have a clue where to start looking until a friend told me about Vision Resources for Independent Living, a new agency in town. I decided to check it out. Phone research revealed that they provided training and counseling for adults with vision loss. It was a small private agency and they were looking for volunteer blind people to teach daily living skills.

Sounds like the "cat's meow" for me.

I made an appointment to tour their center. Arriving at VRIL's front door, I was greeted by Ruth, their receptionist. What a delightful elderly lady—her warmth and charm calmed my nervous apprehensions like a creamy milkshake after a tonsillectomy. She introduced me to both the agency's director, Mr. Gardner, and the Independent Living Supervisor, Dorothy. They were very friendly people. To my surprise, they both took time to help me get acquainted.

Mr. Gardner headed the Transcription Department and gave me a tour of this section. He explained that blind people could submit any print material to this department. A trained core of faithful volunteers would transcribe it into either large print, Braille or a talking book.

Dorothy was director of the agency's second section, the Independent Living Center. That department was designed to help visually impaired adults gain independence. At the end of the tour, I asked Dorothy if they still needed volunteers to teach classes.

I was in luck or I should say, in the middle of a great big blessing! They did need one more class. I offered to teach a class in organization. That was a natural for me and especially beneficial with vision loss. At the same time, the concept of organization often seemed vague and difficult for many people. My goal was to show easy ways to get organized. Dorothy liked my idea. That very day, I signed up and my class went on their calendar of events.

I had no college degree nor any courses in the subject. My two wise scholars were Mom and Dad. It seemed like the very day I got home from the hospital, Dad began my course in Organization 101. How well I remember his words, "Pam, you really need to figure out a place for everything and put it right back as soon as you're done with it. That is something that would help all of us. But, it is especially important for you since you can't just look around and see where you left it."

His suggestion fit like a glove and with practice became my Modus Operandi. The need to be organized became super clear in my college days. It all took place at Carla's. She was in the same Medical Transcription class. On my arrival, there was an obvious delay in the cooking. She asked me if I liked green beans. I answered yes and expected to enjoy a nice helping soon.

Instead, she responded with a delighted, "Good," and promptly handed me a big plastic bowl full of green beans. "I already have a casserole full for dinner. I'll never be able to eat all those. So, if you want, this bowl can go home with you. You see—I was trying to find a can of tomato sauce for the casserole. Each can I opened ended up being green beans. I have six of them opened now."

When asked to help her look in the cupboard for a can of tomato sauce, I was astonished with the disarray. The cupboards had a wide assortment of everything, crammed from bottom to top, resembling the inside of a trash compacter. This experience proved that a little basic organization would be helpful for blind people.

Teaching a class—what an exciting development!

My days off were busy with planning and thinking, thinking and planning. I designed my presentation like an open house walk-through tour and focused on one room of the home at a time. Once my teaching outline was done, I created a handout for the students entitled, "A Guide to Organization." I submitted my handout to the Agency's Transcription Department, which made both Braille and large print copies.

With the hard part done, it was time to spice it up and add some hands-on participation to this lecture. I went through each room gathering samples and displays for the class. It was a time-consuming project, but I loved every minute of it.

Soon my dining room table was covered from one edge to the other. This collection included gadgets, hangers, cleaning items and more.

Now comes the real test of my organizing skill—get some order into this huge mess. I've got to figure out some way to get all this stuff in workable order.

At first, the huge mess totally baffled me. It escaped all my options of order.

Well, guess I could just pile everything in big trash bags and wait to sort things when I get to the classroom.

That sounded way too cumbersome and just didn't set well with the planner in me.

All of a sudden, a brain storm hit. Cardboard boxes! That was it! It was off to Safeway to gather cardboard boxes, one for each room. With the boxes lined up alphabetically in a row on the couch, I began sorting my demos. At last, the dining room table was usable again.

One box was transformed into a kitchen drawer. Lined up in it were different sizes of plastic drawer organizer trays. The longest tray held long handled utensils like rubber spatulas and wooden spoons. The shorter tray had a vegetable peeler and measuring spoons. Tucked in the corner was a smaller square, one to capture miscellaneous little stuff that otherwise could roll around and be lost forever in corners. Adding my sixty-minute Braille timer to this make-shift drawer, I was satisfied with the collection of kitchen demos.

In the bathroom box, I lined up examples of often used items. It was my past experiences that nudged me into the importance of having the bathroom items organized and identifiable. One of my first mornings back at home as a blind girl, I squeezed a big glob of Steve's Brylcreem on my toothbrush. I was so sure it was Crest that I didn't question it until the horrible taste filled my whole mouth. I also learned that a can of hair spray and air freshener were easy to mix up. It was not until I had a generous layer of Glade on my hair that the fragrance alerted me to the blooper. That is why having things unmistakably stored in the bathroom was a must in my book.

Finally, my collection was complete. All my boxes were full: Bathroom, bedroom, den and kitchen. I was teaching-ready and twice as eager.

If thoughts could have feet, mine would have been constantly pacing up and down the calendar. At last, the class day arrived. Mom graciously offered to drive me with all my stuff to VRIL, and was I ever glad of that. About an hour and a half before class, we began unloading the trunk of her car.

Walking from corner to corner of the classroom gave me a general picture of my teaching space. Then, it was time for organization in action. I got busy with my boxes. They were strategically positioned the full length of the head table. I had the boxes in the order of my talk. In each box, the contents were arranged in the order to pass them out. I stood back and smiled at my organization.

It was time to welcome my students. That small class of five was a fun, interactive bunch. One of the most memorable instances happened while showing the students my bathroom demonstration. I passed around two tubes. A regular tube of toothpaste went first followed by an identical sized tube of first aid cream. The only difference was a strip of cloth bandage tape secured to the end of the second one. They were able to distinguish them with ease. That pleased me, but even more so was Greg's response. That middle-aged gentleman hit the table with a loud thump and exclaimed, "Yes, that's perfect!" Waving the first aid cream high above his heads, he said, "No more first aid cream in my comb!"

The next topic was the bedroom closet. The class roared as I related my high school embarrassment. Getting ready for school one morning, I dashed into my bedroom and grabbed a pair of loafers. I rushed and made it just in time to catch the bus. I had been in such a hurry that my goof-up was not noticeable until the end of first period. One of the students announced to everyone that Pam was wearing two different shoes. Both were loafers, but one was patent leather and the other a dull brown. That story broke the ice for a few tips in keeping shoes and outfits matched.

The kitchen make-shift drawer was a hit, too, but not quite as hilarious. Sally's comment made my day, however. "I'm going to stop on my way home and buy some of those plastic trays for my kitchen. I'm darn tired of emptying the whole drawer just to find my potato peeler."

During my desk presentation, the students taught me a new technique. As I passed around a desk organizer tray, Mary got excited. "Hey, Pam," she addressed me with a squeal of delight. "This tray is perfect for me. Look at this! All I have to do is turn mine backwards from yours. The big slot is the perfect place to put my candy stash. I won't have to hunt for runaway M&M's anymore."

"Good idea," Allen added. "I never thought of using my office tray for that, but that's good for business, you know. Without an afternoon pick-me-up, how can you get enough work done?"

Well, it was a majority rule that this "sweet tip" should be added to my den box. A strong stipulation came with that, too. They said I needed to add enough bags of M&M's for each student in the class. My presentation went like clockwork and I had a ball teaching it.

Afterward I spoke to Dorothy and said, "I am very impressed with your agency and what you're doing here. If you ever need to hire more staff, I'd love to join you."

Teaching was an exhilarating experience, but the next day it was back to my typing job. I had to settle into the humdrum of typing again. As my fingers kept racing across the keyboard, I also kept praying.

Dear Father in heaven, it's me again. I'm willing to stay in this job as long as you want me here. I know it's asking a lot, but if you could give me a job working with people, I'd sure appreciate it. Amen. Oh, and by the way, If it lines up with your will, I'd really like to work at Vision Resources.

On the job I sat engrossed, typing a lengthy operative report. I made a point of tuning out everything going on in the office. It took extreme concentration to push for top speed and keep from making mistakes. The reports had to be accurate. They were crucial for the patient's treatment and could even end up in court as a legal document.

Anyway, there I was in my own world of a complicated neurosurgery when our secretary tapped my shoulder. "Pam, there's a phone call for you."

After a mental notation of the last word typed, I headed for the secretary's desk.

"Hi, Pam," a familiar voice greeted me. This is Dorothy at Vision Resources. We have an opening for a Braille teacher, and I want to give you the first opportunity to fill it."

She informed me that an ad had to run in the newspaper for two weeks before they could close the application process. But, in the meantime, she wanted me to go in for an interview. Hanging up the receiver, I shook my head in an attempt to clear the mental cobwebs. I stepped over to Paula's desk and tapped her on the shoulder. "Paula, you won't believe it! I just got a call to go in for an interview. There is an opening for a Braille teacher."

"Wow, Pam, that sounds great!"

Thank goodness it was almost lunchtime. I probably would have burst if I had to wait much longer to share the exciting details with her.

That evening the first thing in the door, I dropped my bags and headed for the phone to call Marv. I filled him in on the phone conversation and the exciting new opportunity. He was not sure it would be wise to make the change since I was so accomplished in my present job. On the other hand, when I explained that it was the chance of a lifetime for me and what I'd been praying for, he willingly agreed.

I did go for the interview and it went well. Truthfully, I figured someone else would be hired. After all, I had no college degree and the job was advertised statewide. It was a nice idea but just a pipe dream for sure. As I was busy with my typing at the hospital, God was busy working behind the scenes. Monday morning had rolled around again. With a gentle tap on my shoulder, the secretary informed me that I had another phone call.

"Hi, Pam, it's Dorothy. How would you like to start teaching Braille tomorrow?" Silence filled the phone line a few seconds before my breath returned. Struggling to untangle both my tongue and thoughts, I answered, "Wow! I'd love to, but I don't know what my boss will think about it."

"Well, Pam, you don't have to worry. I've already talked to her and you're clear to start tomorrow if you choose."

A teacher! I'm going to be a Braille teacher! That's incredible, a miracle for sure.

Well, it wasn't a quiet high-production business office anymore. My squeal of ecstasy disrupted every transcriptionist in the department. Our small staff was close knit, so all the girls gathered around me, eager to hear my news. I was congratulated with a victory hug from each lady. The conversation turned to expressing their regrets about my leaving. After all, I had been there about ten years and had grown to love each of them.

The next few hours were filled with excitement, apprehension and the challenge of maintaining my concentration. At home that evening, my excitement mounted and hit the top of the chart. Of course, waves of apprehension and questions were intermingled with my ecstasy. *Can I really do it?* That fear of facing the unknown created a broken record replaying in my mind.

Thank goodness for my rose garden. It clearly reminded me of God's personal interest and help. Even though everything seemed hopeless without a solution, He was right there when I called out. As I slipped into our bed, Marv snuggled up, holding me tight in his arms. His loving support personalized the reality of God's love. Instead of tossing with worry, my heart beamed as I pictured myself sitting beside a student teaching Braille. What a comfort filled me knowing that my Heavenly Father would be right beside me each step of this new adventure.

Early Tuesday morning I awoke, long before my alarm was due to ring. Getting ready for work was no problem. In fact, the trip to VRIL went like a snap. But, the moment my foot hit the sidewalk of VRIL, a thick fog swallowed up my air of confidence without warning. Fear of the unknown and doubting my ability kept recycling in waves of uneasiness. There I stood, stunned in a mental haze. The reality hit me that I was about five seconds away from opening the door into an unknown realm.

My emotions ran the full gamut. The exhilaration of excitement and anticipation was jumbled together with a hefty dose of fear and nervousness. With a silent prayer and slow deep breath, I reached out and took a firm hold of VRIL's front door.

Ruth was right there to greet me. Her warm caring personality waltzed right into my heart and dispelled the pent up apprehension.

"Good morning, Pam. You're sure here bright and early."

Popping open my watch, I responded, "Oh, my, I really did make good time getting here. I purposely caught one Max earlier than needed so that I'd have plenty of time."

"Good idea. Let me show you to your desk."

Stepping out from behind the reception counter, Ruth offered her arm to guide me and we were touring ready.

Ruth was an excellent guide. She acquainted me with the offices of each staff person.

"Pam, this is an unusually quiet morning as most of the staff are out. As they arrive, I'll make sure you get to meet them."

At the end of the far hall was my office. Stepping into it, Ruth said, "You have a nice large desk right here. And, oh yes, let me show you your bookcase against this same wall. This will give you lots of storage."

I checked it out by sliding my hand along the top shelf from one end to the other.

This thing is huge, taller than me. I don't need all that space.

She turned to show me my phone and explain the intercom buttons. "Dorothy is due in the office about ten o'clock. She'll fill you in on your job and get you set up. In the meantime, feel free to roam around and get acquainted with the office. Just give me a buzz if you need anything or have questions."

"Thanks so much."

After a few minutes of exploring my desk drawers and work space, I began unpacking my bag. That didn't take very long. I had packed light—just a few essentials to get me started. A box of Kleenex and my slate and stylus with notebook were also in place. Feeling settled in, I was off to do some scouting. I turned down the main hall with my ears in surveillance mode. The ominous emptiness of this large building began to wane with the warm chatter and laughter of ladies in the reception area.

As I approached the front desk, Ruth's smiling voice greeted me, "Oh, Pam, good timing. I'd like you to meet Bea. Her desk is right across from mine. She is the executive secretary and head of the Transcription Department."

Following warm hand shakes and a few words of welcome, the telephone called Ruth back to her desk. A second incoming call sent Bea straight to her desk. No sooner had I turned down the hall toward my office when the bell dangling from the handle on the front door jingled. It was Dorothy. She greeted me warmly and welcomed me aboard.

"Pam, give me ten minutes to get settled in and I'll meet with you in your office."

There I sat almost motionless at my desk, but my mind was anything but still. It was teeming with an overflowing bushel basket of questions.

What kind of teaching text will I use to teach Braille? How many students will I have? Is the conference room where I'll be teaching?

To my surprise, the topic of teaching was of little significance on this first encounter. Dorothy was prompt and about ten minutes later entered my office. Pulling up a chair beside me, she began with an overview of their agency.

"You see, Pam, we're a community-based agency. That means most of the teaching and counseling takes place in the homes of our consumers. You will be teaching Braille, but probably not a lot. The people we serve are usually quite new to vision loss. What they need are skills for coping and living independently again in their own homes."

"Do you have a driver that takes us to those places?" I questioned.

"No, Pam, you will need to get there on your own by bus or the Max. Jean does it that way and she is totally blind. Have you met Jean?"

"No, not yet."

"I think she's in her office now. Come on and I'll introduce you. She can give you lots of good information."

A few quick steps down the hall and we were at her door. "Good morning, Jean," Dorothy announced our presence with a warm smile. "I'd like you to meet Pam Jordan, our new Independent Living Counselor. Do you have a few minutes to get acquainted and tell her what you do?"

"Sure, my next appointment is in the office right after lunch."

"Fine, I'll be back about 11:30 to take Pam out to lunch. You can join us, too, if you have time."

With a swish of her flowing dress, Dorothy was on her way down the hall. Taking a seat across the desk from Jean, an uncomfortable silence ensued. We both hesitated, pensively searching for the best way to start. Jean was pleasant but much more matter-of-fact than friendly.

I found out that my job of "Braille Teacher" was almost everything but that. I would be traveling, just like Dorothy said, by myself to places I'd never been before. Once in a home, I would go through a list of assessment questions and then figure out what services they needed from VRIL. Jean and I had covered almost everything when Dorothy appeared at the door. "Ready for lunch?"

"Perfect timing," I responded, and my stomach seconded the motion with a low rumbling growl. Jean declined the offer since her next appointment was due right at noon.

My first day at VRIL was a full one. I spent my time getting acquainted with the building itself, the staff members and the many dedicated volunteers.

I was supposed to be a Braille Teacher, I don't know about this one. Dear Lord, if I weren't sure that you brought me here, I'd be tempted to tell Dorothy no way! I like the people and everything but the part about the buses. The thought of traveling all over Portland by myself is downright terrifying!

No telling how I was going to handle this one. But I did know one thing for sure—if I thought for a moment I'd be traveling out there all by myself, I would have said FORGET IT!

CHAPTER 23
1…2…3—TAKE-OFF!

I think the next part of my life could be compared to racing a sports car on a road course. Years of watching my dad as a professional racer could have something to do with choosing this pictorial comparison. Most of his career was spent on oval tracks. Our whole family thought he would never quit driving around in circles. But it did happen when his boss (owner of a local Lincoln Mercury dealership) twisted Dad's arm. With the promise of a much better income and no problem getting time off work for race events, Dad was sold. He agreed to drive a sports car.

From that moment on, he counted the days down, watching the calendar. Finally, that special package from England arrived at the dealership. Its unveiling was quite the celebration. That same day, all the mechanics, Dad and the boss took an elaborate lunch lasting the whole afternoon. A handful of top mechanics was chosen to be Dad's pit crew. The next few weeks were spent getting acquainted with the McLaren and its performance.

Our family certainly did not take a back seat in all this. We also had a chance to get acquainted with Dad's new racing machine. Typical for our family, we all took a real interest in what each member was doing. That meant active participation and a helping hand where needed. This new chapter in Dad's life was no exception.

Dad made special arrangements for our family to see the new sports car.

Knowing that I would have to have hands on, he cautioned, "You guys be careful not to lean on the car. If you put your elbow on the hood with too much pressure, you could crack it."

Learning about the fragile fiberglass body with even faster speeds than stock car events was not comforting news. Sports car racing was a brand new experience for Dad, and it worried me more than ever.

Then I rode in the McLaren with Dad on a practice lap. My fear turned from frightened to being terrified. It was too fast, too loud, too low to the ground and too fragile. I couldn't help but verbalize my observations. Regardless, none of those concerns slowed him down in the least. During the 1969 Rose Festival season, Dad skillfully motored the McLaren to win the Rose Cup Race at Portland International Raceways.

With all those memories still alive, the scene of a road course was clear and forefront in my view. A standard road course had many challenging S-shaped curves and hills. I had been racing down the straight-away of life and doing quite well despite the challenges presented on my new job. For over ten years, I had been a skilled, confident white cane traveler. My confidence in my faithful partner, Cemore, had not changed. After all, I could "see more" when walking with my white cane.

I seldom had to go anyplace unfamiliar. However, S curves appeared at every turn when I started working at Vision Resources. The new job demanded traveling alone to many parts of the huge tri-county metropolitan area. This meant I had to take public transportation to places where I had never set foot before. Everyday travel had become more difficult. Those scary and unsettling trips were my hairpin S curves.

One morning at my desk, I sat scanning my stack of new referrals. One consumer lived in a very bad part of Portland. Mr. Norton had just lost most of his vision a month ago. Both he and his family were struggling with how to cope. While they were struggling with his vision loss, I was struggling with the fear of making the trip into that section of town.

Following Jean's advice, I did my homework first. This entailed calling the Special Needs dispatcher at the Tri-Met bus company. Bless those folks. They were lifesavers! Those dispatchers had extra information designed to help passengers with disabilities. I told the specialist my starting point and the address I was heading for. They gave me the bus number to catch, where it stopped and when I'd need to board it to reach my destination on time.

With my homework done, I slipped on my coat. An inner shiver of fear snaked up my spine as I rose to my feet and got ready. It was a good thing I didn't have time to sit and stew about it. The next Max was due at 10:15, about ten minutes away. That meant cinch up my track shoes and get moving. Well, the Max was on time, and so was I. Climbing aboard, I sat down and leaned back to catch my breath and rest my brain.

So far so good, I'm making good connections and right on schedule, too. Guess I'd better review my travel notes.

I had just finished reading my directions when the driver announced my stop. Stepping off the bus, I turned to cross the street. I had to walk north four blocks then turn right and find Mr. Norton's house in the middle of that block. According to my phone conversation with his wife, theirs was the second driveway from the corner. I rounded the corner and switched into "driveway search mode." Finding a driveway was not as simple as it sounded.

Driveways, like people, are anything but uniform. Some are gravel, some ruts and others like sunken canals. Today, however, I was fortunate. The easier-to-find driveways lay just ahead. They had uniform depressions with a distinct rise between each.

This is my kind of neighborhood—smooth sidewalks, short lots and sunken driveway entrances.

I was surprised and relieved to find their home with such ease. They were a delightful couple and I enjoyed the time with them. My assessment revealed that Mr. Norton could use several sessions of instruction. He wanted to continue cooking flapjacks every Sunday morning, read novels and sign checks by himself. With an appointment set for next week and a couple of warm hand shakes, I was on my way to catch the bus.

A quick check of my notes revealed a bus shelter was very close, just two blocks away. The next bus was due in just a few minutes. With my white cane tapping left-right, left-right and my short legs trying to mimic Paul Bunyan's sprint, I darted toward the target. All the while, my ears were scanning forward and backward for any sounds of an oncoming bus. I had to get to that shelter before the bus arrived.

The last thing I wanted was to be sitting out there by myself a second longer than necessary. After all, the recent news broadcasts had reported drug busts and gang violence in this very area.

At that moment, inner panic surged and my heartbeat probably could have set a new track record. But I made it and promptly sat on the bench inside the shelter. Entranced in deep concentration, my ears searched for any sound of a bus. The neighborhood was silent with an almost eerie stillness. An uneasy feeling hit me. It was just too quiet. I had always found comfort in the sound of children outdoors playing and the sounds of family activities like people working in their yards. There was no sound of anybody anywhere.

I'm alone, totally alone! Better double check when that bus is due.

Reaching into my backpack, I pulled out my little black book. In Mr. Norton's file, I scanned the page of bus directions. With a horrified gasp, I discovered that in my hurry, I had misread the time. It would be half an hour until the next bus. Sighing, I put my book away and resumed listening. Nervously, I shifted my weight as if it were possible to find a comfortable spot on that hard wooden bench.

My fidgeting was interrupted with the loud slam of a door and angry male voices. By the sound, they were senior high guys and not the best of friends, either.

Their voices mounted to shouting proportion, yelling words that I never wanted to hear, much less repeat. Every muscle in my body stiffened into readiness for a fast get-away. My heart beat like the pounding of a jackhammer.

My adrenaline sky-rocketed as the shouts increased in intensity. Across the street, another angry dude appeared. He was in no way bashful about giving them his piece of mind. And his words were worse than the others. The loud crash of a glass bottle shattering caused a brief interruption and an intense jolt of panic to my bones.

Instantly, the hair on the back of my neck turned into starched Army fatigues. Standing up, I thought about making a fast get-away by sprinting to the next bus stop. But that option was dismissed when I reminded myself that I had no idea where the next bus stop was.

Sitting down again, I trembled and listened, listened and trembled. Another crash of glass sounded followed by more shouting—then silence hit.

Oh no! Where are they now? I hope nobody's coming this way.

Then my mental faculties took charge and rallied to the rescue.

Good grief! What's wrong with me! I'm not alone. God is here with me.

I began talking to my Heavenly Father.

Oh, Father, I'm so glad I am really not alone. You're right here with me.

I want to thank you for your promise of protection. I know this one's just for me right now: 'When I am afraid, I will put my trust in God. In God, whose word I praise, in God I have put my trust. I shall not be afraid. What can mere man do to me?' Oh, Father, just wrap your loving arms around me and hold me tight, please. I'm scared beyond scared.

At that moment, an indescribable peace filled me from head to toe. And, then, the sweetest sound on earth caught my ears—a bus! It wasn't supposed to arrive yet, not for at least ten minutes. Jumping to my feet, I was at the bus before the driver could get the door open. I bounded up those steps with the speed and agility of an adolescent.

"Am I ever glad to see you," I greeted the driver with a huge sigh of relief. "Is my timing off or are you running early?"

"Well, young lady, I don't know how it happened, but yes, I'm about ten minutes ahead of schedule."

With those words, I felt God's reassuring hug as if to say, "See, Pam, I am right here with you all the time."

A little shaken and worse for the wear, I returned to VRIL and settled in to do the pleasantly boring paperwork on my desk. A tall diet Coke and cushioned office chair never seemed so satisfying.

On a different excursion to a consumer's home, I ended up walking down a freeway ramp! I thought I was making a left turn onto a side street. Thank God for nice people. A motorist paused his car to yell out the window, "Lady, did you know you're headed down a freeway onramp?"

I had been comfortable on the straight-aways, but this new road course route was seriously undermining my self-confidence. It was time to consider a different approach.

The other option to cane travel was a guide dog. Although I had known of those special guides for many years, I knew little about them. I never saw the need for a dog in my own life. Getting a guide dog was tucked far back in my mind. My intellect agreed with the benefits a dog could give. But, until this point, I wasn't ready to change my ways.

Having a guide dog was beginning to look pretty good. I began the mental process of weighing the pros and cons. One comment from the past sat heavy like a pregnant hippopotamus on the back of my mind. It came from a dear blind friend. She was a very capable and confident guide dog user. Shortly after my accident, Lana said, "Pam, if you had been walking with a guide dog, you never would have been hit by that van." I tucked that thought in the back of my mulling memory. There it stayed until one day on the job.

That morning, I left work and caught the Max light rail for my first visit to the home of Mrs. Riley. This particular trip seemed like a simple task since I knew the area.

This will be a snap. I know those streets run in order with no cul-de-sacs. No problem.

Sitting on the Max, I pulled my Braille notebook from my backpack. Flipping it open to the page entitled, "Mrs. Riley," I ran my fingers across the Braille to refresh my mind with the particulars about my route and the client's needs. Finishing my review, I leaned back and began assimilating the facts.

Ever since going blind, I had worked with diligence at creating detailed images in my mind. This was my way to keep track of and in touch with the world around me. Both my family and dear husband were very thoughtful in describing things around me. With their description, I would begin painting vivid images on the movie screen of my mind. This way I didn't feel so blind. With time and practice, I became quite accomplished as my own photographer and motion picture producer.

This day was no exception. I sat there creating a detailed map in my mind. I had no sooner completed my diagram when the driver came on the speaker announcing, "102nd Avenue Max Station, next stop." That was my stop. I began walking and counting the streets as I crossed each one.

Right on 97th and two blocks to Ankeny. Watch for coarse gravel. That's what Mrs. Riley told me.

I was moving along smoothly, making good time. My cane tip hit the loose rocks and I turned onto Ankeny. Stepping forward with confidence, I took one, two, three long strides and splash! There I stood with both feet in an ankle-deep cold, very cold, mud puddle.

Mud puddles are difficult to detect with a cane, so I slowed my pace, revved up my concentration and began widely swinging my cane. I had developed my own technique for locating mud puddles. By holding Cemore a few inches above the ground while swinging it wide and fast, I could hear and feel the slosh of water against the tip. Continuing my technique, I proceeded tapping and swinging. I beamed with satisfaction as I maneuvered around one puddle and then made it between two others. Feeling a little too cocky, I guess, I picked up the pace. With the next giant step,

I lit with both feet right in the middle of Lake Superior. Finding my way to shore, I regained my balance and caught my breath.

Oh, great! The perfect way to make an impressive entrance into Mrs. Riley's home. I can see it all now. She probably has a white or very light carpet. Every step I take will leave a big ugly mud print.

Finally, I arrived at her front yard. Stepping up onto the paved sidewalk, I began the fruitless attempt to shake some of the water from my pant cuffs. To my shock and bewilderment, I did not have just wet cuffs. Both pant legs were sopping wet halfway up to my knees.

I can't go in like this! Maybe I should go find a phone booth and cancel our appointment. But, what will I tell her? What if she sees me standing on her front lawn and afterward gets my call that I can't make it today? I'm stuck, stuck in the muck! Dear Lord, I sure hope this lady is really blind. Maybe she won't be able to see what a mess I am.

Fortunately for me, Mrs. Riley was a delightful senior lady with good old-fashioned hospitality. She was much more concerned about serving me than checking my fashion code. After a cup of piping hot tea and cookies, my shivering body was back to normal temperature. By that time, our conversation had warmed up, as well. We laughed and enjoyed the excuse to just sit and visit.

After completing my initial assessment questions, it was time to catch the Max back to work. We parted with a hug and Mrs. Riley invited me to stop in any time, adding, "You know, Pam, I even serve tea and cookies to visitors with dry feet." With a parting belly laugh, she closed her door and I was on my way.

Changes were ahead for me. I was fed up with the hassles of traveling all alone. The combination of Lana's words and my soaked pant legs clenched the deal. I was ready to get a guide dog.

Only six months plus six days had passed since our wedding and already we were getting separated. I was leaving my handsome man for a whole month. The day had come for me to fly to Guide Dogs for the Blind in San Rafael, California. A few twinges of lonesomeness invaded my takeoff, but soon the friendly flight attendants dispelled them with their smiles and trays of refreshments. This soda pop and chips flight was precisely that. It seemed like we merely got up in the clouds and already it was time to land.

An instructor from the Guide Dog School was there to greet me as I stepped out of the plane and into the hot smog-laden air of San Francisco. Almost the moment my foot hit the pavement, a smiling voice met me. "Pleased to meet you, Pam. My name is Ben. I'm an instructor at the Guide Dog Center. I'm here to drive you to the school." He offered his arm to guide me and we headed toward the school's van. Despite the noisy bustle of flight crews and lots of passengers, we chatted the whole way. From the very first "hi," I liked Ben. His personality and speech were comfortably kind. He was about my height, a short, jovial fellow. There were three other students yet to arrive. One student was coming from Ohio, the second from Washington and the third from Nebraska. They were due within the span of an hour and a half.

That wait wasn't so bad and the van was air conditioned with very comfortable seats. What an opportune time this was for all the questions bottled up inside me. We had a good time joking and exchanging information. One by one, the other students were ushered aboard. Each of us were pleasant but obviously laden with a heavy coat of apprehension. Thank goodness for Ben's reassuring ways and good sense of humor. In short order, our laughter and wide smiles replaced our tension.

About forty-five minutes later, we pulled into the Guide Dog Center. What a lovely campus it was. Stepping off the van, it felt so tranquil and fresh compared to the hot asphalt jungle of the noisy airport. Stately tall trees dotted the plush sprawling lawns. Spacious cement pathways wandered through the grounds. Rustic wooden benches beckoned visitors to take a scenic rest in the cool shade. As Ben continued his description of our surroundings, my senses swept me into pleasant oblivion.

"Pam to earth, Pam to earth," Ben teased, coaxing my attention back to the task at hand. A moment later, a stranger appeared at my side.

"Ah, good. Your escort is here. Pam, this is Allen. He's an Eagle Scout volunteering as sighted guide today. He'll carry your bags and escort you to your room. See you in a little bit."

"Hi, Pam," Allen said with a courteous smile in his voice, "Ready to go?"

Across the parking lot and down the long entrance sidewalk we strolled. Just before entering the building, he halted.

"We're about to go through the double doors into the Loading Lounge. This is where we are supposed to meet. Then I will take you to your room."

He guided me to one of several booths. I just got seated and folded up my cane when an instructor walked up.

"I believe you're Pam Jordan. Correct?" But without waiting for my reply, he continued, "I'm Dan, pleased to meet you. By the way, you won't need your white cane for the rest of your stay."

I heard the familiar sound of the cane's sections jostling against each other as he picked it up from the table. This must have brought a worried expression to my face.

"Don't worry, Pam. I'll put your name on it and you can pick it up on your way home."

What on earth's going on? Here I am in a totally foreign place miles from home, and they're taking my most valuable asset. This doesn't look so good to me!

Without waiting for my protest, he stepped away to confiscate another white cane. I was sure this meant doomsday for me. My security was taken away without any warning. I felt vulnerable and insecure. I had become so dependent on the actual contact and input of the cane tip. I could step out with confidence knowing what was just before my feet. My heart quivered with panic as my mind flashed back to Seattle. I couldn't help thinking about the impending possibility of again having to stumble and grope through each day.

Soon the students were assembled, about twenty in all. Mr. Franks, the supervisor, stood up to welcome us as a group and proceeded to explain the reason for hanging up our canes. We would be traveling throughout the safe region of the dormitory. That would give us time to learn how to move around without the input of a cane. They assured me that there were no orchestra pits in the dorm. Mr. Franks ended his speech with another welcome and we were dismissed. It was time, high time, to find my quarters and get settled in. Allen almost magically appeared again at my side with my luggage in hand. He showed me right to my room.

Stepping through the door, a somewhat shy yet pleasant hello greeted me from the far side.

"Hi, I'm Debby. I just beat you to the room by two minutes. Looks like we're going to be roommates for the month. What's your name?"

"I'm Pam, nice to meet you."

I made a quick inventory to be sure my luggage was all there.

"Allen, you're a real lifesaver. I never would have made it this far with my cane and all this stuff. It's been lots of fun getting to spend time with you. I hope your senior year is packed with all your dreams come true and then some."

Reaching out to give him a hearty good-bye hand shake, he short circuited it with a big hug. That made my day!

The time for operation exploration had come. I was eager to get acquainted with my surroundings. Learning the layout of my room was easy, especially with the help of my new roommate. Our small rectangular room was strategically designed to be comfortable and user friendly for both dogs and students.

Each student had their own door opening from the hallway into their side of the room.

Two separate entrances into one little room seemed rather strange to me at first. But its value soon became apparent. Each dog needed to have a specific door to identify as their own home.

Once entering our door, everything of mine lined up along the right wall. First was the closet, then a desk and across the far wall, a twin bed. Debby's living space was identical along the left side. Centered on the wall between the two entrance doors was our bathroom. We each had our own sink with the unique feature of a tiled area directly below. In that space was a water faucet, drain and large metal bowl. It was user-friendly, indeed, no worry about any spills or messes.

We were both settled in and still had an hour left before dinner. It was time to get adventurous and expand our territory. Once out in the hall, the noise of other students congregating nearby caught our attention. We headed that direction and were just in time to join a tour of the Center.

Everything we needed was housed in this spacious, large dormitory building. For relaxing and visiting, there was the music room with stereo and easy chairs or the lounge with television and couches. Just a few doors down the hall was the library, a quiet retreat, well stocked with Braille and audio books. And, of course, there were the more practical places, like the laundry room, spacious dining room and even a snack room.

CHAPTER 24
FLYING HIGH

Busy, busy, busy—that was our schedule. It wasn't due to all the canine interaction. Quite the contrary, there wasn't a hint of one guide dog anywhere. Those days were spent learning hand signals and voice commands. The instructors sure made good dog-substitutes those first two days. An instructor would walk to one side while holding the harness at about the same position of a dog.

It wasn't a matter of just picking up the handle and following an automatic pilot. We had to use one hand for the harness and leash. The other gave the hand signal simultaneously with a voice command. Using inappropriate commands or techniques could ruin the dog's training.

As the pre-dog training continued, the excitement and anticipation heightened. The word, Wednesday, became almost as common as mentioning rain on a cloudburst day. On Tuesday afternoon while walking to class, I saw Debby in the hall.

"Wow, Pam, just think! There are only a few hours left in today, and when we wake up tomorrow, it will be Christmas."

She caught me off guard. Sure it was already November, but Christmas was still over a month away. It took a few seconds to click and I realized that tomorrow would be like Christmas around here. All twenty adult students were filled with excitement and wonder, almost like little boys and girls on the night before Christmas. Debby was right. The big event was just hours away and that fact was increasingly apparent throughout the dorm. Chatter in the halls had increased both in volume and in frequency. Laughter and squeals popped up in unexpected places like firecrackers being tested before the fourth of July.

Wednesday morning came bright and early, even a bit earlier than usual. I'm not sure which of us woke up first, but we were both up and raring to go long before our alarm rang.

"Sure hope I get a German Shepherd. How about you, Pam?"

"I'm partial to Golden Retrievers, but truthfully, a gentle, mild mannered dog is my preference. That's what I told the instructors, too."

"Wonder when our turn will come. I can hardly stand the wait," Debby mumbled as she nervously shuffled through her dresser drawer.

"I hear you. The clock almost seems to be going backward right now. Keeping busy helps the time drag a little less for me."

With a knock on the door, my heart rate doubled. I straightened my blouse, cleared my throat and pole-vaulted to the door. It was Ben.

"Hi, Pam, I brought your dog. This is Marcie. She's a beautiful Golden Retriever with big brown eyes." Handing her leash to me, he said, "Here, you two have some time before dinner to get acquainted. Just don't go outside the dorm with her, okay?"

"You got it! We'll get acquainted right here just fine."

Marcie didn't even need a command for that request. As I knelt down to say hi, her big brown nose met mine followed by a bonus kiss on my eyebrow.

Turning to close the door behind me, I heard a sharp knock. This time, it was on Debby's door. Her record sprint to the door revealed a large German Shepherd wagging and straining at the end of its leash. She squealed with delight when she reached out to touch her guide, Rex. Two little girls sat on the floor admiring their brand-new Christmas presents.

Dinner came sooner than usual that night, so it seemed. Although neither of us noticed any hunger pangs, we were both eager to get to the dining room and show off our dogs.

The very next morning kicked our rigorous training program into full swing. The school's goal was to give us the knowledge and skill needed to travel with competence in a wide variety of settings. They strategically and methodically advanced our training from the basics of grooming our dogs to the ultimate challenges. All work and no play wouldn't cut it in real life, neither did it at Guide Dogs. As the month progressed, many friends were made. Our curriculum and routine had progressed, as well—more routes each day, more challenging escapades and longer lectures.

Our grand test of negotiating crowded foot traffic areas was in the heart of San Francisco's Chinatown. As usual, whenever working on a new or difficult maneuver, an instructor stayed just an arm's length behind the student. That's how it was during our walk in Chinatown. We all stayed aboard the Center's bus and visited while awaiting our turns. There were four instructors. They worked with one student at a time. This gave us a good opportunity to chat, play cards or catch a catnap.

When our turn came, Marcie and I were anxious to stretch our legs. Before leaving the side of the bus, Ben briefed me on what to expect. "It's really busy with shoppers today. I haven't seen it this busy in a long time. The sidewalks are narrow and crowded with people stopping to look at things. Just relax, Pam, and take it easy. You'll do fine."

"Okay, we're ready." With the command, "Marcie left," we turned left and headed down the sidewalk. Marcie's nose and mine were working hardcore. I could tell when she was engrossed in the nearby smells because of the fine, almost jiggling vibrations of her sniffing coming through the harness. I don't know what she smelled, but the odors I caught were unidentifiable. Some were almost appetizing and others came close to triggering my gag reflex. My elf ears were perked up as far as they could stretch while I eavesdropped on every conversation and sound around.

Oh, neat! Feels just like I'm in a foreign land.

For a moment, I was lost in the euphoria of fascination. Then, my dog stopped. With her front paws perched on the edge of the curb, she had halted to let me know a step was ahead. It was my job to check it out by sliding my right foot forward to feel for a step down or curb going up. We were at the end of the first block and ready to cross a side street. Well, at least I guessed it was a side street.

"Good girl. Forward Marcie," I commanded with the corresponding hand signal.

We were a few steps down the second block when Ben burst out laughing and put his hand on my shoulder (a sign that he wanted me to stop). "Pam, there's a dog distraction up ahead. It's the funniest thing. Somebody has gone in a store to shop and tied their dogs outside. Two little Chihuahuas are tied to the suitcase. But the suitcase is on wheels, and every time one of our guides goes by, both dogs go bananas jumping and barking. Each time they do, the suitcase rolls out into the sidewalk a little farther.

"You can make it through, but just barely. Marcie should do just fine. She doesn't seem too distracted by them."

With a "forward" command, we were on our way. Marcie passed by the Chihuahuas with flying colors. In fact, she seemed pleased to strut by with the attitude of being too important and busy to be bothered with them.

We cruised right along. I was so pleased with my dog. She did so well maneuvering us between people and obstacles. Everything was going along super fine until an unexpected curb caught me off guard with a drunk-like stumble. There came that familiar hand on my shoulder again.

"Pam, Marcie just overshot that curb because she was paying more attention to a short Chinese man right in front of you. He had a huge plastic bag of fish slung over his back." Ben informed me with a chuckle in his voice, "You need to go back and make her rework stopping at the curb. We can't let her think it's okay to guide you like that."

For the ultimate test in negotiating stairs, we went to the City Court House in downtown San Francisco. Marcie handled this one much better than me. I still struggled with the gut-gripping fear of falling down stairs. I didn't remember the details of the numerous falls at the University of Washington. Yet, those downstairs incidences indelibly anchored panic in my mind. Whenever standing at the top of a staircase without rails, that fear paralyzed me from the inside out.

We mounted the massive marble stairways with the ease of a breeze. But once at the top, I froze, rigid with fear as I turned and heard the wide open vastness below. It was a long way down with lots of steps and too many opportunities to stumble and fall. My fear delirium was interrupted with an opportunity to tour the ornate ivory columns and other gingerbread sculptures of that grand entrance.

One of the instructors announced that it was time to head back to our bus. A throng of people and dogs began the migration downward. However, Marcie and I were not part of it. I knew fear was in control, so I needed time to gain composure and courage.

Easy, Pam, take a deep breath. You can do it.

That sounded good, but I was far from convinced. I reminded myself that I did not have to do it alone.

Oh, Lord hold my hand. Here we go.

With the last syllable of my prayer, the fear dwindled. With a newfound steady surefootedness, I made my descent. We did it! Once reaching the bottom, I praised and hugged my dog big time and then almost collapsed from exhaustion.

Each day was filled to overflowing with classes, outings and more classes. Every evening, we had a short time to catch our breaths before dinner. A real highlight then was the mail delivery. One of the office staff would hand deliver the day's mail to each room. How eagerly we waited for that hoping to be among the lucky to receive something. If we did get mail, we then had to wait for a social worker to read it.

Of all the correspondence, one letter stood out above the rest. It came one afternoon when we made it back to the dorm just in time for Mail Call. I had no sooner set my pack down when there was a knock on my door. The social worker, Susan, handed me a letter, read the return address and left.

Debby's curiosity popped out with, "Hey, you got some mail. How neat. Do you know who it's from?"

"Yes, yes, it's from my husband."

"Bet you can hardly wait for Susan to come back and read it."

"Not really, I'm reading it right now." Debby was stunned to silence. She couldn't figure it out.

She knew Marv was sighted and she knew I didn't see enough to read print.

"Pam, you must have lots better vision than I thought. Didn't you tell me you only have light perception?"

"Well, it doesn't have anything to do with my vision. The letter's in Braille."

"What! You're kidding! Marv is fully sighted and he wrote it in Braille, himself?"

"Yes, he sure did. Now I know why he wanted a copy of the Braille alphabet before I left home. I'm so lucky, I mean blessed, to have a wonderful husband like Marv."

Holding that letter gently in my hands, I hugged it close to my heart and beamed with the thought of each endearing dot.

Most sighted people know Braille exists, but that is the limit of their knowledge. It is rarer than rare to get something written in Braille by a sighted individual.

It was such a treat to get mail that I could read myself. I sat at my desk beaming and purring with pleasant contentment as I read Marv's love letter.

As the last week drew near, a small group of students decided that more fun was in order. I don't know the instigator's name, but her initials were Pamela Lee Jordan.

I was so impressed by our excellent instructors and their dedication to our success. Somehow we had to let them know how much we appreciated them. I found two gals who shared my feelings and we went to work. Although my focus was primarily on showing appreciation, theirs was a bit wilder. Several secret meetings and hours of work later, we got it together. Everything was ready for the last week's events.

We had a tailor-made prank ready for each instructor. Candy was the victim of a laundry thief. One evening after dinner, two of our threesome created a distraction. Meanwhile, the third member tiptoed into Candy's room and removed all her clothes except for one pair of pajamas. This wouldn't seem so bad if she hadn't been the faithful one to meet us outdoors at 6:30 sharp every morning for leashing relieving. Whether pouring rain or blustery winter wind, she stood waiting until the last dog did its duty. Almost the instant a pile was down, she was there with scoop in action. The morning after that robbery, Candy searched everywhere for her clothes. With no success, she was forced to go outdoors in her pajamas. We made sure a special basket of fresh laundry was delivered to her right after breakfast.

That evening, Mr. Franks was paged right in the middle of dinner. The call was so important that he had to go to the office and answer it immediately. Bubbles was on the other end and in her romantic French voice flirted with him. Although not according to plan, that member of our threesome was discovered before she could step away from the only pay phone in the dorm. Mr. Franks was a good sport and took it in stride with lots of laughter.

As for Ben, he probably thought he had escaped the plague. But that was the calm before his storm. The next evening, also in the middle of dinner, a special visitor came just to see Ben. The wild side of our group insisted on this event. In the middle of enjoying his steak, the stereo's volume mounted and switched from country music to a romantic instrumental. Then the special event in Ben's honor was announced and a stripper took the spotlight. At that moment, I think I was more embarrassed than Ben. Nevertheless, our mission was accomplished for the moment.

The week was almost over and our shenanigans were over, as well. But the best part, the staff tribute, was about to be unveiled.

We wanted to honor the instructors for serving us in so many different ways. Another coconspirator of mine worked with me to put this item together. We designed and made a wall hanger to be awarded to the staff on graduation day. It was challenging to gather all the materials needed since no craft store was accessible. Nevertheless, two wire coat hangers, a skein of yarn, a local variety store and lots of creativity did the trick.

That award was designed to display the many different hats they wore. The hangers were shaped in a circle, then covered with a hand knitted bright wrapping. Right across the middle was a shiny red plastic pooper scooper. On the outer circle were attached paper party hats with a title on each. It was far from a gold engraved plaque or marble based trophy, but the instructors valued it even more.

The musicians in our group had written a school song to the tune of Camp Grenada. We all had learned the words. In the middle of singing it to the staff, several students carried our handmade wall hanger to the front. At that instant, the remainder stood up and shouted, "Hats Off to You!" Right after our presentation, each instructor came to the front and expressed their appreciation. That was the finale of our graduation. The only thing left to do was to load up our belongings and circulate the goodbyes.

My emotions were mixed. The victory of graduating and completing the course was sweet, very sweet. But I knew this flight would leave many dear friends far behind and for good.

As the tears formed, I switched into Pollyanna mode, creating a crocodile smile in my heart and on my face. I was going home to be with this rare Braille-writing sighted husband of mine and a new life of help from my dog.

I decided to sleep through the plane ride so that I'd be fresher than a dew drenched rose when arriving home. My nap plan was successful until the plane hit an air pocket and took a sharp dip. My mild-mannered sleeping guide was no longer at my feet. Her two front paws plopped right in my lap followed by a wet nose touching mine. At the school, we were warned that the dogs had never flown and could be unnerved, but would do fine with calming words and reassuring pets.

An important fact this flight taught me was that Marcie had a sweet, oh so gentle, spirit. A hug from me was much more therapeutic than any strokes or petting. She loved to stand on her hind feet with paws almost to my shoulders and get a snug hug right around her middle. This plane trip was just the beginning of our hug tradition, and it was something we both needed.

Marcie and I had just settled into a short daydream when over the intercom came, "Please fasten your seatbelts and prepare for landing."

The descent brought Marcie up for another hug, and before long, she and I were leading the procession of passengers off the plane. Marv was right there to greet us. A family hug was in order but not until Marcie's harness came off. We were warned and warned again not to let anyone else pet or visit with our dog while the harness was in place.

Once inside the airport terminal, I couldn't contain my joy any longer. Turning to Marv, I said, "Honey, watch this!" With one soft, "Marcie, forward," she and I were off and almost running. She took me down a long ramp and stopped at the curb's edge. At the curb, I gave her a left-left command to get us turned around. Obediently waiting for my next command, she stood by my side. I listened for any sounds of a nearby crowd. When the ramp had cleared, I said, "Marcie, forward," and up we went right back to Marv.

"Oh, Honey, isn't she great! I feel like I'm flying!"

"That's super, Dear. You know what—you looked like you were both flying, too."

I was more than eager to settle in at home and then introduce Marcie to all my family and friends. We were home, home sweet home!

CHAPTER 25
STRETCH, SNAP, POP!

Just as good as it felt to be home, it felt good to be back on the job. One footstep into VRIL's front lobby and Marcie became a star. Everyone was happy to see both my dog and me. I spread Marcie's plush rug under my desk and she looked so cute there. We busied ourselves with getting my things unpacked and finding places for all the new Guide dog paraphernalia. My concentration on getting settled in was interrupted as I heard Jean's talking watch announce 9:50 a.m.

Oh for goodness sake! My first student is due in ten minutes.

I scurried to find the cupboard where the Braille teaching texts were kept. I was ready in plenty of time. I sat poised at the table trying to relax as I listened for my student to arrive. Daniel, a young man in his mid twenties, was right on time.

Before delving into the actual dots of Braille, I needed to clear up a common myth. I chuckled inwardly as I thought about this absurd advice given by well-meaning sighted folks. The two "fix-all solutions" for blind people are getting a Guide Dog or learning Braille. Braille is a very helpful skill, but difficult to master. I needed to make sure Daniel understood that and had a realistic way to use Braille before investing lots of time and energy in the learning process.

"Daniel, let's talk about ways Braille could help you. I am not a bookworm, so I seldom sit down with a Braille novel as a pastime. However, there are many who enjoy that. For me, Braille is an invaluable tool in everyday life."

"Well, Pam, I'm not an avid reader, either," he said. "What is really hard for me is keeping track of my appointments and figuring out what stuff is in my cupboards. It would be nice to get my albums labeled, too. I get kind of tired listening to the same music several times in a row."

We both agreed that Daniel had plenty of ways to use Braille. Next came testing his finger sensitivity. Daniel was able to feel the dots well as I helped him position his right forefinger on a variety of different dot configurations. "Congratulations, Daniel, you did extremely well. This week I would like you to work at home on learning the first five alphabet letters."

In the beginning, I was probably more nervous than my student. But that first lesson went like well-greased gears. I was excited about having a student like Daniel, so eager to excel and gain independence. I was pleased with the day's events and oh so thankful to be in the office all day.

My initial concept of being a "Braille Teacher" was less than the tip of this job's iceberg. In less than two months, my job description had grown beyond Braille and way beyond teaching. It expanded to include cooking, writing skills, home management and leisure time activities. Soon I was also counseling, getting people connected with community resources and doing public speaking. Although that had broadened my list of duties considerably, much more stretching was yet to come.

Another glimpse of my proverbial "iceberg" came into view when I was assigned a new consumer. Mrs. Elderquist had been referred to VRIL by another agency with the request for adjustment counseling. This was a common request, but as usual, gave no clue as to her needs. That meant I'd have to start from scratch and identify the real issues.

Mrs. Elderquist lived alone with some serious health concerns in addition to her vision loss. She lived within walking distance of the office. This was a tailor-made trip for Marcie and me. With a soft "Marcie," my dog was out from under my desk with tail wagging. She was just as eager to go as I was. With a stop at the restroom to give Marcie a big drink of cold water, we were out the door and into the fresh air. The sun was shining with soothing warmth on this spring afternoon. What a perfect day it was for a twelve-block walk through our neighborhood.

With smooth sidewalks and beautiful surroundings, our trip seemed to fly by almost too fast. Soon I was knocking at Mrs. Elderquist's door. I stood there a long time and began to wonder if she was home. I decided to linger a few more minutes, and sure enough, she opened the door with a genuine warm welcome.

"Sorry I kept you waiting so long. It takes me forever to get anywhere with this walker." We sat and chatted casually at first. After awhile, it was time to go through my intake assessment questions. They were an essential tool to assist in identifying the person's current situation and needs for service.

Mrs. Elderquist asked me to please call her Elsie. She had one thing on her mind which preoccupied both her thoughts and our conversation. Interestingly enough, it had nothing to do with vision loss and was not on VRIL's list of services.

She could think of nothing other than her dilemma of oxygen tubes strewn across the floor. This concern was understandable as she was very unsteady moving about with her walker. The fear of either falling or crushing those plastic oxygen tubes possessed her thinking so completely that any other topic fell on two deaf ears. Whenever I asked about her ability to live with such poor eyesight, she always switched right back to the oxygen tube problem.

"Pam, I just don't know what to do. I've talked to all the professionals that come out here. They just tell me to lift my walker over the tube. That would be no problem if I could see the darn things."

"Elsie, I have an idea. Is there a handyman in your family or a neighbor nearby?"

"No, Pam, I'm pretty much all by myself. The oxygen men said I just have to live with it. This is how they do it for everyone."

"Well, Elsie, if we could get someone in here to screw a few eye bolts into your ceiling, I think we could get them off your floor. This is not part of my job at Vision Resources, but it looks like you need this resolved before you can do much else. Does that sound right?"

"Are you serious? Do you really think there's a way to do that?"

"I can't promise anything, but let me talk to my husband tonight. He's a terrific handyman with a really kind heart. I have your number so if it's okay with you, I'll give you a call this evening."

"Oh yes, yes, please do."

That evening, the first topic at the dinner table was, of course, Elsie and the oxygen tubes. When I explained my idea to Marv, he said it should be easy to put a few eye bolts in the ceiling. Then came the punch line.

"Well, Marv, there is another piece to this puzzle. She doesn't have anyone to do it for her. Do you think it will take a lot of time and energy?"

"No, half an hour or so, I'd guess."

"I know this is asking a lot, but would you be willing to do it? She's in a real dilemma, and get this! The 'professionals' all say that's the only way they do it, so they won't even try to help her."

Without even twisting one elbow, Marv was agreeable to pitching in.

"Oh, Babe, you're a lifesaver! Thanks so much! I've got to go call Elsie. She'll be ecstatic!"

I set up an appointment with Elsie and the next week, Marv and I were in her home. With his power drill and a handful of eye bolts, the job was done much sooner than I expected. After that, Elsie was like a whole different lady. Her fear of moving about her home had vanished. She actually was able to concentrate on learning the new techniques of preparing simple meals, dialing her phone and so on.

With independence and confidence achieved in her daily life, it was time to move on to my new referrals.

A new referral came from Bob and his mother. They made a special request for counseling from me as I had met them in the past at different social gatherings. I agreed to do it and set an appointment for our first counseling session.

The next Monday morning, I had hung up the phone after a lengthy conversation with a caseworker at Aging Services. My mind was still sorting those facts when the intercom buzzed. It was Ruth informing me that Bob and his mother had just arrived.

Dear Father in Heaven, you promise that if anyone lacks wisdom, they just have to ask, and you will give it abundantly. I know it's going to take your wisdom and love to make a difference in Bob. I don't have a clue how to help him. It's up to you, Lord.

With a fresh batch of confidence, I swung my chair around and headed for the lobby to greet Bob and his mother. The first session went well and we parted with the agreement to meet each week for one hour.

Todd, Dorothy's assistant, was my immediate supervisor and it was normal protocol for him to monitor all the counselors' case loads. A few minutes after that first session, Todd called me into his office.

"Pam, I noticed you just met with Bob. What's going on with him?"

I filled Todd in on the request from Bob and his mother along with my plan of counseling. Todd's harsh manner had always made me feel a bit intimidated. However, this time, his disgust-charged statement was more than intimidating.

"The audacity of you to think you could counsel anyone! Do you have a BS degree in anything?"

My first response was silent. *Thank goodness I don't. You have enough BS for both of us!*

The only response I could muster up was a sheepish, faint "no."

Continuing with harsh exasperation, he asked, "Do you know that Bob has already seen a myriad of professional psychiatrists, psychologists and clinical counselors most of his life?"

Todd punched the word "professional" with a very unmistakable dart to my ability. I informed him that I had no clue about Bob's past history. But, what I did know was that both Bob and his mother decided prior to calling me that I was someone he could relate to.

With a gruff sigh, he said that he would give me one month to meet with Bob. That meant I was limited to three more one-hour sessions.

I stepped out of his office feeling as though I'd just been hit and flattened by an overloaded cement truck. At that moment, I was anything but appreciative of Todd's intrusion. But it benefited me more than he would ever have guessed. It catapulted me into mega prayer and reliance upon God. Each time before stepping into the counseling room with Bob, I prayed earnestly and specifically.

On each visit, I was amazed at the words of wise counsel I had. Bob was making great strides in improving his attitude of anger and bitterness.

The end of the month and the fourth session had arrived much too soon, it seemed. Neither Bob nor I wanted the sessions to end. In fact, he was feeling depressed about that. I encouraged him that we could still work together by phone. Hearing that, he smiled and we parted on a positive note.

Exiting the room after our fourth counseling session, I headed down the hall and toward my office. Deep in thought, I walked and wondered how to convince Todd that things were going well. But before I could reach my office, Todd's voice halted my steps.

"Pam, have a minute?" His voice seemed friendly and much more mellow than usual.

"About ten minutes. Then I have to catch the Max."

"Well, I have to say, there is a difference in Bob since you started working with him. Both the staff and I have seen a real change in him. Congratulations."

"Oh, wow! That's great news. Does that mean we'll be able to extend his counseling a bit longer?"

"Give me an update on his Independent Living Plan, and we'll consider it."

"Will do, and thanks. I'd better get my things together and head out of here. I am doing in-service training for the rehab nurses at Good Samaritan Hospital this afternoon. I should be returning about 4:00."

Oh my goodness, I never expected that! It's a miracle! And, dear Heavenly Father, it's you! It's you! What an awesome God you are!

My career at VRIL was enjoyable, rewarding and challenging but physically, it wore me out.

STRETCH, SNAP, POP—that's how I'd sum up those almost eleven years.

I loved my work which super-stretched me in many areas. It broadened both my personal growth and skills immensely. Two different services listed on our brochure were not yet in existence. Mr. Gardner, our Executive Director, asked me to develop each of them from scratch, put them into action and then take the position of supervising the whole thing.

One afternoon, he asked me to step into his office and said, "Pam, I was looking over our brochure. Leisure Time Skills is listed as a service we provide, but so far we have no program to fill it. Since you're the craftiest lady around here, I would like you to design a program and head it up."

Vision loss often robs a person of enjoyment in life. When that happens, most people have no clue how to continue doing those enjoyable activities without good eyesight. I have to confess that phrase, "Leisure Time Skills," had been puzzling to me. So first, I went to work figuring out the definition of leisure time activities and what it encompassed. My list grew to include hobbies, crafts, games, social outings, dining out and so on. Next came the brain gear-stripping task. How was I going to help my consumers regain enjoyment within their lives?

My assessment tool this time was not a lengthy list of questions. Instead, I had a few short questions and a bag full of hand craft materials to test manual dexterity and eye-hand coordination.

It was challenging to get all the pieces together, but right down my alley of interest. I loved the opportunity to be creative and loved to do crafts. Mr. Gardner was right on target when he determined that I had a heart for crafts.

With the Leisure Time Skills Program up and running, Mr. Gardner hit me with another "stretch, snap, pop" request. He told me about the need for a program that would provide sighted volunteers to help individual blind adults. Our office had already received many requests from blind people throughout the Tri-County area. They asked where they could find help with all kinds of things, like reading their mail, handyman repairs, doing shopping, and so on.

Well, that meant back to the creative drawing board—one of my favorite places to be. Although it stirred my creative juices, both my brain and my heart were pounding with ebbs of nervousness and fear. All kinds of questions raced through my mind, crashing into each other like the cars in a huge demolition derby.

Where will I find enough sighted people who are willing to volunteer their time? How can I figure out which request best fits which volunteer, if I even get any? Then, there's evaluation and followup to consider. Oh man! I don't even know where to start.

The instant that thought registered, I knew the answer. I would go straight to my Heavenly Father and get an abundant supply of wisdom just as He promises.

That's precisely what I did. Right there, in my office, sitting at my desk I prayed in silence. With the last syllable of my prayer, a vivid view of my rose garden popped into mind. What a crystal clear reminder of his desire to be my partner. I knew that God would walk hand in hand with me through this one, too.

With the winds of confidence filling my sails, I began this new voyage. The first challenge was working out the step-by-step mechanics of the actual process. It was easy to line up the different steps of this process. The tricky part for me was designing on paper the forms. I could still picture how the layout looked. That was helpful but didn't give me solid confidence in my forms. Thank goodness for Bea and Ruth. They were always so willing and helpful in times like that. With their final approval and editing, I knew everything was top notch. With that piece of the project finished, it was time to present it to the agency head.

Every available moment was spent planning and pouring over my creation. At long last, it was done! Reviewing the process from beginning to end, I smiled with a sigh of satisfaction and relief. It was ready to present to Mr. Gardner.

Wednesday morning dragged on like a bad headache, but finally the time had come to meet with Mr. Gardner. As he perused my proposal for the Volunteer Program, my insides paced in nervous spasms. To my surprise, little change was needed before it met his approval.

It was time to start recruiting and advertising. Response to my first neighborhood ad came much quicker than anticipated. Carter, age 65, had responded and expressed an interest in doing some volunteer work. And, he was due for an interview right after lunch.

Coming back from the nearby deli, Ruth greeted me. "My goodness, Pam, you just left a couple minutes ago. I thought you were signed out for lunch."

"Yes, I was, but wanted to be back at my desk well before Carter arrives." Although all my paperwork was thoughtfully arranged and set out well before lunch, I wanted to double (or triple) check the efficiency of my layout. By that time, my lunch had turned into a large bowling ball rolling around in the pit of my stomach. Quite frankly, on that first interview, I was more nervous than my interviewee.

"Carter, I need to apologize. This program is brand new, and you are the first person I've interviewed. I'm so nervous."

Carter, however, was a jovial fellow and very easy to talk to. He took it in stride. With a chuckle in his voice, he responded, "Hey, what do you know! We found something in common right off the bat. I'm nervous, myself."

This new position gave me more skills and confidence. One of the best benefits was that it brought me in contact with some of the nicest people. One of the downsides was that I seemed to face almost continual rejection from the other staff members.

Even though the secretary encouraged me to "toot my own horn," I chose not to. Instead, I turned to the One who gives the praise worth having.

Dear Father, you know how much I hurt and all the tears I push down everyday during my work. It's so hard to be rejected by all the staff and left out of the fun things. I know I'm not supposed to boast in anything but You, Lord. But this is getting old, really old. I haven't followed Bea's advice and bragged about myself. So, Father, it's up to you. In the meantime, help me feel your praise and be satisfied with approval from you.

That same request was made often, and all the more, as rejection by the staff continued. In the midst of the rejection months, I had become quite depressed. I decided it would be wise to talk to one of my peers about it. That conversation was the total opposite of encouraging. She said I just wasn't "professional" enough and weird, to boot.

This time, my prayer was much longer and a rather soggy one. The tears of heartache just couldn't be stuffed any longer. But the important part to remember was not what my colleagues did, but how God stepped in.

A real highlight of my work was a delightful sighted lady who volunteered as my teaching assistant. Susie was the daughter of one of my students. She had been a full-time teacher with a Master's Degree. Susie and I shared much in common and had a ball teaching the classes together.

Near the end of a cooking class one Friday afternoon, Marv came to pick me up. Susie and I were just cleaning up after the class. I was called away to answer the phone. In my absence, Susie visited with Marv and talked about me.

Thank the dear Lord for giving me such a caring, supportive husband. The same evening at dinner, Marv said, "Honey, remember when you left the classroom this afternoon? Well, while you were gone, Susie said this to me: 'Marv, your wife is a real teacher. She has all the credentials of a Master's Degree. The only thing she's lacking is the piece of paper.'"

Hooray! Three points for our team, Father!

That was the first exhilaration and praise, but certainly not the last.

That next week at staff meeting, we were told about this terrific team-building consultant. VRIL had hired him to spend an afternoon with "all of the staff" in a training session. Both my supervisors raved about this consultant's ability and were excited about having this opportunity.

Stewart was highly acclaimed in his field and would be meeting one-on-one with each staff member prior to our workshop. My turn came to meet with Stewart. I was a little nervous. This unprofessional misfit would be face to face with an outstanding "professional"! To my relief, Stewart was a regular human being, very down to earth and anything but haughty. The conversation was brief, but went well.

The very next week, the whole staff went out to lunch followed by a full afternoon of training. Stewart began with a very conventional lecture. After that brief block of general facts, he addressed the specific needs of our team. Stewart informed us that the best team-building approach was to recognize the good qualities of each person.

He had us take turns mentioning good qualities about one another. This was an encouraging time for all. Stewart then took the floor with comments that almost jolted me into orbit. He proceeded to tell the whole group that during his one-on-one sessions, he found me to have lots of wisdom. Stewart suggested they consult with me often for problem solving.

Wow! All I asked my Father to do was to give me a little toot of praise to help me not feel like a worthless worm. But I never expected a trumpet blast of praise like that.

Oh, Father, I knew you'd come through with some kind of praise, but a whole band of trumpets! You are incredible, amazing! Thank you, thank you! As usual, you knew just what I needed.

After such a mountaintop experience, I was expecting a real letdown once I walked though VRIL's front door the next work day. Unbelievable— the tables had turned 180 degrees. The icy air of rejection was gone. In its place were smiles, appreciation and genuine acceptance. What a wonderful change!

Oh, how I loved my job. With teaching classes, public speaking, networking with other community agencies and taking buses all over town, it never got boring. I poured my heart and soul into it everyday. Indeed, my heart was 200 percent committed, but my health was going downhill and couldn't take much more. Getting soaked and chilled to the bone while waiting for buses out on the streets certainly didn't help matters at all. I was hospitalized for pneumonia two winters in a row. That next summer, a trek across town in the beating afternoon sun wilted my body to near heatstroke.

Dear Lord, You know I love my job. But, I don't think I can last much longer if things don't change. I want to do your will, so please give me wisdom.

I knew there was a total of two choices—keep my job and check out of life ahead of God's schedule or resign. Oh, how I hated the thought of quitting. But, in the fall of 1991, I turned in my resignation.

Although those years exhausted me physically, spiritually they were more effective than the most potent energy drink on the market today. The vision of my spiritual eyes was sharpened and clearer than I ever thought possible. I experienced for myself the incredible power of prayer.

There were so many, many times when I had no clue what I could or should do. But, I made it a consistent habit to pray before every appointment or activity. Although riding the buses all over town was not my favorite task, it did prove most beneficial. It gave me time to talk with my Heavenly Father. In silence, I asked Him for wisdom to help that person in the best way possible. And, literally "out of the blue," I would get a brilliant idea, often unorthodox, but the perfect solution for that individual.

Those days taught me one valuable fact. God is our loving daddy who longs to be personally involved in the life of each child of His. What I never knew before was the fact that He is just waiting for us to ask. He wants to enrich each moment of our every day.

I was amazed to watch Him in action in my life. I had no college degree and was often put down as not being professional. At times, I was even ostracized and rejected by the VRIL staff. Despite all of that, God showed Himself to be more than faithful.

My resignation turned the triumphant trumpets of the work world into the nervous pacing of a waiting room. I was about to step into God's waiting room. Waiting and wondering—that's how it is when stuck in a waiting room. This is never a comfortable place for human beings. The impending financial loss combined with ongoing cabin fever looked most uninviting and worrisome. But, here again, God's peace prevailed in the midst of uncertainty and waiting. I had no clue as to what I would be doing with my life nor how long I'd be wandering. But one thing I did know—God was still walking with me. He had never let me down before, and I knew He never would.

This time, as the question marks and concerns bombarded my mind—I just shook my head and took a walk in my rose garden.

CHAPTER 26
MY PHOTO ALBUM

It was time to do some major gear shifting again. This time I was reluctantly ready. The mere thought of changing from a professional career to full-time homemaker brought surges of subtle depression. I feared boredom and dissatisfaction with my new role. That concern began mushrooming out of proportion the first week of non-VRIL days. In very short order, my attitude began slipping downhill. I knew just what to do—dial the hotline to Heaven, of course.

Dear Heavenly Father, I know I've talked to you about this many times before. I don't want to think like the world around me who downplay stay-at-home mothers. I keep telling myself that my worth does not depend upon having a professional position. But, the truth is, I sure don't feel worth much just staying home and taking care of this small apartment. I just can't seem to change my attitude about my new role in life. Please help me to see things from your perspective. I need your thoughts to fill my mind.

Once I began focusing on the good stuff in my life, my attitude soared upward. Soon, variety was present at home. And, the best part was—I had some time and energy to enjoy the good things as they came.

A real spark of variety and ongoing blessings arrived September 24, 1984. Fran and Steve gave birth to their second child, a baby boy. A proud aunt times two—that was me. What a broad smile of deep happiness spread across my heart with that little miracle from God snuggled in my arms. Oh, how I could have sat for hours just holding Jarin and enjoying his tiny little fingers, soft grunts and every movement.

Another delight close by was Bria. What a vibrant four-year-old livewire she was. She tickled my heart and mind with an ongoing flow of cute words and ways. That was my kind of variety—yes, indeed.

Fond remembrances like these brought to life a saying I heard years ago.

It went something like this: No one is alone when accompanied by noble memories.

For some reason, that saying was implanted in my mind deeper than the roots of a hearty old Sequoia tree. With time, I realized the powerful impact of good memories.

Bria's unique style of playing Hide and Go Seek was one of those special memories. One afternoon, at age three, she decided that Auntie Pam should play Hide and Go Seek. My first response to this idea was far from enthusiastic. Being blind and trying to find a silent hideaway was near impossible and definitely not fun. I had tried that more times than I cared to remember.

Oh darn, I might as well. She's not going to give up until I play with her. Hopefully, it won't last long anyway. I doubt she can stay still more than a minute at best.

With impatient exasperation, I agreed. With the speed of a champion quarter horse, she bounded up the short flight of stairs giggling all the way. I heard her turn into our bedroom. *This is good. At least I know where she went, and our little bedroom will make it easy to find her.*

At the bottom of the stairway, I counted to ten and said, "Ready or not, here I come." With each upward step, I listened intently for any sound of the slightest movement. Then came the surprise as my ears were greeted with "I'm hiding. You can't find me." Hey, this was looking better all the time.

Rounding the corner into the upstairs hall, Bria announced with a drum roll of giggles, "I'm hiding in the closet. You can't find me!"

"Oh my, where could she be? I wonder if she's behind the door or maybe under the bed."

With the announcement of each guess, a burst of giggles sounded from the closet.

Turning, I opened the closet door. Bria bounced out of the closet and delivered a flying hug right into my arms and heart. Ever since going blind, I had hated Hide and Go Seek. It was humiliating to be the only one who couldn't find the rest of the kids. They would sneak right past me and later brag about it. But, Bria's version—that was my kind of game.

A few days later, Bria introduced Marv to Hide and Go Seek. He got a real kick out of her cute ways. Ever since that day, our lives have been enriched by its youthful joy. One morning in the middle of our get ready for work routine, Marv sang out with a teasing tune, "I'm hiding behind the shower curtain, you can't find me." One unwritten rule that has always been followed to the letter is the reward: Hugs and giggles, smiles and light-hearted fun.

Simple and silly. Yet, it perked up our hearts with a youthful happy flare that got our day off with an upbeat attitude.

As Jarin entered his toddler years, he also began adding mental snapshots to our album of special memories. What a cute picture that made with Jarin straddling the living room rail as he pretended to be a bus driver. It all took place one afternoon when Mom and I were babysitting him at my parents' home in Gresham. The family room was bordered by a sunken living room. The smooth wooden rail dividing those two rooms turned into the driver's seat of a large tour bus. Our driver was a charmer, too, and quite the comedian.

He kept us well entertained and laughing for quite awhile. His most memorable stunt happened when he came running through the front room and attempted a Roy Roger mount. He overshot the rail and slid down the other side almost landing in Mom's lap. That didn't faze him in the least. He bounced up like a kangaroo and sat atop the rail. With a gasping chuckle, he said, "Wow, this is a tricky bus!"

Ever since that bus trip, the small word, "tricky," popped up in our conversation often. Along with its remembrance came warm smiles and light-hearted laughter.

"Oh my goodness, Dear, I don't know how your ball of yarn got way over there," Marv stated with a puzzle in his voice.

"Well, that figures. After all, it's a tricky ball of yarn."

The possibility of irritation had no chance to escalate once hit with the laughter and smiles accompanying that word, "tricky."

Flipping back a few more pages, I found another gem. The actual event happened during my school years. Returning home from the races exhausted and hungry, Dad would often head for a quick refueling snack. One of his favorites was toast with peanut butter and jelly. That was no big event until the day Dad discovered someone else was getting into the jar of peanut butter. At first, he casually mentioned, "somebody's been in the peanut butter."

Mom, Steve and I all denied eating any. With a low disgusted grumble of disbelief, Dad walked out of the kitchen. On the next return from racing, his comment was the same, but delivered with a punch of irritating disgust. Next time, he called the three of us together and said, "I don't care if you eat the peanut butter. What really bothers me is that somebody's lying about it." Still, none of us could remember eating any peanut butter. With this pattern of tension building, I was getting worried.

Oh boy, this isn't good. Dad actually sounded angry today. Seems like every time he comes back from the races and opens the peanut butter, he gets madder.

Another weekend had come, and Dad was off to the races for three days. After he left, I was watching TV when a Skippy Peanut Butter commercial came on. It showed two elephants in bed. Mrs. Elephant was scolding Mr. Elephant. He was eating peanuts and making so much noise crunching that it kept her awake.

"Melvin," she said, "why don't you eat Skippy Peanut Butter? It has the real peanut flavor."

That's it!

Off to my bedroom I ran to find my little plastic white elephant. With prize in hand, I dashed to the kitchen. I opened the cupboard and found the jar. Carefully, I smeared a big glob of peanut butter on his tusks and mouth. Satisfied with my decorating, I set it right on top of the Skippy Peanut Butter jar.

Sunday evening, Dad came home and I was ready. Setting down his luggage, he greeted each of us with a cheerful hi and a big hug. With his welcoming rounds completed, he headed to the kitchen. Standing out of view just around the corner, I listened for sounds of toast being made. Sure enough, he was going for it. With the ding of the toaster, I rounded the corner.

"Hi, Dad, how's it going?"

"Pretty good, just fixing a snack. Let's sit down and catch up. Would you like a snack, too?"

"No, thanks, I'm still full from dinner."

Setting down the butter knife, Dad opened the cupboard.

"Oh my gosh! That's who's been eating my peanut butter!"

Stepping closer to look in the cupboard, I exclaimed, "Oh, Melvin, shame on you! You know better than that!"

I was flabbergasted by Dad's response. He was not angry at all. Instead, he was genuinely amused and even chuckled. From that moment on, Dad never growled about the peanut butter.

Instead, he laughed. "My gosh, Pam, Elmer's been in the peanut butter again."

"Oh, you mean Melvin," I corrected.

"Yes, that's the one. It's bad enough that he's into my peanut butter, but now the darn elephant keeps changing his name."

We both roared with laughter and clenched our discovery with an arm wrapped around each other and wink in our eyes. Melvin never left our home.

It became not uncommon to hear comments like, "That block of cheese sure went fast. Guess Melvin came by when we weren't looking."

With a tee-hee from every ear close by, the concern never became a problem. Instead, we scolded that ravenous elephant and went on about our business. Good thing for such big shoulders because Melvin's position of all-purpose scapegoat lifted tons off our shoulders.

Continuing to thumb through our memory album, another special snapshot caught my attention. That took me way back to my teenage years. It was Steve and me skiing down the snowy slopes of Mount Hood. What an exhilarating experience that was! My brother was the kind of skier people turned around to watch as he slalomed down the slopes. He wanted me to get a true feel of downhill skiing. Our day was perfect with sunshine and fresh powder snow. At the top of the slope, he had me hold onto his waist and put my two skies just inside his.

"Pam, the slope is really steep. The best way to ski this is to make wide sweeping turns back and forth. First, we'll make a wide sweeping turn off to our left and then slalom down. You should be able to feel me shift my weight as we turn. Ready?" He paused for my response. With a jittery "yes" from me, we were on our way. Once the initial panic subsided, I was able to indulge in the super sensations. He was right. The change in his body movements was evident. I had no problem detecting his shift in weight from flat skis to the cutting edge on turns. His movement was so smooth and flowing that it almost seemed as though we were skiing on air. He had total control, breathtaking speed and a gracefulness that appeared effortless. The only drawback is that the bottom of the slope came too fast for me. Slowing to a gentle stop, I gripped Steve even tighter with a victory hug in thankful ecstasy.

And there on the next page, another snapshot caught my attention. It was the broad dark green leaves of the grape arbor in the back yard of my brother and his wife, Fran. The common phrase of someone having "a green thumb" reminded me of Fran, although in Fran's case, it was more like two green thumbs. God's creation always intrigued and amazed me. Any opportunity to experience its beauty was better than a Dairy Queen Royal Treat.

Fran was always kind in taking time out of her busy lifestyle to give me a tactile tour of their garden. She also made sure I got to see the gorgeous floral arrangements that she created for special occasions. She made it possible for me to "see" the beautiful floral display as she guided my fingertips to examine the flowers, candles and greenery. Knowing my enjoyment of sweet smells, she would pause longer at each fragrant blossom. With her extra description of the colors and special features, the arrangement was captured in brilliant clarity. That was my family—super, supportive and caring. Time with them was always special with many fond memories.

Turning a couple pages and a few years back, another special memory jumped into my heart. How well it portrayed the wealth God has given me in real quality friends. Yes, there was Paulette beaming with the most pleasant expression of laughter. It all started one evening with a seemingly insignificant chat on the phone. As we started sharing events of our day, the morning shower kicked off the lineup.

"Paulette, you are so lucky that you can shower every morning and don't have dry skin problems. Man, if I showered everyday, I'd look like a scaly fish. As it is, I have to lather myself all over with handfuls of lotion after each shower. Well, I might as well face it, I'm just a weirdo."

"No, Pam, you are not a weirdo. It just proves you're a walking miracle." That always made my heart swell with inner warmth and satisfaction as those words echoed in my mind. God used Paulette to whisper a reminder of his unconditional love for Pam.

What a simple statement that was. Yet its impact was more than profound. It changed the mental portrait of myself so much that it was hard to see any resemblance. The shabby looking woman in shades of gray had been transformed. The new portrait of Pam displayed a gorgeous dame with vibrant countenance in a regal gown. Bright warm sunshine beamed over her shoulder and the fragrance of sweet lilacs graced her presence.

From that moment on, I was able to view myself in a whole new light. In the past, I had clothed the image of myself with garments of failure, shortcomings and negative stuff. Both the Bible and pastors had told me that in God's eyes, I was beautiful. But finally, I got the picture. Being a child of God makes an everyday human beautiful.

Marv and I have found recalling special memories to be an excellent habit. This simple tradition has brought a youthful vibrancy and heightened enjoyment to our lives.

CHAPTER 27
CONSISTENT INCONSISTENCY

The winds of change began blowing again. It all started with our good neighbors, Russ and Colette. They lived in the same apartment complex just two doors away. We bonded with them, sharing many of the same interests and were close in age, as well. We gals were go getters and our husbands both more laid back fellows. A major common interest was our love for children.

Marv and I taught Sunday school at our church. Those vivacious four-year-olds were a tremendous source of enjoyment. Russ and Colette, on the other hand, showed this love for children by serving as foster parents for teenage kids. They worked with The Boys and Girls Aid Society. This small local agency removed teens from an unsafe environment and provided temporary shelter. The State gave them a limit of three months to work out permanent placement in a home or in some kind of therapy program. The agency's goal was to have the young people stay with a family rather than in the juvenile detention home.

As we spent time with our neighbors, we also interacted with their teenage guests. We got along so well with the teens, we often gave Russ and Colette a break by having the kids spend time in our home. Marcie, of course, was a big ice breaker. She drew people like a magnet.

I learned interesting things about each guest as they petted and talked to my dog. And dear Marcie never tired of that attention. As she stood there soaking in their affection, it gave me prime time to get a look at their character. Kind kids were easy to detect as they talked gently to her. The more hard core kids spent less time petting and usually made at least one derogatory comment.

As Marcie warmly welcomed the kids into our home, she became an open door sign for lots of questions. They were most eager to learn how Marcie helped me. With their guide dog questions answered, curiosity juices began to flow.

My deck of Braille playing cards and Scrabble game with Braille overlay came in handy. The surprising thing is that the kids often seemed even more eager to see how I did everyday things around our apartment. Just little activities that were so mundane to me fascinated them. It was fun for me, too, as I showed them how I wrote with my Braillewriter, cooked, color coordinated my outfits and so on. Their wide range of questions kept me guessing and challenged my ability to think on my feet.

One afternoon, in the middle of preparing a green salad, there was a knock at our door. Making sure not to leave my knife in a precarious place, I positioned it with its sharp edge snug against the back of the counter. That kept it well out of finger cutting range. Then, straightening my apron, I went to the door. It was Brad, our neighbor's fifteen-year-old foster son.

"Hi, Pam, Colette wants to know if she can borrow a cup of sugar from you."

"Sure thing, come on in. Just let me wipe the chopped onion off the counter and I'll get the sugar." With a teasing giggle, I said, "Colette probably doesn't want onion mixed in with her sugar." I could sense he was awestruck standing right behind me in stunned silence. My perception proved correct as he asked, "Did you do that all by yourself?"

"You mean chop the onions?"

"Yes, how did you get them chopped so fine?"

"Lots of practice—I do all the cooking. I'm making a taco salad for dinner tonight. Here's how I do it. My left hand does the looking. Of course, that means feeling for the spot to be cut, and I keep my left forefinger there as a marker. Then I put the flat side of the knife blade against that finger. I always make sure to move my left hand out of cutting range before applying pressure. Notice this nifty knife?"

"Yes, I've never seen anything like that. Sure looks funny with the handle sitting on top of the blade."

"I imagine so, but with the handle there, it's much easier for me to tell exactly where the blade is. Watch this."

"Wow, you sure are fast. How do you keep from cutting your fingers?"

"The key is knowing exactly where my knife blade and fingers are at all times."

He must have liked cooking because his list of questions seemed endless. My Braille timer, measuring spoons and spices with Braille labels fascinated him. But, it wasn't enough just to look at them. He wanted to know how they worked.

"Let's do some measuring here. It's really hard to pour liquid into a small measuring spoon without making a mess but with these measuring spoons shaped like miniature ladles, I can just dip and get an exact fourth teaspoon or whatever. Any liquid ingredients like vanilla, cooking oil or vinegar, I pour into a wide mouth container so that I can just dip out the amount I need."

I filled a glass halfway with water and showed him how easy it was to get an exact tablespoon.

"Here, Brad, would you like to try it? You can be blind for a minute." I instructed him to hold the handle straight, dip it into the water and pull straight up. Opening his eyes, he was pleased with the results—one exact tablespoonful of water. Then, my talking clock shocked us both with the late hour as it announced 5:00 p.m. Trying to be kind and still nudge him out the door, I suggested that Colette might be waiting for that cup of sugar.

Well, that evening Marv had extra time to read the newspaper since dinner was much later than planned. He was such a good sport, though. We had already both agreed that spending time with the teens was a good investment, so he patiently waited with no complaints.

We were spending more and more time with our neighbors. Colette and I enjoyed shopping together, pot-lucking meals and orchestrating summer outings for both families. Pizza and teens seemed to be a winning combination. It wasn't long before pizza potlucks became a common occurrence. We teased Colette about having a pizza parlor just two doors from our apartment.

Pizza night again—there Marv and I sat in her homey dining room. The long worn school-like table had lost its slick finish from many years of use. Strewn from one end to the other were many souvenirs of the day's activities. The kitchen bustled with dinner preparation and the frequent interruptions of her young children. It was far from an elegant setting or gourmet cuisine, but some of the greatest dining experiences happened right there.

It was on one of those evenings, right in the middle of a piping hot Hawaiian pizza, that Russ informed us of a real shortage in foster parents. Both Russ and Colette felt we would be just right for the job. I could almost hear Marv's eyebrows raise at the same time mine did—what an unexpected offer. We agreed to talk it over and get back to them. As soon as we got home that evening, we sat together on the couch in a pensive whir. There the Lord, Marv and I talked it over. After all, we did have a two-bedroom apartment and we both loved kids, so why not? The decision light was blazing in a brilliant racing green.

It took just one visit to the Boys and Girls Agency along with reams of paperwork and we were in. Our first few youngsters were mild mannered, quiet guests. Getting used to the newcomer was a challenge at best. Understandably, the teens were on guard. Most of the time, they entered our home with distrust and an attitude of "bucking the system." Even though their stay was short, God helped me to see value in each of them. Some were easy to love, others not, but I grew to love them all. Within the first day or two, it was common to see an obvious change. How refreshing to witness the harsh gruff exteriors turn to smiling voices and even a kind word now and then.

Eric had the annoying habit of making a crude comment about Marv or me and then stating, "Ah hah, burnt you!" He was proud of his ability to be obnoxious. What tickled me was Marv's response. In a snap, he turned that negative adjective into a compliment. I could hear the almost silent groan of disgust in Eric's throat. This kid took a little longer to soften than most but within a short time, Eric began teasing like Marv. What a change in our home's atmosphere. Positivity was bouncing around our home like the ball in a feverish ping pong match. With each teen, there was some degree of bonding. The longer they stayed, the deeper the attachment became.

The hardest part of all came when we had to say goodbye. Each goodbye came much sooner than any of us wanted. The agency had a time limit of three months. In that time frame, a plan had to be designed to meet the needs of that teenager. This meant either placement in another home or enrollment in a therapy program. In most cases, however, the kids were with us just two or three weeks. It was heart wrenching to watch them warm up to us just in time to be torn away.

Comments like "I just wish they'd let me stay in one place," were made often when they had to leave. Words like those hit my heart with tears upon tears. Hugs and tears were commonplace as they were ushered on to their next placement. That was a hard time for all.

My saving grace was knowing that God loved each child more than I ever could. Real relief and comfort settled in my heart as I committed each child into God's care. Whenever the sad remembrances came, which did happen often, I reminded myself that they were in God's hands. After all, they couldn't be in any better hands than His.

With so many years of survival under my belt, it would seem like I should be well conditioned to the fact that one constant thing in life is change. Ever since we signed up to be foster parents, change was constant and much more frequent than I liked.

With each new teenage guest, we had to regroup and adapt. At first, they felt a bit awkward being around a blind person. But God's love intervened so well. Once they felt our genuine love for them, it did not take long before they warmed up to me. On the other hand, getting them to cooperate and comply was met with icy glares. Issues popped up over simple things like sharp knives pointing up in the dishwasher and shoes left in the middle of the floor. Little things mounted into big obstacles for my everyday routine.

It took a few hair-raising episodes before I wised up.

I know what…I'll give myself an extra fifteen minutes to get ready for work each morning. That should be enough time to deal with those surprise glitches.

It was essential to plan ahead for the consistent inconsistencies. There were many small, time-robbing, messes that often met me upon arising.

Despite all that, I still was in no way prepared for the challenge that was about to step through our doorway.

CHAPTER 28
CHALLENGES EXPLODING

It was just a few days after our third foster teenager left when the phone rang.

"Hi, Pam, it's Julie from Boys and Girls Aid. We are in desperate need of a home for a thirteen-year-old boy." Then she began fiiling me in on all the details. "His name is Jeff and he has a history of being violent. Parrot Creek Boys Ranch, his home for the past two months, kicked him out because he started too many fights. Jeff actually broke some bones and hurt the other kid so bad that he had to be hospitalized. They just can't keep him there any longer.

Since you and Marv don't have any children in your home, we felt your place would be best. Jeff seems to have the most difficulty getting along with other kids. This kid's a stick of dynamite with a real short fuse. So, Pam, let me warn you—whatever you do, don't demand that Jeff do anything. He's likely to haul off and punch you."

"Oh my, I don't know about this one. Marv is still at work. I'll talk to him as soon as he gets home. Can I let you know first thing tomorrow morning?" I gingerly placed the receiver back on the phone. Shaking my head, I prayed.

Dear Lord, I don't know about Jeff, sounds dangerous. We sure need your wisdom.

That night, Marv barely stepped through the front door from work when I informed him of the call. We sat down to dinner and I filled him in on the conversation with Julie. After praying and discussing our options, we agreed to take Jeff.

The very next day, a caseworker and Jeff arrived on our doorstep. The caseworker stayed just long enough to make an official introduction. Then she disappeared as quickly as dry autumn leaves swept away by the wind.

That first afternoon was quite the encounter. Of course, neither Jeff nor I knew what to think of the other. We kept our distance much like two boxers, apprehensively sizing each other up while pacing back and forth inside the ring. I busied myself with dinner preparations. Yet amidst frying hamburger and peeling potatoes, a silent tenseness filled our kitchen. My feeble attempts to create conversation and show interest in him still resulted in awkward near silence.

While I was cooking, my ears were carefully watching Jeff's every move. My gut was churning as I felt his icy stare in my direction. Although all was quiet on the home front, it was the opposite of a calm, comfortable environment. The minutes dragged slower than a slug caught in a wintry traffic jam. I continued to try to keep busy and ignore him.

Finally, Marv was home. What a relief. A few pleasantries were exchanged, and then, Jeff spilled his anger.

"Hey, man, what's the deal! They told me your wife is blind. That's a bunch of crock. I know she can see—she looks right at me when I talk to her. She finds everything in the kitchen and cooks and does all that stuff by herself. What are you guys trying to pull? There's no way I'll be staying in a home with a bunch of liars that can't be trusted. I'm going to call Boys and Girls Aid."

I figured Jeff needed a little explanation, so I motioned for him to step closer to me. "I can understand what you're saying, Jeff, and it sounds like you have a good case. But, please give me just a couple minutes now. I think you'll have a better picture of what's going on once you get the whole story. My eyes look normal because they are normal. It's the nerves behind them that don't work."

"You see, it's like this, Jeff, the doctors told me I had to move my eyes. If I don't use those muscles, they will weaken. Then, I'd end up having surgery to take out my real eyes and put in glass ones. No way did I want that! I thought the doctors were crazy! How did they expect me to move my eyes all the time when I couldn't see? So, I decided the best way to do that would be to act like I could see. So, I made a habit of looking at a person's voice as soon as I hear them talk. I also look toward any noises, just like I did when I could see. That's why I don't look blind."

I could hear hesitance in his thinking. He kind of grasped that, but still seemed puzzled. Then, I brought my Braille cookbook out to check on a recipe. Purposely sitting right across from him at the kitchen table, I began reading my favorite Au Gratin Potato recipe out loud. That clenched it. He was satisfied and no longer felt the need to report us.

Well, we cleared hurdle number one. That was as easy as going across a speed bump compared to the next challenge. It was Jeff's third day with us. Dinner was good and the dishes done. The three of us set off in different directions. Marv was headed for bed and Jeff seemed content reading his paperback book in the living room. Sitting alone at my desk in the den, I was comfortably engrossed in a project until loud angry voices from the kitchen jarred me out of my cozy corner. With a quick bound, I sprang up, knocking the wooden desk chair backwards.

Oh, forget it, can't take time to pick it up now. Got to get to the kitchen.

Down the hall I flew and around the corner. An ice cold steel wall of silent tension hit me as I came to the kitchen doorway. Listening intently for any hint of movement, I inched my way into the kitchen. Nothing was audible, not even a hint of movement. Then Marv's keys jingled slightly as he shifted his weight.

Ah, Marv's over there at the counter by the sink.

Then a low heavy sigh revealed Jeff standing with staunch defiance in the center of the room. There in the kitchen doorway I stood, frozen. Like the sharp thorns of a desert cactus, cold shivers went up and down my spine. I whispered a silent prayer: "Father in Heaven, HELP!"

Okay, Pam, you're the mediator, it's up to you. March!

"Hi, guys." I made my entrance attempting to be nonchalant. "What's going on?"

The frightening silence continued. At first, my presence seemed invisible. Yet, within less than two seconds, its affect hit like pressing the power button on an action packed video game. The battle was on.

"Touch me again like that and you've had it," Marv warned with a harshness I'd never heard before.

"Yah, old man, come and get me. I'll show you a fight."

"Hey, guys! What's the deal here! I haven't a clue, why are you both so angry? I can't imagine you know each other well enough that you need to fight it out."

I waited for some kind of explanation. Marv began by describing how Jeff walked up and grabbed his earlobe with a sharp painful tug.

"Oh, no!" I shrieked. "It's all my fault! Jeff and I were talking in the den. Both of us were bored and restless. So, I said, 'guess we'll just have to grab Marv by the ear and go do something.' I sure didn't mean for him to literally do it. That phrase was used by our family in a teasing way. It simply meant to get someone's attention."

"I just did what you said," Jeff spouted.

"Well, it better not happen again. That's all I have to say," Marv sternly warned.

I gasped and tried to hold my breath in so as to keep Jeff from noticing my fear. The tension was heightened to a red flag state with no sign of anyone yielding even a millimeter.

Oh, Father in Heaven, SOS, please! I don't even know what to ask of you, but I do know things are way out of control, beyond our control.

In an attempt to separate the two impending wrestlers, I motioned Jeff in my direction. "How about helping me in the den?"

Jeff sluggishly made his way to the den. It was obvious that he was still too hot under the collar to talk rationally. But, it was also obvious that it took divine intervention to get him that far. Keeping the conversation brief, I asked if his book was a good one. He said it was.

"How about reading for awhile to help get your mind off the problem? Do you think that will help?" I asked with genuine concern. He acknowledged my suggestion and headed for the couch in the living room. Then, as he left, I motioned Marcie to follow him.

She was a true peace ambassador in our home. Jeff had grown up with dogs and really loved them. My dear Marcie was a real hit with him. That night, she was the perfect therapy for Jeff as she snuggled up beside him soaking up ear rubs and caring strokes. I was more than happy that Marv worked such an early shift. Thank goodness he had to go to bed immediately.

Phew! That was way too volatile for anybody's good! At least Marv's safely sacked out in our bedroom, and Jeff is on the couch engrained in his book.

Slumping in my chair, I exhaled a huge sigh of relief as I soaked in the present peace and quiet of my sanctuary.

Good thing I was capturing the moment, because that's precisely how long it lasted. Soft footsteps were headed my way. I listened intently with the hope that they would walk past my door and down the hall to the bathroom. No such luck—Jeff stepped through the door and right into My Sanctuary.

"Hi, Jeff, how's your book coming along?"

With sluggish heavy steps, he moved even closer. "Have you ever heard the word, mincemeat?"

"I have. Are you referring to Marv?" I asked in a sheepish tone.

"Yes," he snarled with deep seated anger. "I feel like pounding him to a pulp and then some."

Stunned into silence, I sat motionless for a few seconds.

"Why ever would you want to do that? What has Marv done to hurt you?"

Oh, Lord, help me. Reach out and hug Jeff, please.

The real shock came when I heard tears in his voice. This macho hunk was actually sniffling.

"Jeff, it's okay," I said, attempting to comfort him as I stepped in his direction. The tug at my heart pulled me like a magnet even closer and before I knew it, I was holding this sobbing youngster tightly in my arms.

"Pam, the last thing I wanted to do was to hurt Marv, but the first thing that popped into my head was to pulverize him!"

"But Jeff, you didn't. You just proved you can control yourself. That's a real accomplishment."

With a deep remorseful sigh, he stretched his arms toward me, turned his large hands palm up and said, "Pam, here, touch my hands. Feel them. See how strong and big they are. I'm really good with my hands, but the only way I know to use them is to fight."

"That is a problem, all right. I'm sure there are other things besides fighting you can do with your strong skillful hands. Hey, I've got an idea. Let's go talk to my friend. He's the one I always go to whenever I haven't a clue what to do next. That's where I get the best advice."

"Just so I don't have to talk to any man with an attitude. Men and I don't get along. It's always been men that I have real trouble with."

"I see. I'm sure you'll like him. And, if you don't, you'll never have to speak to him again."

We did visit my friend and had a good conversation. However, Jeff let me do most of the talking since he was not at all used to praying.

"Thanks, Jeff, for praying with me. I know God will help us find some way you can use your strong hands to do good. Just wait. You'll see. But, for now, we'd better get ready for the coming week. Do you have your alarm set to get up for school?"

He assured me he did, so I headed to my bedroom and Jeff went upstairs to his. Slumber was sweet, at least initially. Then, directly above Marv and my bed, came a thundering crash followed by two more foundation-shaking thumps. Instantly, I sat straight up and tapped my slumbering husband. "What was that?"

While still more than half asleep, he replied, "Don't worry, Dear, it's just Jeff."

Almost more amazing than the triple crashes was Marv's nonchalant response. To think that he actually heard it but was nearly oblivious to this midnight interruption boggled my senses. Within a few seconds, Marv had returned to softly snoring. As for me, it took a bit of time for my nerves to uncoil. Meanwhile, I lay there with both ears switched into radar mode anticipating more of the same.

Things were quieter on the home front after that. For the first few weeks, Marv, Jeff and I were going through our routines in almost normal fashion. But truthfully, I wouldn't say any of us were comfortable. There was the subtle, but ever present, tension of each person being in their on-guard mode. We carefully watched every move made by the other. This was especially the case with the two guys.

Jeff and I were actually getting along quite well. After that night when he let down his guard and bared his soul to me, we had a kindred spirit and strong bond. I was praying harder and more often than ever and at the same time, watching for creative alternatives to fist fights.

Early on, it was apparent that Jeff loved to help others. Thank the Lord for my blindness—boy did it ever come in handy. He was always, well almost always, willing and eager to help me. With teasing and laughter, we found lots of projects to do together. My praise and appreciation set very well with Jeff. Praise seemed to be a new experience for him and he was thriving on it.

One project we both enjoyed was baking. Soon it was apparent that baking cakes was his favorite thing to do. After several successful Betty Crocker sessions together in the kitchen, Jeff was ready for a solo run. I helped him get set up. With the assurance that he was cooking-ready, I disappeared until the timer rang.

Ring-g-g, my timer sounded. Setting down my dust rag, I was off to find the baker. "Jeff, it's time to check your cake. Here, take this toothpick and poke it right in the middle. If it comes out clean, the cake's done."

I, of course, inspected it with my tactile vision. Gently touching the edges, I checked for slight crusting and then slid my fingertips toward the middle to see if it had raised enough. And, yes, it was baked to perfection. We both agreed that it smelled and looked scrumptious.

As we beamed at his success, I asked if he wanted Marv to see it before we cut it. To my surprise, he answered that he did not want to eat it that night but would like to take it to school the next day.

The Boys and Girls Aid Society had a high school in the basement of their agency. This was for a select few teenagers who couldn't handle public schooling. That is the school Jeff attended. The next morning, Jeff had no problem getting out of bed on time. In fact, he was up and ready for school way ahead of time. Being a light sleeper, the extra noise in the kitchen at such an early hour awoke me with a start. I was on my feet with a dash to my robe. I had to check it out. There Jeff was busy gathering his cake, napkins and paper plates. With the utmost of care, he positioned his masterpiece in his backpack to insure its safe travel to school. That moist chocolate cake with an extra thick layer of cream cheese frosting was a real hit. All the staff and students were delighted with Jeff's thoughtfulness and delicious gift. In fact, just a few cakes later, he was known by the whole school and agency as, "The Baker."

Even sweeter than that was his new accomplishment. He made star student of the week. That title was awarded to the teenager exhibiting the best behavior in the whole school. This new title and success convinced him that there was, indeed, a way to use his strong hands for good. He also got his first glimpse of God's personal interest and love. Those busy hands and heart that loved to help others blossomed even more one night in our home. That evening, I came home from work totally exhausted. I told Jeff that I'd have to lie down for a quick nap before I could start cooking dinner. Passed out on my bed, I knew nothing until Marv's gentle touch on my leg woke me.

"Time to get up, Sleeping Beauty. Dinner's ready."

To my surprise and sheer delight, Jeff had prepared dinner. It consisted of baked chicken, Rice-A-Roni and carrot sticks. Although the rice was way overcooked, it tasted good, filling both my stomach and heart with a heaping helping of smiles.

While things had settled down in the home, outside those walls, it wasn't all that calm. It didn't take long before we learned that Jeff was more dangerous to himself than to anyone else. Every morning, as he left home, there was a drastic rise in both my blood pressure and eyebrows. When out on the streets, he was a walking time bomb. His frustration and anger often wounded the best of him.

After a long ride on his bicycle, he came home. As he stepped through the front door, he sounded sicker than a dog. And, boy, was he ever worse for the wear. His bike didn't look so hot, either. The front of it was bent beyond repair.

"Jeff, are you okay? You don't sound so good."

"I'm a little bruised and sore, but that's all."

"How did that happen?"

"I was riding my bike down Powell when a young boy came barreling toward me on his skateboard. He left me no room. I either had to go out in the street or hit the kid. So, I swerved to miss him and literally went through the bus shelter."

"You rode your bike through a bus shelter?"

"Yeah. The bike stopped at the bus shelter, but my body kept going. I crashed through one pane of Plexiglas, flew across and crashed through the other side."

"No way! Are you bleeding? How about your head, any scrapes or lumps?"

I couldn't believe how tough that kid was. He had just a few bruises and scratches. That was the first episode but far from the last.

I knew that God provided a guardian angel to watch out for each child of His.

In Jeff's case, however, I'm sure He kept a whole band of angels busy full time.

I learned to count my blessings each day that he arrived home safe and sound. His being accident-prone, a time bomb and a juvenile was quite the combination. In fact, this kept our home more action packed than Marv and I had ever imagined.

Jeff wasn't all accidents and no fun. Once the three of us settled into the comfort level, Jeff brought plenty of fun our way, as well.

CHAPTER 29
THE DOUBLE "D" DAYS

Three months whizzed faster than NASCAR at full throttle and Jeff was still with us. The counselor at Boys and Girls Aid Society had not figured out a good placement for him yet. With a resourceful approach and caring heart, she was able to extend his stay one more month, but that was the absolute limit. Then, he would have to be moved somewhere else.

The previous three months were anything but stress or problem free. Jeff came into our home filled with harsh bitterness. He often tried to offend and upset us with his coarse comments. His heart gradually softened as he found that we still loved and cared for him despite his behavior. The ongoing opportunities to help me and care for Marcie proved to be a positive force that began building up his self worth. By the end of his four-month stay, a positive bond of caring and love had grown strong in our home.

Along came the season of disappointment, and discouragement hit in major league proportion.

Marv was unemployed for the twelfth month. He had grown so hopeless that he was sullen around the clock.

What happened to the teasing punster I married? Nothing I do seems to pull him out of this rut.

I kept praying and even scolded God for not helping Marv. Grandma's words bolstered my faith and hope for a brighter tomorrow. They rang clear again and again in my mind. They kept me looking up. It had already been thirty years since I went blind in the hospital where she gave me those words of encouragement. "Pam, here's a passage in the Bible written just for you. It says that God will work out everything for good because you love Him."

I certainly knew from past experience this promise was true, tried and true. God worked my blindness out for good. He could do it again. I just couldn't figure out what He was waiting for. Watching Marv continue to be so miserable just heightened my worry and inner aching. I did a lot more worrying and agonizing than praying. I just didn't know how much longer I would have a husband if things didn't change for the better, and in short order, too.

My plate of worry soon grew to a turkey-sized platter. It mushroomed and mounded to gigantic proportion when Marv and I took in two more foster boys. Jay and Joseph hit the top of the chart when it came to defiance and bad behavior. They both came preprogrammed with a full vocabulary of foul words and open disrespect. I just couldn't do a thing with them. They took advantage of my being blind. Whenever I asked them to do even the simplest thing, they swore and refused. Any hint of discipline from me resulted in, "You can't make me," and out the front door they ran.

To make this double D season even worse, Marv continued to be indifferent to everyone and everything. He refused to exert his authority even though I pleaded for his help with the kids.

Thank goodness Jeff was still with us. He was our saving grace. The moment he witnessed Jay and Joseph talking back to me, he went to bat. He took both boys out to the nearby park. There, far from my hearing, he set them straight. Jeff told them, "Marv and Pam are good people. You two hellions had better start treating them right. You do anything to hurt either of them, and you're dead meat. Count on it!"

The very next day, there was a drastic change in both boys' language and attitudes.

Later that evening, Jeff came home. As usual, I welcomed him home and asked how his day was. After filling me in on his day, it was my turn. I told him about the shocking transformation in Jay and Joseph. It was then that Jeff informed me of the park episode. He was older, much huskier and stronger than the other two. When he meant business, they knew it. There was no doubt Jeff would do just as he said.

I was struggling in my attempt to relate to our two new boys. I wanted so much to let them know they had value and that I loved them. But it was difficult to have any kind of meaningful conversation with either of them.

Jeff, on the other hand, enjoyed doing things with me and took it upon himself to be my protector.

One afternoon, Joseph and I were the only ones home. I needed to take cake to work for a party the next day. Since Jeff was not available to bake, it was a good opportunity to do something with Joseph. To my surprise and delight, he was willing to do it. He wanted to set the oven for me and I consented. The cake went in the oven and the timer was set. We actually did quite well together in the kitchen. After cleanup was finished, we both headed out in different directions. Joseph wanted to go outside and ride his bike. I agreed to stay inside and watch the cake. It was agreed that once the cake was out, I'd hang a blue dish cloth on the front doorknob. That would be Joseph's sign to come inside and frost the cake.

With the home front void of turmoil and interruptions, I switched the stereo on to soft easy-listening music and picked up my crocheting. That had long been a favorite indoor pastime. Although I enjoyed it a lot, I did it so little. Our busy city lifestyle seldom had spots for quiet reflection or hobbies. That day, I had a good excuse just to sit a bit and crochet. I needed to stay in earshot of the kitchen timer.

As long as I could remember, Dad had complained with real disgust about how dry his mother's cakes always were. I, too, had become very fond of light, extra moist cakes. As a result, I developed the habit of setting the timer for less than the recipe said.

There I sat basking in peace and relaxation with a real treat in my hands. I had not a care in the world. It was my ears on alert, keeping a watch out for the ring of the timer. But instead, my nose sounded the alarm.

Something's burning. Probably just a little batter on the oven rack. It has ten minutes left.

Turning full attention again to my crochet project, I began picturing the pattern of my afghan. This one was extra fun to make. It was for my soon-to-arrive niece. Steve and Fran's new little bundle was due next month. These lime green, beige, pink and lavender pastels, I hoped would be a bright welcome to her arrival.

Carefully protecting my peaceful oblivion, I ignored all potential disruptors like the jingle of Marcie's collar, children playing outside and everything within the home. But to my dismay, the ole nose was no respecter of peace and quiet. This time it set off an alarm—a four alarm blast. I tossed my crocheting in the seat of my comfortable rocking chair and raced for the kitchen.

The stench of burnt food increased with every step.

Putting on my oven mitts, I braved the heat. Slowly, and oh-so cautiously, I opened the oven door. A ravage black smoke panther sprang straight out and lit full force right in my face. With wide frantic swings, I attempted fanning my face as I gasped for air. I pulled the 9 x 13 inch pan out and set it on the nearby cooling rack. I dashed to the back door and swung it wide open. Thank goodness for the cavalry of fresh air. It galloped through the door to my rescue.

Should I hang out the blue signal now for Joseph or not? Seems pointless to interrupt his bike riding for this disaster. Guess I'll just wait. He's bound to come inside sooner or later.

In the meantime, the air had cleared and the cake was cool. I forced myself to go assess the damage.

Bending down for a close-up sniff, not even the slightest aroma of cake was detectable. Fingertip inspection was next. It was bad, worse than bad. A nice dome was present, but the surface resembled asphalt.

In the midst of wiping up crumbs, my ears picked up the sound of footsteps on our front porch. Sure enough, Joseph came bursting through the door.

"What happened to the blue flag? I kept watching for it. Pam, something's burning!"

"You're right and guess what!"

"Oh, no, my cake," he cried as he ran into the kitchen. "Oh, crud! It's black, totally black! What happened?"

"That's a good question. I checked it before the time was up, and this is what I found. By the way, what is the oven dial set at?"

Joseph walked over to the oven and studied it carefully. "Looks like 475 or 500."

Well, that solved the mystery. We had managed to charbroil one yellow cake. Before another word could be uttered, the front door banged open. It was Jay, and just a couple steps behind him was Jeff. The first thing they noticed was that deformed ebony blob.

Jay commented first. "Phew! What a mess!"

Jeff stepped up next. I asked him to see if it could be saved by trimming off the burnt layer. He cut a piece and informed me that it was black at least half way through. With this discovery, tension started brewing with crude comments and sharp darts of blame fired back and forth at each other.

Jay piped up, "Forget it! That's a total waste. Nobody will eat that cake!"

I turned and snatched our tall plastic trash can. Placing one hand on each side of the rounded lid, I danced it across the floor toward the cake. Moving its push-in flap back and forth, I said, "Hi guys, my name's Herkimer. I love burnt cake. Just watch this—I'll swallow the whole thing in one gulp."

After downing the entire charcoal brick, Herkimer let out a loud belch with Jay's help.

Fortunately for all of us, this zany display caught everyone off guard and created a round of laughter. The feud was off, thoroughly dispelled by fun.

The cake disappointment was forgotten, but the despair of my hubby lingered longer and stronger. I was on my knees when another "out of the blue" idea came to me. Marv's fortieth birthday was only a couple weeks away. A birthday party would be just the ticket.

Planning parties was one of my favorite things to do, and I had done lots of them. One of my duties in teaching Sunday School and Kids Club was to plan parties for each holiday and special occasion. I had lots of fun decorating the room and dreaming up activities. I think sometimes I had more fun planning the party than the kids did participating in it.

It was party planning time again, and this time I was extra eager to make it a success. I called all of our friends and invited them to it. Almost every person asked what kind of gift Marv would like. My answer was that the best gift would be a personal note telling something they appreciated about Marv.

The party was an incredible success and was Marv ever surprised. Our home was full to overflowing with family and friends. Marv's self-worth went from minus one hundred to way above ground level. What a major relief—I had my husband back. Even more astonishing to me were the responses from each person I called. They were never wishy-washy saying maybe they could make it. Instead, comments were made like, "You bet, I'll be there!" or, "A birthday party for Marv—I wouldn't miss it for the world!"

I'd never had such enthusiastic and positive responses like that before.

Marv thanked me many times for this special party. Afterward, I told him about the extra enthusiasm shown by his friends when invited. He said that information meant even more than the party, itself.

This incident taught me a most useful and valuable lesson in communication. Had I failed to tell Marv this detail, he would have been deprived of the most important gift of the whole shindig. From then on, I knew it was essential to consistently communicate the good things that I experienced each day.

Despite all my worrying and hopelessness, God did work it out for our good. The boys rallied to the cause, as well. They helped me clean the house, bake an "unbroiled" spice cake and hang bright streamers and balloons. They learned first hand the powerful difference kindness and positive comments could make.

Another capital D hit us when Jeff's fourth month came to an end. It was more than heart piercing to part. And even though we knew it was coming, its actual arrival was devastating. Jay and Joseph were with us for the short stay of one week. And the time had come for Jeff to go, as well. All three boys were out of our home. The quiet hours took many days to adjust to, but having more foster kids was questionable. After discussion and prayer, both Marv and I agreed that our home was not the best place for these teens.

We let the Boys and Girls Aid Society know of our decision.

"Oh, Pam," Julie said, "I'm so sorry to hear that. You and Marv are some of our best foster parents. The fact that you are blind and so upbeat is real therapy for the kids."

I was sorry, too, but knew that decision was best for all. Even though our home was teen-less, Jeff kept in close contact. He called once or twice a week. Whenever things got too stressful, he would call me. That meant it was urgent to have some quality Mom-Son time. Often, we would meet for lunch or just go out with Marcie to the park. The frequency of our get-togethers dropped to almost zero once Jeff went out of town for training at Job Corps.

After Jeff graduated from Job Corps, he was at our doorstep. At that point, he was old enough to be on his own, so he moved back in with us. Soon after, Jeff brought a most unexpected, totally awesome gift.

That was Shelly, soon to become our daughter. Shelly had attended Job Corps the same time Jeff did. He brought her home to meet his parents. Our first visit was a good one. Near the end of that visit, Jeff's statement to Shelly caught me off guard. "You can call her Mom. Everybody else does."

That simple comment from Jeff was the start of such a beautiful relationship. Shelly fit so well into our family and our hearts. She soon became our dear Shelly, a loving daughter. At that time in their lives, both kids were in real need of parents to love and guide them. Their need was the perfect thing to fill the empty spot in Marv's heart and in mine.

Both our kids tease me, saying, "Mom, you sure lucked out. You got your kids and didn't have to go through the diaper stage." Jeff and Shelly have blessed Marv and me so.

Extra special family fun happened each year in the Christmas season. I have always loved Christmas with its shopping, baking, bright decorations and gift giving. That was the good part, but not without a big drawback, as well. The busy Christmas season always posed a major balancing act for me. Every year, about two months before Christmas, my two hundred percent inner drive kicked into high, high gear. I wanted to do and to be a part of everything possible. The balancing act came in when my list of things to do was much greater than my supply of physical energy.

My kids knew this only too well. One Christmas, Marv and I had just come home with our fresh-cut Christmas tree. Already exhausted from the day's activities, I plopped down on the couch feeling frustrated and glum. There was not an ounce of energy left in me. The Christmas tree stood there just begging for me to decorate it. Tears no sooner began to well up than when the door bell rang.

"Merry Christmas, Mom and Dad, Santa's elves are here to help you decorate the tree."

My heart flooded with joy. That evening, the festive event unfolded with the greatest of ease—that is, super easy on me. Jeff and Shelly made sure I maintained the position of Director while they and Marv did the rest. Christmas trees like that are the most gorgeous ever. Their decorations please more than just the eye. They sparkle with much richer ornaments— lavish love and hidden treasures of the heart.

The caring ways and helping hands of my kids continued often, not just at Christmas, but the whole year through. We were all happy campers in the city, smack-dab in the middle of the city.

Well, that's proof again of God's promises being absolutely true. Having a family had long been a desire deep within my heart. And, now we had a son and a daughter.

CHAPTER 30
SOUPED UP

I had moved out of a career and into full time homemaking and it was a monumental change to my system.

My worth is not measured by my job nor production. What really makes me valuable is the fact that I am God's child. Got to remind myself that the most important accomplishment in the whole world is to love my Heavenly Father and have a heart that seeks after Him.

This truth did recycle through my brain periodically, but not as often as needed. I had already been a homemaker for some time, but still the feelings of worthlessness recurred. This time, it hit me head-on. Life just didn't seem meaningful or exhilarating like it used to. The ongoing routine of doing dirty dishes, ever mounting piles of laundry and housecleaning just didn't satisfy. Despite purposeful reminders of my true worth, I just wasn't content.

This isn't working. Okay, Pam, it's hotline time again. Your attitude stinks!

On my knees I went. Fortunately for me, the solution was a simple one. After talking with God, I realized that what I needed was a shift in my focus. Without realizing it, I had allowed my thoughts to dwell on all the negatives. I knew better than that. A favorite saying I'd heard years ago became my homemaker motto: "True contentment in life comes by enjoying what we have, not what we think we should have." With that new motto, I determined to shift my focus to the good all around me.

I began to have fun every day just by searching for the "good stuff" in my world. A common occurrence I had taken for granted was my morning walk to Jack in the Box. I made it a routine to go while the morning air was fresh and not yet smog-laden by the rush hour traffic.

Our apartment building was nestled in a park-like setting. We were surrounded by plush green lawns, lofty leaf trees, bushes and flowers. Early each morning, with white cane in hand, I was out my front door. I had no more than swung it open when Mr. Breeze greeted me with a cool eye-opening kiss. That welcome friend never failed to curve my lips into a broad smile as I breathed in the freshness. The leafy trees high above greeted me next with their soothing "good morning" tune. Amidst their branches, the birds serenaded my new day. Oh, how I loved to slow my pace and bask in its beauty.

Just a few blocks away was my destination. A nice cushioned booth at Jack in the Box awaited me. I had a favorite spot there. A booth in the corner with large windows on both sides caught the morning sunshine in full glory. Sitting there in its warmth and enjoying my diet Coke, I spent time with the Lord. I talked to Him in prayer—then He talked to me as I read my Braille Bible. After getting a fresh batch of wisdom, it was time to review the menu, shopping list and activities for the day.

A deep heart's desire of mine was to have a family of my own. And although I had never experienced childbirth, this came true.

Jeff and Shelly were our kids without a doubt. Their respect and genuine love for us was incredible. These two kids were born into our family as teenagers. Both of them loved to help me around our home. Even the mundane household tasks became supercharged with fun, laughter and teasing as we did them together. The drudgery of folding laundry was transformed into fabric gone animated. Washcloths sprouted wings and socks went wild. Thanks to Marv, both kids had mastered the skill of flinging socks with a sharp-shooter blow.

Almost every morning, my sweetheart whipped me into shape with his pair of socks. The blows were so harsh that Marv had to be sure to proclaim his attack. "Sock! Sock!" he announced with a youthful flare. It's a good thing he did, or I would never have noticed that I'd been socked. Being socked actually paid off in my favor. Since he had punished me, I wailed and needed consoling with a great big hug. This merriment jumped started our day and our hearts with enthusiasm and love. Jeff was first to witness this morning routine. He loved it and made sure that no pairs of socks from the dryer went un-flung. Of course, when Shelly became Mom's helper, she, too, had to learn this fine art.

What a miracle of love and goodness filled our hearts and our home. That would have been plenty good enough, but here comes the real shocker. They enjoyed walking with me in public and were proud to call me 'Mom.'

What an incredible dream come true—Marv and I had family, our kids. And the goodness just kept going. Shelly brought her beau into our family. Steve, a tall, strong young man was encouraged by her to call us Mom and Dad, too. He was hesitant at first, and that was understandable. But, Marv and I just kept treating him like one of the family.

And then we gained another son. With time, Steve let down his guard and the Lord bonded us together as family.

Staying young at heart is something Marv and I have found to be most beneficial. But, perhaps, there are times when we are too dedicated to it. One such occasion was a summer afternoon when I was too hot and tired to cook. I talked Marv into taking the four of us to Izzy's for dinner. We all chose to have the full buffet. Shelly guided me through the buffet line. Marv and Steve soon appeared at our booth with their plates full of savory selections. Marv had no sooner finished praying when I heard a fresh batch of mischief brewing right across the table. It was a very quiet, almost muffled chuckle. But still, I could detect a hint of mischief in it.

I didn't even have time to speak a single syllable before Shelly said, "Mom, watch out!" In less than a New York Second, a UFO hit my bare forearm.

"All right!" I tried to sound stern in my protest. "What was that and where did it come from?"

Shelly giggled as she gulped to clear her throat for an urgent report. "That was Steve. He shot you with a green pea."

And Marv, exhibiting his mature behavior, sat beside Steve roaring with laughter. Marv's amusement didn't surprise me, but the next one really shocked my socks off. As another pea lit in my lap, Shelly broadcasted the event with a giggle, "Mom, you'll never guess where that pea came from! Dad did it!"

Two peas confined to our table would not have been concerning, but there was more to come. Both boys, and I do mean boys, were laughing and announcing their sharp-shooting feats.

"Did you see that, Dad? I shot it clear into the kitchen."

Again, setting a mature example, Marv chimed in. "Way to go!"

With each new shot, Shelly and I turned a shade redder. When Marv shot his pea over ten feet and hit me in the leg, it was past time to exit the battlefield. Shelly and I found it prime time to visit the ladies room. Interestingly enough, we never found our way back to the booth, but headed straight to the parking lot. Well, that day we girls learned a valuable lesson. Avoid any establishment that features "flying pea" salad.

Our hearts swelled with love and pride as those endearing words, "Mom" and "Dad" were heard often.

As our family was expanding, Marv's and my relationship was deepening. The unwritten code of keeping all negativity out of our speech and home was paying off big time. The simple two-word phrase, "Let's pray" proved to be a huge pressure reliever. I noticed tension at the moment of its onset. It was normal for me to want to short-circuit trouble by nipping it in the bud. I knew that ignored tension meant trouble.

Whenever I noticed tension in our midst, I would come alongside my man and say, "Honey, let's pray." This was not an easy thing for Marv at first, especially since he was unaware of any problem. We have often chuckled at the remembrance of that very first incident.

The two of us were in our car headed for a weekend in Eugene. Several irritations had cropped up in the process of getting ready for the trip. That detained us which resulted in getting a much later start than planned. Then, in the midst of battling downtown traffic, Marv thought of something that didn't get packed. The anger leaped out full force in his sharp comment, "Oh, forget it! We might as well just turn around and call off the trip."

This exasperated outburst was anticipated well before it happened. Previously throughout our morning of getting ready, unexpected problems cropped up. With each occurrence, he grumbled. The complaints grew harsher as the day and delays continued. I reached across to his leg, and with a reassuring squeeze said, "Honey, let's pray." That's when the jolting shock hit my gut. With loud harsh words, he blurted out, "What do you mean pray? I don't need to pray!"

I sat there stunned to silence, and that's an oddity for me. I dialed my hotline to heaven.

Oh Father, SOS, please help Marv let down his wall and pray. You are the only one who can give us the peace in the midst of this stress mess.

A few moments later, Marv began to pray. He finished praying and said, "Thanks so much for getting me to pray." Later he added, "I don't know how to explain it, but after praying, I felt such a relief—like a ton of bricks were lifted off me." He explained that he had no idea there was so much stress. But when he heard those angry words come out of his mouth, he said to himself, "Boy, you'd better pray and right now!"

After awhile, Marv did get used to and comfortable with that quick phrase. It sure paid off to have such a strong godly leader. I thrived on Marv's thoughtful way of expressing appreciation of me. He would often comment on how much he enjoyed just being with me.

We teamed up to attack the buildup of stress. Our main weapon for this warfare was laughter and teasing. It proved most effective, too. My dear Master Punster created spontaneous bouts of giggles and laughing. He often used that as a means to turn a negative occurrence into something cute or positive.

A classic example happened just three months into our marriage. I had to use Bag Balm on my hands everyday to keep eczema from recurring. And ever since a friend remarked that it smelled like shoe polish, I was extremely self-conscious about wearing it within smelling range of anybody. But, I had solved that concern with my routine of applying it just before going to bed. That worked so well until I got married. It was my good fortune that Marv fell asleep almost the instant he pulled the sheets over his shoulders. On the other hand, I had to fight with my pillow, then toss and turn a lot before my muscles unwound enough to relax into sleep. At first, I was a bit irritated that I couldn't fall asleep quickly like him. But, that proved to be a blessing. I would lie in bed until Marv started snoring. That was my cue to head for the can of Bag Balm.

One night, I was doing my usual slip-out-of-bed routine. I stood at the bathroom counter putting my hair in rollers. I had just finished that and was rubbing Bag Balm on my hands. Quick as a wink and twice as quiet as a mouse, the bathroom door popped open. Before I could even greet him, Marv stood right behind me and took in a very loud, deep breath. "Ah," he sighed with an air of sheer satisfaction, "Aroma de Bagboma!"

I squealed with delight as I spun around and reached out to give him a great big "thank you, thank you" hug! From that day forth, I never wore that stinky Bag Balm again. It was transformed into the exquisite French fragrance of Aroma de Bagboma.

Another marriage culture shock was wrapped around my need to wear curlers to bed. This was another unpleasant thing that I'd rather Marv didn't have to experience. But, in his fun-loving way, he thoroughly resolved that concern, too. He often called me his princess and queen. Stepping into our bedroom with my peacock display of pink and blue rollers one night, I gasped.

Oh, no! He's still awake!

He turned from the closet and wrapped his loving arms around me. "See, that proves you're a queen." And as usual, he paused a few lengthy seconds to let my mind ponder and puzzle his shenanigans. Gently tapping my rollers, he said, "You're wearing a crown on your head this very minute."

Well, that did it! There was no more rolling around in the embarrassment of nighttime curlers. After all, I was not ugly. I was beautiful. The king had just decreed that. Well, I couldn't prove Marv's royalty by the curlers in his hair, but I did find another avenue. His long arms, combined with being nine inches taller than me, gave him a long upward reach. In fact, he could stand flat on the floor and reach heights that were out of limits for me even atop my stepstool.

Marv was always so kind about reaching things for me so I wouldn't have to waste energy dragging out the stepstool. One day while standing at the grocery checkout counter, I came across the cleverest phrase. The instant I heard it, I knew it was going home with me. The next evening, Marv and I were in the kitchen just before dinner. I needed something from the top shelf in our cupboard.

Oh perfect, now is the time!

"Honey, I sure could use your high-ness."

Of course, being a genuine punster, he caught this one in style with an applauding chuckle.

Shattering stress and negativity with our humor hammer proved to be a most beneficial activity. Yet, another key element was that of enjoying and capturing the good things around us. We didn't have to wait for the once-a-year cruise or even the weekend for our enjoyment. Good little things abounded around us, and we determined they were not to be overlooked.

Nature provided just the ticket and a prolific supply of goodness for us. I have always been fascinated by God's intricate designs and breathtaking colors. As a youngster, I loved to watch spring unfold. That spectacular display vanished with the onset of my blindness.

Even more remarkable than the beauty of nature was the fact that Marv jumped in with all four feet, as well. He did not just stand by and observe me as I used my "unique" techniques of seeing. He got right in there and had fun with me. His participation and enjoyment added pizzazz to each little good thing that came my way.

The good things seemed to almost jump out of the woodwork every time we were together. It didn't matter what we were doing, fun and good stuff abounded.

CHAPTER 31
MIRACLE MOUNTAIN

Special memories, an upbeat outlook and good things all around added up to year after year of true wedded bliss. Of course, life here on planet earth is never perfect. And, without a doubt, my life was no exception. I was carrying a lot of baggage from my past. That plague was not visible on the outside, but internally, it was a killer. It had been with me so long with such subtle lingering that it went unnoticed much of the time. Although, when it did surface, the pain cut sharp and deep with a killing blow to my emotions and self-worth.

It was devastating to be blind, but this rejection from my dad over my weight cut even deeper. Since my pituitary gland no longer produced needed hormones, I had to take cortisone and my weight doubled as a result. My dad's comments about my weight continue to hurt me to this day.

One summer afternoon, I was typing a business letter for Dad. I had just pulled it out of my typewriter and handed it across the desk to him. As usual, he would read through it for content and accuracy.

"Pam, this letter is top-notch. But there's one thing you've got to face up to. Your performance can be excellent, but as long as you're overweight, you'll never get very far. So, if you don't lose weight, you might as well crawl off in a corner and die. You'll never amount to anything."

Cringing with shock and tightening my muscles as firm as possible, I walled off the tears and managed to mumble a civil response.

"Well, Dad, if there's no more dictation, I have things upstairs to do." Once alone in my bedroom, the gusher burst forth resembling Oregon's six hundred foot Multnomah Falls during the spring snow runoff.

Long ago I had forgiven him for the many hurts. But, my intellectual storage compartment was at times too keen.

I wish I could forget all those derogatory names like hippo, blimp and tank, but no such luck! They would surface at any moment with the powerful blow of an open-clawed tiger paw. Much like a lion trainer with outstretched chair and whip, I fought that relentless beast every time it snarled at me. But, despite my constant counterattacks, that kind of pain always lingered with stubborn resistance.

With many years of practice, I had become quite successful in forcing that dark gloom back from my immediate thoughts. Yet, its effect was always haunting me. Like a big dark cloud threatening to ruin a gala outdoor picnic, it hung over my head. No matter how well I had done, there was always the damper.

Good job, Pam, but not nearly as good as it should be, Madam Hippo. If only I were thin, then I'd really be successful.

I pleaded with my doctor to do something. He told me that the cortisone definitely caused the weight gain. He added, "Your body just doesn't manufacture those essential hormones. Pam, if you don't take them, you'll die."

Well, that didn't lessen my weight by even an ounce, but it did ease my mind a little. These facts didn't penetrate Dad's thinking, however. He continued to state that I was just using cortisone as an excuse. Quite frankly, I had considered throwing all those prescriptions away and just take my chances. Although I was tempted many times to do that, each time my Heavenly Father whispered his love to me. He reminded me that in his eyes, I was beautiful. That's what kept me from plummeting to the depths of depression.

I worked with constant diligence to keep this black cloud in my own sky. No one, not even my beloved husband, knew about that. I figured it was bad enough to have that black cloud raining on my picnic. I certainly didn't want anyone else overtaken by its gloom.

There, right in the midst of wedded bliss, I struggled to keep this dark cloud from blocking our sunshine. Another saving grace was Marv's love and affection that continued to flood my life with sunshine and happy thoughts. He often called me beautiful and even whistled at me as I stepped out of the shower.

A hard nut to crack, that was me for sure. But, thank God, nothing is impossible for Him! One afternoon while cleaning in our apartment, I was dusting and dancing to the music of our radio. I felt an unusual sense of wellbeing and inner joy, even smiling way down deep in my heart. It was then that I realized my black cloud was gone, G-O-N-E!

And the remedy? It was God's love with skin on. Marv's unfailing, unconditional love and acceptance did it! He was and always shall be my knight in shining armor. With his powerful sword and gentle embrace, he slew that fierce black cloud beast.

I was free! Free to be me to the fullest. It made such an incredible difference in every part of my life. My overall outlook was more upbeat. The spontaneity of my humor and expressions was unlocked, as well. No longer a repulsive worm imprisoned in a cocoon—I was flying, flying! Gliding freely, my wings spread wide in the warm sunshine. No wonder I still was in the "honeymoon stage" after almost twenty five years of married life.

For most of my life, I had two lingering dreams—going to a tropical island and swimming with dolphins, and these were grandiose wishes for sure. Perhaps, I had mentioned to Marv once or twice my deep desire to experience a tropical island. However, those big hopes grew more insignificant in the midst of the enjoyment and romance of my marriage.

Relaxing together on our loveseat one evening, we were recounting the blessings of our day and week. I was so pleased to hear Marv say, "Honey, you know this coming May Day will be our twenty-fifth? Sure would like to do something special for it, but I don't think we'll be able to afford much."

"Oh, my goodness, you're right. That's not very far away, either."

I was surprised he would even remember, much less want to celebrate it. *Imagine, just six short months and it will be our silver anniversary. That really is something worth celebrating.*

I knew Marv was right. We had struggled financially all our married life. But, still, I drooled with the thought of going somewhere extra-special. My mind began to lapse into a paradise setting. Soft warm sand massaged my bare feet while warm gentle breezes blew a hint of coolness to the soothing rhythm of crashing waves.

Then the timer rang and my daydream was snatched. It was back to disappointing reality. I had to get my clothes out of the dryer. My daydream was disrupted, but the importance of the upcoming May Day lingered on. I was determined to find some way to celebrate our anniversary with a flare.

I couldn't sit around wishing any longer. It was a call to action. I began my search by talking to the most reputable travel agent.

Oh, Father, I know you're aware of my thoughts and all my hopes. You have blessed, blessed me with such a wonderful husband and marriage. I'm thankful for all your generous gifts. But, if it's not being too greedy, we'd sure love to be able to do something extra special for our anniversary. Please help me get something together that's extra special and within our budget. Amen.

A week went by, and I was still in the pondering pool with nothing more innovative than a live concert or theater show. Either of those would have constituted a special outing since they were considered extravagant and not within our means. But somehow, that didn't settle with me—it was just too commonplace.

A few days later, I answered the phone. On the other end was a fast talking stranger. She was trying my patience and wasting my time until I heard that magic phrase, "special deal on a vacation get-away." Instantly, both ears switched to the same wavelength of that "vacation channel" with intent concentration. Even with the straining of my ears, it was hard to believe what I heard! They were offering me a trip to Florida, five days and four nights at an upscale hotel on the beach.

The price was lower than reasonable, so I said yes. Despite my ecstasy, I managed to keep it a secret. First of all, the financial details had to be fine tuned. I knew Marv's response would be "and how are we going to pay for it?"

"Oh, Daddy!" I exclaimed with the squeal and jump of a youngster at Christmas, "You've done it again! Almighty God, I don't know why you love this microscopic spot in your vast universe, but I'm so, so glad you do! What a great answer to my prayer. Thank you! Thank you!" This spontaneous outburst came the moment I discovered that the amount of our renter's refund covered the whole cost of that vacation package with a dollar to spare.

I still had five months to save for the plane fare and meals. That would be a challenge, but it was going to happen somehow. At best, it would be tight with barely enough money for eating out much less renting a car or taking in the sights. But, that was okay with me.

Just relaxing together on the Atlantic Coast with its warm water and sunshine would be plenty special. I knew my Father in Heaven was working behind the scenes, but little did I know how very busy He was. That was exciting, but just the beginning of an avalanche of miracles.

If a jump and a squeal of joy signified that first blessed phone call, the ensuing months created one bouncing kangaroo on a pogo stick. I could scarcely believe all that was happening! Within just a few days, another phone call dazzled my ears. This time, the fast talking vacation specialist didn't try my patience at all. They were offering us a two-day cruise to the Bahamas as a bonus to our Florida package.

The avalanche gained in momentum. Our name must have been on the vacation hit list. The next phone call came in with another irresistible package deal. They offered us one full week in a condo right on the white sands of the Florida gulf. That took my breath away for sure. But, I almost passed out when hit with the next miracle just around the corner. It happened in the middle of a casual conversation with my brother as I filled him in on the latest happenings. I told him how excited I was since Marv and I had never done anything lavish like this before.

"I know," Steve said, "but, there's another thing you should consider. You'll be really close to Disney World. You should go there. Fran and I sure enjoyed it."

"That sounds good, but it's way, way out of our price range. As it is, we'll be scraping the bottom of the barrel to afford this much."

"You know, this is a trip of a lifetime. The family business will pay for time at Disney World if you want to do it. Just talk it over with Marv and let me know."

Well, I couldn't keep all of this a secret any longer. It was time to tell my sweetheart. Marv was so surprised and appreciated my diligence in putting it all together. With my explanation of each new miracle, Marv's eyes and excitement grew bigger. And before long, there were two kangaroos pogo sticking right in the middle of our living room that night.

On April 28, 2007, Marv and I were flying much higher than the plane, itself. I had lost track of how many miracles were in our blessing avalanche, but another was already waiting at our layover in Houston, Texas.

Our dear daughter, Shelly, had moved to San Antonio, Texas. That left a real empty spot in our lives for sure. Nevertheless, we sent her with our blessings because we knew that move would be best for her. She was living there with her birth mother, her Aunt Nancy and their service dog, Didi Boo.

Here again, God's promise of working out all things for good kicked into gear. About a year previously, Shelly's mother flew into Portland to help her daughter move. During Sky's short overnight stay in our home, we bonded with her like Super Glue and twice as fast. Marv and I ended up not losing a daughter but gaining a sister. Our family was growing in the most delightful way.

Our flight itinerary included a three hour layover in Houston, Texas. When I informed Shelly of this, there was nothing stopping that foursome from making an eight hour road trip. Marv and I had just embarked on an exciting tropical trip, but all we could think about was our airport layover.

What a greeting we received—bear hugs and kisses, bear hugs and kisses with streaming tears of joy! That Houston dinner satisfied so much more than growling stomachs. Our hearts were bursting with happiness to see how well Shelly and her mother, Sky, were doing. That would have been more than abundance, but God's gifts just kept flowing. It was such a treat to hug Nancy, too, who until then was just a friendly voice on the other end of the phone line. We also got to meet little Didi Boo, Sky's service dog, trained to predict her epileptic seizures before they began.

What at first sounded like a long gap between planes ended up being what seemed like the quickest three hour layover on record. And, we stretched it to the maximum, too, almost too far, in fact. Marv and I had to jaunt to the loading gate. We were sweating it all the way, but did make our flight.

"Fasten your seatbelts and prepare for landing," the flight attendant announced. "We are approaching the Fort Lauderdale Airport."

And, prepared we were. Marv took hold of my hand with a long warm squeeze. We were ready—ready to celebrate big time!

Off the plane and into the airport we went. It was quite a lengthy process. What a good feeling—we were in the comfortable air-conditioned rental car with all the heavy bags off our shoulders and in the trunk. As Marv started the car, a giant beam spread across my face. Everything was going according to plan, and boy, did I ever spend hours juggling and planning to get all this together. We were off to the Ramada Hotel.

"Honey, we're in Florida!" Marv announced with a burst of enthusiasm in his voice as he punched the gas and sped onto the busy boulevard. "Man, it's warm, and there are lots of palm trees."

We no more got parked in the hotel's lot and out of our car when the familiar fun-packed words caught my attention, "Oh, Honey, you've got to see this!"

Over the curb and across the bark dust we went. Marv guided me to the cutest little palm tree. Standing a mere four feet high, it was just right for me to get hands on. He pointed out the interesting features and gave my fingertips a chance to take in the details. What perfect timing that was. It had been fifty years since I'd seen a palm tree. That meant my recollection of what a palm tree looked like was vague at best. Right at the beginning of our tropical celebration, his thoughtful ways refreshed my mental picture and gave life to all the scenic beauty surrounding us. That meant so much to me.

That first night in our luxurious hotel was a pleasant one. However, on awakening the next morning, the first downer hit full force. One small detail that Madam Planner had overlooked was that we had to take a tour of their vacation timeshare. This was the way I got such a good price on our trip. Oh well, at the time of planning, I considered it a small price to pay.

But, once at the Hotel, the price of that tour had grown larger. The only time that we could take that tour was the day I had planned to swim with the dolphins. But we had to take that disgusting tour to get the voucher for our Bahaman cruise. This new development was not in my plans. It dealt a heavy blow of disappointment to my heart and enthusiasm. I was so close to the dolphins, so close, but it wasn't going to happen.

I closed the bathroom door behind me and let the tears gush. I had to get it out of my system. I couldn't let that downer continue. The whole trip would be spoiled if I held onto this attitude. I dried my tears and tried to convince myself that it was no big deal. That was a good idea, but I couldn't get my brain and my heart to agree, no matter how hard I tried.

Marv, as usual, was factual about the whole thing, which meant it was no big deal to him. At that point, he knew nothing of my dolphin dream that had been tucked deep inside my heart since childhood. It was hotline time again.

Oh, Father, it's me again. You know all about my feelings and this big disappointment. It hurts so bad that I just can't get rid of it. Please help me get over this and have real happiness in my heart.

Miracles again! Once I turned my attitude upward, the whole picture changed. My heart smiled when I thought about all the dolphins my Father has in heaven waiting for me. It was then that I knew I could enjoy our vacation thoroughly even without the dolphins. After all, the cruise was just a day away, and that's where we would be on May first. Now, that was something to be excited about!

It was the next morning and the time to board the Imperial Princess had come quickly. Settling into our tiny cabin, we were treated like royalty. On the end of our bed, a unique gift awaited us. Two towels were twisted together and cleverly shaped into a swan. For me, this special greeter was better than any expensive Rembrandt hanging on the wall. Marv was impressed, too, and got a real kick out of surprising me with it.

Our cruise was off to a great start. That is, until downer number two intruded our agenda. April 30th was a beautiful sunny day on the ocean, but not so sunny in our cabin. That morning, I awoke with the miserable symptoms of a sinus infection. This was no minor development. A sinus infection was not uncommon for me. But because of the hormones my body could not produce, if it was left untreated, it could put me in the hospital with bronchitis or pneumonia. And, of course, that was an event Madam Planner had not scheduled. There I was in the middle of the ocean with no treatment for it.

Oh great! What a time to get sick! It would have to happen now, right at the beginning of our vacation.

Fortunately, I wasn't sick enough yet to feel miserable, just wiped out. Ever since the brain surgery, I'd been faced with less than average stamina. Even though I knew this fact, my 200 percent inner drive refused to acknowledge it. As a result, I was quite accustomed to the experience of feeling wiped out. At times like that, it was mind over matter. I would tell myself, "Of course, you're tired. But that's no excuse. Just don't think about it and keep going."

So, that's what I did. For sure, things were not as enjoyable as they could have been. But, I chose to focus on the good that remained. One good thing was that we were there to relax, so relax we did. What a blast it was, just touring the boat, relaxing and taking it all in.

It seemed as though we had just started touring when the words "all ashore" came over the loudspeaker.

Hand in hand, we stepped off the boat and into Nassau, capital of the Bahamas. My feet were on an island, a genuine tropical island! This bustling tourist trap certainly did not match my "monkeys and palm trees" picture. But, that didn't upset me in the least. I was too busy to dwell on it.

No time to tarry—we were off to explore Nassau. It surprised me to see the strong American influence. Some of the first businesses Marv spotted were Burger King, McDonald's and Subway. I, of course, was chomping at the bit to know everything that was there.

Marv was his wonderful self and began to describe in detail everything around us. One large building took up the whole block with several shops in it.

As he was explaining, my ears absorbed every syllable. And at the same time, my sensory scanners were on supercharge. In between Marv's scenic narration, my ears stared at the by-passers. Street venders were everywhere. "Beach towels," one young man yelled. "Get a beautiful beach towel right here." Just a few steps later and a strange item brushed against my bare arm. High above my right shoulder a rather gruff, much older voice asked, "Would you like to buy a necklace or bracelet?"

"No thanks," I answered, and as quickly as she appeared, she vanished into the crowds.

Turning the corner, we headed toward the center of town, one short block. The Tortuga Rum Cake Shop was in sight and most definitely in smelling range. This small store was crammed full of shoppers, cakes, samples and busy bakers. Its small, crowded quarters enabled me to experience the kitchen atmosphere all the better. I could hear the bakers stirring and clanging in the kitchen just a few feet away. What a sensation trip that was for me—oh, the aroma, sounds and tastes!

The gift shops were not as numerous as I expected. Although sparse in number, each shop was a self-contained miniature traffic jam almost overloaded with merchandise. Tactile tantalizers were everywhere and literally right at my fingertips. We took time to browse thoroughly. As we started to make our exit, Marv pointed out another fun piece of the local sights.

"Honey, look. You'll like this."

Before he could even get one more word out, the little girl in me jumped with jubilance and excitement. With a gentle touch, he guided my hand forward and said, "Each tile has a raised flower in the center. It's interesting how different their colors are here, mainly pastels with bright orange and yellow."

"Oh, my! I do feel the flowers. Neat! That's my kind of decoration."

Good thing there was a time limit. That kept us from spending too much. We had chosen to go to the Breezes Super Club as our afternoon activity. With prize in hand, we dashed to catch our shuttle to the club. It was both a shuttle and tour bus. The phrase "scenic tour" was not something I liked to hear. More often than not, it meant a long, boring ride for Pam. That was not the case on this bus. The driver was very entertaining and informative.

About ten minutes later, the bus pulled up to the entrance of that mammoth resort. What a classy place it was. The indoor amenities couldn't hold us very long. Warm sunshine and ocean waters were calling. We headed outdoors and down the marble steps.

We walked beyond the resort and headed toward the ocean in search of the soft white sands. At the edge of the resort's property, we finally reached the beach. Marv announced the upcoming sand with an interesting comment. "What do you mean, white sand? This ain't white. It's a light tan!" With my first step off the cement, my bare feet said it wasn't soft, either. The coarse sand was almost prickly for such a tenderfoot. Marv, again, brought the seashore into MY view. He explained that much of the sand was made up of crushed shells. As we walked, I listened intently for the crashing waves.

"Are we very far from the surf?"

"Only five miles away," Marv teased. "I mean about five feet in front of your toes."

"You're kidding! Where are the waves?"

"Here comes one right now. Could you hear it?"

"That sounds more like a ripple on a lake."

It was so different from our Pacific Ocean. It didn't crash or foam at all. The cool ocean breezes were not there, either. Instead, warm sauna puffs lazed by whenever they wished, which wasn't very often. There certainly was a world of difference in the water's temperature. Eighty degree water was a shock to our toes, but not a chilling one. We both sighed with delightful satisfaction as we stood waist deep in the gentle warm waves.

Then Marv's loving ways began adding detailed brush strokes of beauty to my picture as he described how the water looked. "I can see all the way to the bottom for miles. You know your solid turquoise T shirt? It would resemble that with lighter bleach spots here and there."

"Oh, Babe!" I exclaimed, "what a picturesque way to describe it. Thanks a bunch!"

There we stood chest deep in the tropical sea hugging and rejoicing.

Tropical, pleasant and romantic was our short Bahaman excursion. The time went faster than flying, and already May second had arrived. It was all aboard the cruise ship. The enjoyable environment and smooth sailing made the trip super short. The cruise would be ending in just a few minutes, but that didn't sadden us at all. We, instead, were eagerly anticipating the next part of our adventure, Disney World. At the same time, quietly tucked beneath all that enthusiasm was the nagging concern about my declining health and probable sinus infection.

I had been begging God to keep me from getting really sick and ruining our trip. However, the increased aching between my eyes with the all over "not so good" feeling told me things were not getting better. As soon as we hit land, I was on the phone to my doctor. I figured it would be a simple request to have him call a prescription into the nearby Walgreen's pharmacy. But, he said he could not do that. With a disheartened thud, my cell phone dropped to the floor of the car as I slumped down in the front seat.

Now what! Oh, Father, please give me wisdom. You know how bad I need that prescription.

No sooner had I finished praying when I had an idea. Maybe my doctor could call it into my regular pharmacy and they could transfer it. It took considerable time on the phone for sure, but it worked. God express delivered that prescription. As we pulled up to the drivethrough at Walgreen's, another blessing popped out that window and lit right in our laps. The antibiotics cost less than twenty five dollars—unbelievable! I was amazed and relieved all in the same second. I had expected we'd be spending a good chunk of our food money to get my medication.

We did, however, spend a good chunk of that day in Fort Lauderdale which delayed our trip to Orlando. Nevertheless, we dauntless travelers pressed on.

CHAPTER 32
PLEASURE ISLAND

The long wait in Fort Lauderdale for my medication put a big crunch in our schedule. We had planned and hoped to get to Orlando much earlier, but that was far from reality. Nevertheless, we worked hard at keeping our chins up. Finally, the prescription bottle was in my hand. By that time, we had resigned ourselves to the idea that arriving at the hotel in time for a good night's sleep was not so bad after all.

Well, another good plan, but that was not how things went. We had no real difficulty getting into Orlando, but in the pitch blackness, the Ramada Hotel was more than illusive. Marv's map did not show enough details to help us see the lay of the land. Despite that, he charted our course with diligence. He even checked with the local yokels for landmarks. Like brave pioneers, we proceeded with confidence and optimism. Little did we know that there were repeats of the same restaurants, two Hyatt Hotels and several Ramada Hotels along that same strip.

An hour had passed with two unsuccessful attempts to find it. By that time, our supply of patience was drained way below the empty mark. Like two ravenous raccoons squabbling over one crust of bread, we snarled at each other and everything else. After three long hours of wandering in that asphalt wilderness, we pulled into the hotel. At one o'clock in the morning, we collapsed in our room, physically and emotionally exhausted.

On arising the next morning, we were still haunted by the last night's ordeal. Thank goodness, one thing we did remember to pack was our grumble eraser. Instead of continuing to dwell on all the bad stuff, we held hands and prayed. As we turned our hearts and views upward, the gloomy residue began lifting. We were recharged and ready for Disney World. Well, I should say, I was recharged as much as possible. The antibiotics had not kicked in quite yet, so I was still very weak. We had already purchased our all day passes for Disney World, so feeling well or not, I was going.

When I informed Marv how weak I still was, his loving response uplifted my spirits thirty fold.

"You know what we could do. We could rent a wheelchair. That way you could still get around everywhere and save your strength for enjoying the sights. What do you think about that?"

I was thrilled and flabbergasted all at the same time.

"That would work! But, Babe, are you sure that won't be too taxing on you?"

He assured me that he would let me know if it got to be too much. With that confirming statement, it was off to Disney World.

My brother was right. Disney World was fabulous and definitely worth visiting. We had two days to spend there. The Epcot Theme Park was our first choice. So day one, we headed there. Marv's thoughtful idea worked! Riding in a wheelchair was just the ticket and what a relief, too. By not walking, I had enough energy left to feel halfway decent despite the sinus infection. I was able to really enjoy all the interesting sights and sensations.

Marv's four years of military service in England drew us straight to the United Kingdom area. Touring Little England was delightful despite that obstinate wheelchair. The darn thing refused to stay a straight course. At least, that was Marv's rationale for swerving off the main path so often. Those kinds of detours, of course, were tailor-made for me. And, boy, did they ever tickle my fancy.

My curiosity prompted me to ask him what made the buildings look English. Before he could even get a word out, that crazy wheelchair cut a donut and came to a screeching halt with my toes against a very solid something.

"Reach out and feel the shakes on this building. They're just bare wood that's gray from age. The roof is very English, too. It's thatched, just like I remember. Hold on. I think I can get you close enough to touch some thatching."

"Oooh, that's neat! Thanks so much! Now I can see England."

Lunch at the English pub was next on our list. As Marv rested his heels, our jaws went to work double time. Nothing would do but an authentic English beer and meal. With his charming Cockney accent, he stunned the waitress and ordered a tall bitters and a platter of Bangers and mash. Along with the delicious food came a generous helping of hospitality from the young waitress. I've always loved listening to people with an English accent. Her enchanting accent and pleasant personality turned my simple Fish & Chips into a seven course prime rib platter. Having our physical batteries recharged and our tummies smiling, we were off to another country.

My four years of French in high school had given me a real love for the language and an intrigue into their culture. That, like a magnet, drew us to Little France. Marv blazed a trail right toward the first store in France, a fragrance shop.

"Oh, Honey, do you suppose they'd say something in French for us?"

"That sounds very reasonable. We'll ask them."

Hot wheeling it through the boutique's front door, he ushered me right up to the counter. The delightful young clerk behind the glass display case greeted us cordially. She was so much fun to visit with. To make things even better, Marv and I were her only customers. She had come from her home in Paris just one month previously. What a treat to hear her eloquent French and have a chance to speak French, myself. The real exhilarating moment came with her comment about my French. She stated that I spoke it so much better than most four-year French students right out of high school.

Then, Marv added a giant "a la mode" that topped off this French treat. He bought a bottle of French perfume for me. I'd never ever imagined spending so much for a little bottle of fragrance, but this time it was worth every penny spent. Floating out of that shop on cloud 99, we found a bench and sat together.

"Wow, my love, what a superb day!" I sighed with contentment as I rested my head on his shoulder. Marv reached out to hold my hand in tender agreement, "You know, it's almost as though we'd traveled abroad, don't you think?"

Snuggling a little closer, I looked into his eyes and answered with a purr of pure satisfaction.

"Oh yes, and what a perfect ending to this perfect day. Here we sit with our hearts entwined as we savor this gorgeous setting. The air is so warm, what a balmy evening."

The sweltering heat hit early in the day and accentuated my weakness and sick feeling. We had chosen three theme parks as our favorites. Blizzard Beach with its white water rafting, inner-tubing downstream and wave pool was a real hit and most refreshing. The rest of the day was spent in roasting misery with shattered plans. As my strength dwindled, my level of anger rose.

By the end of the day, I was about to go ballistic and fire all kinds of negativity at Marv. Fortunately, that is not how our Disney World experience ended. There I sat grumbling to myself with my angry ammunition ready. The moment Marv returned, I was prepared to let him have it with both barrels. My pity party was interrupted with the soft words, "Honey, reach out."

Into my hands, he placed a frilly something. This one I couldn't figure out. With an undertone of disgust, I asked, "Okay, what is it?"

As I heard his description, I melted into a pool of humility and guilt.

"It's a bridal veil with pink sequined Minnie Mouse ears. It's a crown for my queen. I thought it would be a nice crowning touch for our twenty-fifth wedding anniversary. Hope you like it."

At that moment, I made the conscious choice to remember this afternoon not as discomfort and disappointments, but as my new crown of glory. With that resolve, I thanked God for the day. Turning my eyes to the Lord always helped me "see" things in a much better light.

The next morning, the detective in me awoke first. Lying in bed, restless and impatient, I listened for Marv to awaken. I couldn't stay in bed a second longer. Marv's alarm that morning was not a clock at all. He awoke to the noise of the telephone and Madam Detective on the case. Clunk went the receiver as I bounced with a loud squeal.

"Honey, are you awake? Guess what! I found some dolphins!"

With a yawning stretch, he said, "Oh, really?"

"Yes, yes, there's a place right here in Orlando. I called them, and it sounds like the very thing I've been looking for."

With an air of anticipation and excitement, it was pedal to the metal again. Breakfast was gulped down, luggage tossed in the trunk, and we were off to Discovery Cove.

Stepping into their cove was like spending the day on a tropical island.

Hand in hand, with bare feet in the soft warm sand, we were off to explore. First came the aviary with the friendliest birds. This gorgeous setting was filled with plush tropical foliage and ear dazzling waterfalls. The pleasant staff no sooner welcomed us when not just one, but two, birds lit on my head.

Trying my best to stand still while giggling with glee, I absorbed every pleasant detail of my best hat ever. I could feel each bird moving in my hair and hear their unique chatter. As one flew away, its wing brushed against my cheek with a wonderful good-bye wave. Marv took my hand and began walking with slow deliberate steps. That was my clue something special was coming.

"Feel this. What do you think it is?"

"The silky tassel of that elephant grass?"

Just then that silky fluff moved, and I backed away with a start.

"Honey, your blooming tassel just turned into the tail of a live peacock."

The plush tropical greenery was everywhere. It presented me with so many different textures and shapes for my enjoyment, and enjoy I did. My sweetheart was right there marveling and taking it all in right along with me. We kept one eye on the clock to make sure we didn't miss our next attraction, their stingray pool.

Oh, good, I get to go wading and cool off.

One of the Cove's staff assistants was in the pool. She was very gracious and assisted me in getting right up to the stingrays. They had such a unique feel, much like wet satin. That thing was so big that when I tried to check out its size, I couldn't even get my outstretched arms from one end to the other. Turning to the staff assistant, I asked how big they were. She said they range five to eight feet in length. I was shocked. My mental picture was in for a brand new view. I thought they were but twelve inches long or at the best, eighteen.

After the stingray pool, Marv took me to the gift shop and handed me a life-like miniature figurine of a stingray. How ideal—it was as though Marv just handed me a snapshot of that unique creature. Until that figurine, I had no realistic picture of what had been in the pool with me.

"Oh, Honey," Marv interrupted my browsing, "it's almost dolphin time. We'd better head for the dolphin swim."

Being my non-bashful self, I marched right up to the dolphin trainer. Introducing myself, I let him know about my visual impairment and desire to have as much contact with the dolphin as possible.

Phil was an excellent trainer and very much a people person, too. He made sure I experienced everything to the fullest. Along the water's edge, we lined up in groups of eight. There were four groups, each entertained by their own dolphin. Natasha was our dolphin, and she was perfect for the job. This nine-and-a-half-foot long, 530 pound mammal was no small catch, but catch her, I did!

As an ice breaker, Natasha swam slowly in front of each person. Phil coached us on stroking and petting her. Then that genuine clown gave each of us a kiss. One by one, we went with Phil out into the twelve foot water. Phil had me put my hand on his shoulder and follow right behind him. The wet suit vests let each person comfortably tread in the water while awaiting their turn. With excited anticipation, my ears worked overtime trying to take it all in. I strained to hear Phil's every word of instruction and the surrounding splashes of the next dolphin rider.

"Pam, are you ready?" Phil asked with a chuckle, knowing that I was much more than ready. He instructed me to lock one hand around her dorsal fin and the other hand on her side fin. With a quiet hand gesture from Phil, we were off. Zoom—1, 2, 3 and my feet touched the shore.

"Wow! What an awesome ride!" With my arm wrapped around her, I hugged her tightly to my side. Boy, did I ever get the treat of a lifetime! I got to feel her graceful movements and experience her speed and sheer power. There was just one drawback. That ride was way too short. Phil came up beside me and asked, "You'd like to take her home, wouldn't you?"

With a twinge of embarrassment, I giggled, "You bet I would, but she'd never fit in my bathtub."

It's a good thing another group was advancing for their swim. Otherwise, I probably would have invited myself to spend the night with Natasha. That was one of the shortest days in history—at least in my life's history.

Fortunately for us, more fun and adventure lay ahead. We were off to the gulf side of West Florida. Our next stop was Clearwater. If our little rental car could have run on the adrenalin energy of the copilot, we'd have reached the white sands faster than a lightning bolt. To my surprise, the drive took no time at all as we recaptured the many exciting "firsts" of our Discovery Cove day.

Florida's white sands had a special appeal to both of us. Several times throughout our marriage, Marv had mentioned that he would love some day to take me to see those soft white sands. And, that some day was about to happen. Our journey was sweet and smooth. Soon we were settled in our cozy condo. No chance to get cabin fever that day—we had no sooner unpacked when the urge to explore overtook both of us. In the true spirit of adventure, we began our week. It was most enjoyable just relaxing, dining out and browsing through the gift shops. But, as usual, certain moments were most memorable.

One of those was our day of sailing. It thrilled me so that Marv got a chance to do one of his favorite things. Sailing was a real love of his. He had often mentioned how much fun it would be to sail out to an island. We rented a Hobby Cat and sailed in Clearwater Bay. Sailing a Hobby Cat was a brand-new experience for us both. Marv was impressed with how well it handled.

While Captain Marv was sailing with true exhilaration, I was a lady of leisure basking in the sun. In the middle of the trampoline like mesh floor was a wide slit. How perfect for me—I could reach through it to the water. Feeling the force of the water rushing against my hand gave me an excellent sense of our speed. I felt like I was surfing the wave tops.

We hadn't been sailing very long when he spotted a nearby island. And, there was no stopping the Hobby Cat from heading straight to it. We were just cruising along when the boat halted with an abrupt thump against something very solid. Being unaware that there was an island, I gasped with panic.

Oh, no! What was that! Dear Lord, hold onto us tight, please, I pleaded.

"In the middle of an island, in the middle of an ocean, just the monkeys and the palm trees in a paradise for two," Marv sang in a loud voice of victory.

I jumped up with a squeal of glee while wondering whether to thank him for a special treat or scold him for scaring the wits out of me. I went with the first choice and was glad I did. We strolled hand in hand on that small island, laughing and soaking in the sights and sounds.

Retiring to bed came earlier than usual that night. We wanted to get a jump start on the next day. With a close watch on the weather forecasts, we decided that the sixth day of our week in Clearwater looked like the best time for beachcombing. Up to this point, we had not seen any trace of the long-awaited white sands. When making our reservations, I thought the condo was right on the white sandy beach. However, that whole stretch of beach had just been restored. About six months earlier, the Coast Guard had pumped tons of sand from the ocean floor onto this coastal stretch. It was more like the Oregon

Coast's tan grit. That didn't dishearten us since the landlord told us the traditional stuff was just a few miles north. The coming day was our day for that.

Snuggling in for the night, I could hardly wait for the sunny blaze of "good morning."

About half an hour before the alarm was due to ring, I was wide eyed and counting the seconds. I tried to lie still and not disturb Marv. The harder I tried, the more I wiggled. My elbow just happened to jab him in the ribs.

Yea, he's awake!

Rubbing the sleep from his eyes, he yawned his way to the bedroom window for a check on the weather.

"Oh my gosh! What's going on?" Marv exclaimed as he raced to the front door.

He cracked it open, and the smoky stench almost gagged us.

"Marv, that's awful! Let's turn the news on. Maybe we can find out what's happening."

The news was not good for sure. Major forest fires north of Clearwater were raging out of control. The whole area was blanketed with thick smoke. Another huge downer was right in our faces. It seemed even more depressing and blacker than the smoke. We were getting aced out of our main goal for going clear across the States—walking barefoot in the warm white sand.

"Well, that ruins our beach combing," Marv grumbled with disgust as he shut the car door. "It looks like our last day here is going to be a total washout. It would have to happen on the one day we wanted to be out on the beach."

"You're right. This is a real bummer. That smoke is so bad we can't do anything outdoors. Let's find some shops or interesting places to browse around."

Resigned to this new plan, we decided to explore the local gift shops. That turned out to be a special event for both of us. Marv became both an explorer and hunter as he scanned the aisles for a dolphin figure resembling Natasha. This was no easy quest, but it was a fun one. Although there were many dolphin figurines to choose from, most of them were hard to distinguish with my twenty-twenty fingertips. The dolphins were surrounded by too much confusing clutter. I couldn't figure out which glob was what, much less distinguish a dolphin in the conglomeration. With patience and a heart of love for me, Marv hunted on. Just like a great white hunter, he stalked up and down the aisles with eyes sharply peeled for any hint of the prize catch.

The first shop was interesting but presented no prize catch. That was okay. We dauntless hunters were off to find another hunting ground. And, we were in luck! There was just such a place right next door. This shop was perfect for us, almost too perfect. There were so many nifty souvenirs that we had a hard time choosing which to buy.

Marv diligently searched for the dolphin. And, voila! He found one that looked like Natasha and that my fingers could clearly see. Delighted with this trophy, we stepped down the aisle. Within just a few paces, Marv found a second prize. Again, we had almost too many choices. Perusing through the unique picture frames, we found just the perfect one. It had delightful touchables surrounding the glass pane. The flat base was covered with white sand. To one side was a pair of wooden flip-flops and a lawn chair. A wooden palm tree stood tall on the opposite side.

That did it! We exited the gift shop with two trophies. It was a good morning after all. By the time we had finished a leisurely lunch, the air had cleared considerably. We were off to the beach.

A short drive took us to a lovely beach access. As we stepped out of the car, a Pollyanna thought whispered in my brain.

"You know, Babe, there is a good thing about the forest fire smoke," I said. "We don't have to battle the crowds or drive round and round just to find a parking spot."

"You're right about that one, for sure. The place looks pretty deserted."

Arm in arm, we strolled down the path. One step off the asphalt and Marv announced, "No sandals permitted beyond this point."

He didn't have to say that twice. In an instant, both sets of feet were bare and sandals stowed in the backpack. We were off to the surf.

Well, that was the plan. But, I couldn't walk much farther without a close inspection of the white stuff underfoot. Marv's description of it was right on, it closely resembled salt. Thoroughly intrigued with its unique soft beauty, out came the beach blanket. We were down for the count, or more truthfully, the feel of super soft sand. Oh how I loved to let it sift through my fingers and massage my busy sand-digger toes.

That afternoon was superb as we walked hand in hand and waded in the waves. With the onset of twilight and our backs to the ocean, we walked to the asphalt edge. Marv set the backpack on the ground and wrapped his loving arms around me. We beamed from ear to ear as we thought about another dream come true. It had been fifty years since Marv spent childhood days on these beaches. In the middle of that romantic embrace, I knew why he had so longed to return and show it to me.

We wholeheartedly agreed that our twenty-fifth wedding anniversary celebration was a victorious tribute. Even the unpleasant smoke had its good point. That made it much easier to leave this wonderful beach land. As we packed our bags, sadness wrapped itself around my heart chords.

Sure wish this didn't have to end! Well, guess it's true—all good things must come to an end.

As I contemplated that fact, I tried reasoning with myself. I began counting all the blessings I had waiting for me at home, like my family, the Christian bookstore I had started online and so on.

Yes, I do have wonderful things back home, but still wish I didn't have to leave this warm climate and the warm ocean waters.

Battling the glum syndrome, I continued packing our luggage. I was just about to shut the lid when I scolded myself.

Wait just a minute here. Good things do come to an end here on earth, but not in heaven. Heaven's paradise is thousands of times better than this place and it will never end.

With a giant beam on my face and a bounce in my step, I now sang as I packed.

Knowing the truth that each day spent on earth is just one step closer to heaven kept my heart a-singing all the way home.

CHAPTER 33
AGAINST ALL ODDS

It was time to settle back into everyday life at home. That, of course, meant unpacking our baggage, and there was a lot of it. I left the small suitcase of souvenirs until last. My choice would have been to delve into the souvenirs first, but I wanted to save them until I knew I would not have to rush through it. As I emptied the other suitcases, one at a time, anticipation of the coming treasures spurred me on.

At last, everything was unpacked and put away except for that small suitcase. Opening the lid, my fingers gingerly surveyed the cram-jammed contents. From the back corner, I retrieved a small paper wrapped bundle.

Ah, my dark blue earrings from Dolphin Cove. I can remember so well how carefully Marv searched for just the right color, shape and length. And, they're even highlighted with shimmering silver. How elegant!

That was just the beginning of a true treasure chest. As I unwrapped each thing, my countenance brightened a little more. That trip was a fantastic salute to our twenty-five years together. I sat reflecting on all the love, laughter and enjoyment of life represented by that celebration. At the same time, there was a slight letdown undertone in the aftermath of our trip. It would have been easy to slip into dolphin withdrawals as I thought of all that warm water, sunshine and fun, fun, fun.

Instead of sinking into the doldrums and focusing on all the fun that was gone forever, I chose a different route. I began to follow a pattern Marv and I have benefited from again and again. I began recalling God's goodness. His blessings didn't exist just during those exhilarating days of celebration. God's love in action has been and is the strong energizing force in our lives.

We recall special memories and remind each other of all the enjoyment in our past. Those memories are like a deep well that never runs dry. We frequent it for sips that refresh both the attitude and soul.

One key we've found is staying young at heart. Laughter has proven to be good medicine for the attitude and a very effective anti-aging formula, as well. The sad fact is many adults close the door on this, calling it too childish or immature.

I love how Marv teases in such a positive way. He's become an expert at hyperbole and puns. Just reflecting on his positive comments helps me get my focus back where it belongs. One comment that always perks me up happened many years ago. Marv, Mom and I had just finished running a lengthy series of errands. On the way home, Mom thanked me for doing all the planning and directing. At that point, I turned and said, "Well, since I can't jog or run marathons, I can at least help in this small way."

Next, the driver took the floor. "Oh, Honey, that's no problem. You may not run marathons, but you sure do run brain-a-thons."

I never get tired of that playback. What a morale booster it is and with each recollection, revs up my self-worth. Laughter and teasing are most effective in lessening stress. The reality is that our world is full of sad, negative, stressful stuff. That garbage is dumped on us in overload proportions. It bombards us all the time from every direction. To ignore it leaves the door wide open—open to an avalanche that can end up burying the wholesome "good" life. If left unchecked, this ongoing input can dampen our spirits and accentuate the problems.

A very effective way to counteract negativity is to focus on the positive. Another smile maker came from a short conversation one morning. I greeted Marv with a big smile and informed him that I had just finished writing another chapter in my book.

He responded, "Oh neat—you're screaming right along."

My normal feeling of being a low production gal had tainted my attitude. And, of course, that came out full force in my response.

"Yeah, screaming right along at a snail's pace."

"Well, Honey, as long as you have red flames painted on your snail shell, you're screaming."

"Oh, Babe, how perfect," I squealed with a jump of enthusiasm. In less than a split second, my emotions were elevated from Gloomsville to genuine joy.

Concentrating on and remembering the funny things helps defray the negative stream. One of those fun-filled moments happened at the beauty salon. I have been blessed with a wonderful beautician. She is excellent at her work and a neat friend who adds more good stuff to my life. One afternoon, I sat waiting for my turn to get a permanent. Not wanting to waste time, I pulled out my Braille & Speak. This small word processor had no screen, just a Braille keyboard and speech output. I sat engrossed writing my presentation for the upcoming ladies retreat. Thoroughly preoccupied in this, I tuned out everything around me. I had just finished drafting my introduction and turned the speech on to hear what I had written.

The speech sounds very computerized, much like a Star Wars robot. With both ears staring intently at my manuscript, the beautician called out, "Hey, you, this is America. You need to speak English." At first, I thought she was talking to another customer. Then she said, "Pam, sounds like you brought an alien in here."

The whole salon full of customers roared with laughter. That created another pleasant memory to brighten my days.

Hunting for the good things seems to be a lost sport today. Practicing the Pollyanna mentality has helped me develop a habit of hunting for the good in everything. God is the creator of every good thing in the universe. In everyday life, we are surrounded by myriads of good things. Yet, they often go by without notice and are tagged as common insignificant stuff. Enjoyment of the surrounding good things is heightened as I recognize that my Father in Heaven made them for me to enjoy.

What a definite difference He makes in the life of one solitary, insignificant person. The absolute truth is—I am enjoying life to the hilt. But, how can that be?

According to the world's standards, I should be one of the most miserable people alive. In no way do I come close to meeting society's mandate for being successful or happy. To meet that standard, I'd have to be wealthy, popular, beautiful or a high-speed producer. The fact is—I score a strong F minus in every area. Living just above the low-income level certainly doesn't put me in the bracket of being wealthy. Being blind automatically places me on the bottom of society's popular list.

Attractive? The only thin thing about me is my white cane. Thanks to cortisone, I am alive—but never to be thin again. And fast? Fat chance of that! This report card does not look so good. The truth remains that I still struggle with the handicaps of being blind and physically challenged with just fifty percent of normal stamina. What a balancing act that poses—so little energy and 200 percent inner drive. Despite all these odds stacked against me, my enjoyment of life scores a wholesome double A plus.

I can see the bigger picture. I know that true paradise is waiting for me. It will be thousands of times better than the most beautiful spot on earth. And I can hardly wait to see how many dolphins are up there ready for me to ride. That saying, "All good things must come to an end" is not true in heaven—it will last forever. What a hope, what a perfect future to look forward to.

That is how I can cope and handle today so much better. How about you? Do you have a clear view of the real picture? It doesn't take twenty-twenty vision, eye glasses or lots of carrots. Our trials and failures can become just steppingstones to victory when we have our eyes on Jesus. As for me, I know I am "racing in the slow lane" on this earth. But, that is okay. I know where I'm going. And, it doesn't take lots of speed to get there.

As I'm inching along, I'm enjoying life to the hilt. How about you? Are you experiencing the kind of satisfaction that fills your heart with overflowing contentment?

God has that waiting for us and is reaching out to hand it to each one who asks Him for it.

A Note from the Author:

Today my friends remark how much they admire my ability to cope. Here is what I remember as I cope—and thrive.

Hard times are guaranteed.

True, they come, but they do not have to devastate us. Failures and difficulties are just steppingstones to success. Viewing them in that way makes going through hard times much easier.

Enjoy what you have now and not what you think you should have.

Keep watching for and enjoying all the good things. They are abundant and everywhere, just waiting to be discovered.

God is in control.

I know who is in control today and forever. Adding the assurance that He also has my best at heart gives me peace for today and tomorrow. God promises to work everything together for good for those who love Him. There was no way I could believe that when first blind, but today let me tell you, I KNOW—I KNOW IT'S TRUE!

Hold God's hand.

I have a constant, trustworthy partner to walk through life with. There is no need to fear being all alone nor lacking wisdom. It's no wonder I can step out with confidence and that people call me a "gutsy lady."

My future is secure and the very brightest—and yours can be, too.
Eternal life awaits. Time on earth is just a passage to eternity. Where we spend it is our choice. Accepting Christ as Savior guarantees never-ending paradise in Heaven with the One who loves us the most. The only other choice is to join the opposite, Satan. Choosing not to choose sides is an automatic default to the devil's team. It all boils down to just two choices. Do you want to spend the major chunk of your existence in darkness, pain and misery or in the beautiful luxury of paradise?

If you have questions about your eternal life, or if I can pray for you, please contact me through my website at www.PamelaLeeJordan.com. Also on my website is information about my speaking services.